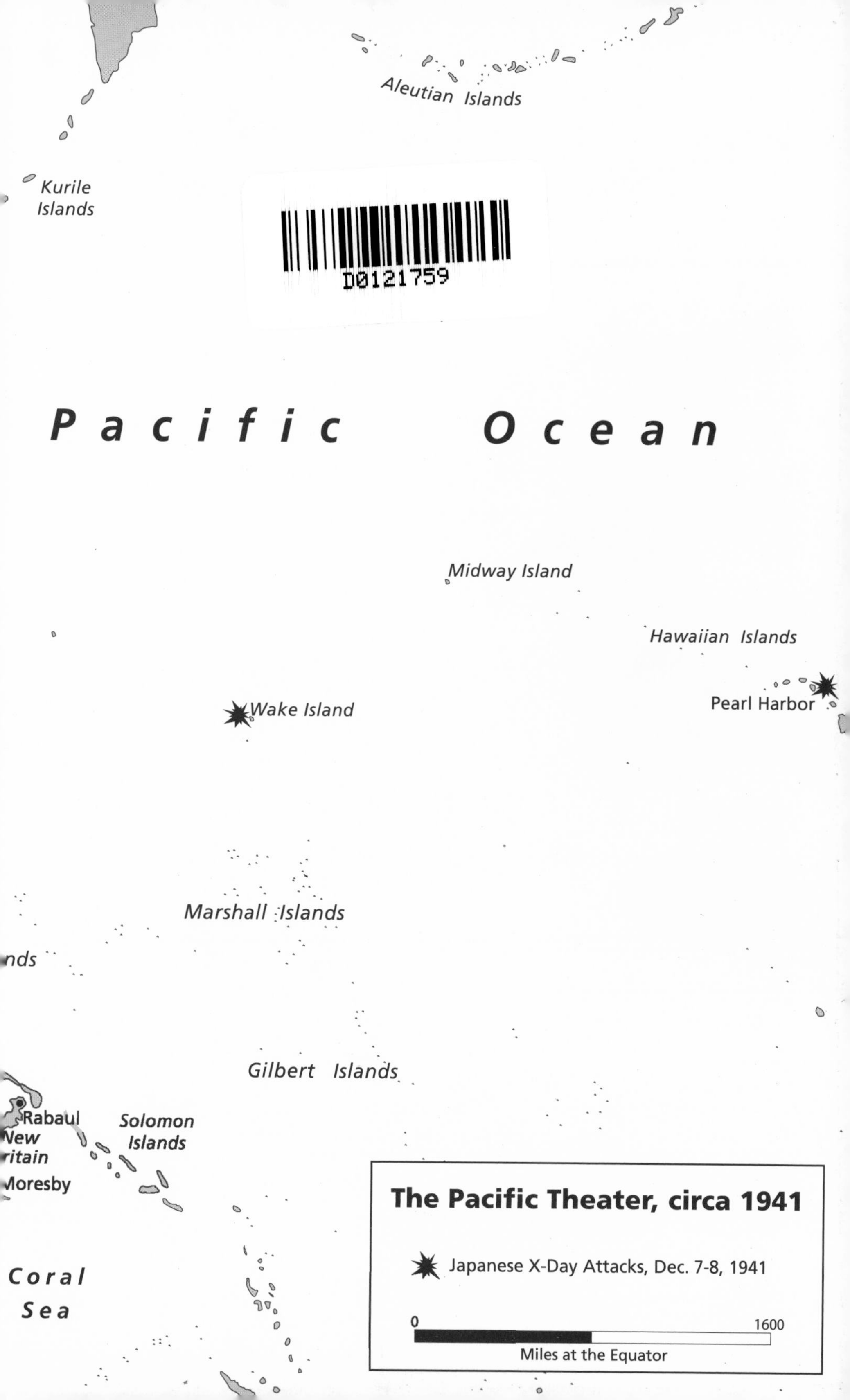

Aleutian Islands

Kurile Islands

Pacific Ocean

Midway Island

Hawaiian Islands

Wake Island

Pearl Harbor

Marshall Islands

nds

Gilbert Islands

Rabaul

New
ritain

Moresby

Solomon Islands

Coral Sea

The Pacific Theater, circa 1941

Japanese X-Day Attacks, Dec. 7-8, 1941

0 1600

Miles at the Equator

Soldier SLAVES

Our debt to the heroic men and valiant women in the service of our country can never be repaid. They have earned our undying gratitude. America will never forget their sacrifices.

—President Harry S. Truman

Quoted in a display at the World War II Memorial in Washington, D.C.

Abandoned by the White House, Courts, and Congress

Soldier SLAVES

James W. Parkinson and Lee Benson

Naval Institute Press
Annapolis, Maryland

Naval Institute Press
291 Wood Road
Annapolis, MD 21402

Library of Congress Cataloging-in-Publication Data
Parkinson, James W., 1949–
Soldier slaves : abandoned by the White House, Courts, and Congress / James W. Parkinson and Lee Benson.
p. cm.
Includes bibliographical references and index.
ISBN 1-59114-204-0 (alk. paper)
1. Ex-prisoners of war—Legal status, laws, etc.—United States. 2. World War, 1939–1945—Prisoners and prisons, Japanese. 3. Bataan Death March, Philippines, 1942. I. Benson, Lee, 1948– II. Title.
KF228.J36P37 2006
640.54'05—dc22

2005037960

Printed in the United States of America on acid-free paper ♾

13 12 11 10 09 08 07 06 9 8 7 6 5 4 3 2

The map on the endpapers was created by Christopher Robinson.

This book is dedicated to the men
of the 20th Pursuit Squadron, United States Army Air Corps—
to those who came home, and those who did not.

Fire is the test of gold,
Adversity, of strong men.

—Seneca

CONTENTS

FOREWORD

THE SOBERING REALITY of World War II is that many great Americans suffered and died so that the rest of us could live in peace. The U.S. soldiers of the Bataan Death March were among the most valiant, and the most unheralded, of these remarkable souls. This outstanding book is a splendid reminder of what happened on that mostly forgotten Philippine peninsula in the spring of 1942 and the hellish years that followed.

More than ten thousand American GIs started that forced eighty-five-mile march at the hands of a merciless Japanese army; nearly a thousand were dead at the end of the march, and the dying continued at a rate of one an hour for two more months. Those who didn't perish led what to us is one of the most heroic and remarkable stories of survival in the annals of warfare. Theirs was a test of endurance, loyalty, and courage in the face of the harshest of conditions and the slimmest of odds. They suffered quietly, they suffered bravely, and they remained resolutely true to their American ideals. Those who were strong and lucky enough returned in honor.

But the late 1940s in postwar America had its priorities, and giving these remarkable men their rightful due was not among them. Those held prisoners by the Japanese came home, mostly unnoticed, to a rebuilding America, and they resumed doing what they had done as soldiers: living lives of quiet honor. They bought cars, were married, found work, had children, and got on with their lives. By 2005, fewer than five thousand of them remained.

Thanks to the dedicated work of some very selfless lawyers, these forgotten soldiers came forcefully to the attention of the United States

Congress as the twenty-first century dawned on America. These former prisoners of war deserved more, it was asserted, from the giant Japanese companies for whom they worked as slave laborers during the war, and even more from the United States itself. With this argument we heartily agree. It is difficult to imagine more deserving, truly American heroes.

The stories told in this book from the war, from the courtrooms of America, and from the State Department and the halls of Congress are stories that need to be heard. They are entertaining, informative, historically important, at times hopeful, at times disappointing, and always inspirational.

The Battling Bastards of Bataan, and all others who paid a dear price for freedom as Pacific Theater prisoners of war, deserve and need to be remembered. Not just for them, but for us. What they did is too important, too awe inspiring, too valuable as an example of the best of the American character to just fade away. And these gentlemen deserve not just our praise and our remembrance of what they did. Most of all, they deserve our thanks.

Senators Orrin Hatch and Joe Biden

ACKNOWLEDGMENTS

SO MANY PEOPLE, in so many ways, contributed to the telling of this story. We would like to thank them all, including those we are sure to unavoidably and unintentionally overlook.

To the gallant veterans of World War II and their families, including, but not limited to, the following: Harold Poole, Lester Tenney, V. O. "Johnny" Johnson, Fran Agnes, Marlene Agnes, Gene Jacobsen, Al Berest, Mo Mazer, Frank Bigelow, Frank Dillman, Olga Bjork, Ed Jackfert, John Bristow, Jim Huff, George Idlett, Bill Mitchell, Don Newbold, Grant McDonald, Joe Moore, Manny Eneriz, Homer Boren, and Tom Nixon.

To the legal team and colleagues in the law: David Casey Jr., Bonnie Kane, Mike Goldstein, Maury Herman, Russ Herman, Tom Boggs, Jonathan Yarowsky, Karen Marangi, Mike Nardotti, Sarah Groothuis, Joe Reeder, Ron Kleinman, Allen Foster, Steve Schneebaum, Jim Kitchen, Charles Mathis, Ed Konieczny, Jessica Valtros Meyer, Elizabeth Rutledge, Venus Soltan, Eli Wallach, Paul Wainwright, David Fox, Steve Herman, Harold Miner, Lenny Davis, Gayle Blatt, Linda Goetz Holmes, Ann Polomo, Betty Hill, David Emig, Wendy Behan, Nancy Taylor, Carol Hemingway, and James Graff-Radford.

To the public servants who always found time to help: Senator Orrin Hatch, Congressman Mike Honda, Senator Joe Biden, Senator Dianne Feinstein, Senator Bob Smith, Congressman Dana Rohrabacher, Congressman Duncan Hunter, Congressman John Dolittle, Congresswoman Sheila Jackson Lee, Congressman Chris Cannon, Bob Sakaniwa, Isaac Yamagata, Ruth Montoya, Makan Delrahim, Rebecca Seidel, Michael Schiffer, Jonathan Meyer, Larissa Bounds, Trish Knight, and Dennis Toner.

To Bill Nixon and Jeff Child at Policy Impact.

To family and friends, including many who helped by reading the manuscript and making innumerable improvements: James Parkinson's wife, Sue, father and mother, Dr. Richard P. and Marilyn Parkinson, and children, Krista, Brett, Brooke, and Matthew; Dr. Richard W. and Mavis Parkinson; Dr. Brett T. and Kelly Parkinson; Laurie Parkinson; Phil Ferranti; Jackie Guerra; Bill Torres; Monroe McKay; Doug Miller; Omer Mohamed; Irma Mohamed; Woody Germany; Steve Root; Carl Ingram; David Raines; Kerri Benson; Dee Benson; Eric Benson; Tori Gagnon; Tanner Gagnon; Kay Green; Tam Green; Dr. Steve Lake; Dr. Lin Lilly; Paul and Linda Warner; Mac Christensen; Rod Basehore; Judy Basehore; Steve Hill; Saleem Coobtee; John Dehlin; Joel Dehlin; Eric Mwenda; Wilbur Colom; Russ Handy; Clark Arrington; Ty and Mindy McRae; Joe Cotchett; Denis French; James Parkinson's great staff, Lupe Pasillas and Ann Hermanson, along with Mike Montgomery, Joe Wojcik, and Robert Davis; and Benji, who drove us through the Philippines without mishap and in style.

And finally, to those in the literary world whose support, encouragement, and expertise have been invaluable: Mark Gatlin, Pat Pascale, Linda O'Doughda, Susan Artigiani, Chris Onrubia, and Tom Harnish at the Naval Institute Press; Lari Bishop and Jay Hodges at Greenleaf Book Group; cartographer Christopher Robinson; and the inimitable Rich Barber, a literary agent with a keen appreciation of history—not to mention the patience of Job—whose suggestions and shepherding of this story enabled it to become a published reality.

Soldier SLAVES

PROLOGUE

IN JANUARY 1944, news reports from the Pacific shocked an America that was at war and thus not easily shocked.

In newspapers, magazines, and a book, an army pilot from Texas named William E. Dyess told of the brutal treatment inflicted on Allied servicemen held as prisoners of war by the Japanese in the Philippines. He described starvation rations, squalid living conditions, almost total medical neglect, and long hours of forced labor.

And that was the fate of those who had first somehow managed to survive a brutal forced-march with virtually no food or water through the steaming jungles of the Philippine peninsula of Bataan.

"A Japanese soldier took my canteen, gave the water to a horse, and threw the canteen away," Dyess, a captain in the Army Air Corps, said in describing the start of that ordeal. "I made that march of about eighty-five miles in six days on one mess kit of rice."

Many, Dyess observed, did not make it: "Totally done in, American and Filipino prisoners fell out frequently, and threw themselves moaning beside the roadside. The stronger were not permitted to help the weaker. We then would hear shots behind us."

It was the first time what Dyess termed the "Bataan Death March" entered the American consciousness.

The pilot went on to describe post–Death March prison camp conditions in the Philippines. He detailed savage beatings, rampant disease, sadistic tortures, and constant harsh physical demands that pushed prisoners to the point of exhaustion and beyond. "Men were literally worked to death," he reported. "It was not unusual for 20 percent of a work detail to be worked to death." Of the prisoners who survived, he wrote, many were "sent to Japan to work in factories."

What made the news harder yet for America to stomach was the fact that the events Dyess described had happened almost two years earlier, dating back to the early days of World War II when the Philippines, and twenty thousand U.S. servicemen, fell to Japan.

For those still imprisoned by the Japanese, no one was betting that conditions had improved.

Part of the reason for the long delay in the news reaching the American public was due to the time Dyess personally spent in captivity. It took him 361 days to make it through the Death March and subsequent stays at three different prison camps in the Philippines before he managed to escape, along with two other officers, Lt. Cdr. Melvin McCoy and Lt. Col. Stephen Mellnick, when they found themselves unguarded while on a farm work detail. They disappeared into the jungle and the arms of rebel guerrilla fighters, who smuggled them onto an Allied submarine that took them to Australia, where they delivered their reports to General MacArthur's headquarters in July 1943.

The other part of the reason was the War Department's decision not to make the news public right away. The details reported by the ex-POWs were so outrageous that they were done in by their own outrageousness. Fearing the news would take the focus off America's concerted war front in Europe, by inciting demands that the problems with Japan be addressed immediately, the reports from the Philippines were slapped with an official War Department censor. Through the summer and fall of 1943, not a word about the situation was spoken. Meanwhile, Dyess voluntarily returned to active duty, determined to resume fighting in the Pacific Theater. In a cruel irony, he was killed on December 22, 1943, in a training-flight crash in Burbank, California. He never lived to see *The Dyess Story: The Complete Eye-Witness Account of the Death March from Bataan* published by G. P. Putnam & Sons. Nor did he live to witness more than one hundred newspapers and magazines, all of them sitting on his story, threaten a First Amendment lawsuit until Secretary of State Cordell Hull finally relented to lift the censor in early 1944.

The War Department was right. American outrage was extreme. Newspaper editorials, reflecting the public outcry, screamed for retribution.

Politicians demanded action. Such atrocities could not be tolerated in a civilized world, not even in wartime.

Speaking on behalf of the War Department, Joseph C. Grew, a former U.S. ambassador to Japan and special assistant to the Secretary of State, said in an official statement: "The Japanese people as a whole would, if they knew the facts, be utterly ashamed . . . I doubt whether the perpetrators themselves will have any feeling whatever of repentance. But others, including perhaps some of their highest leaders, may and probably will feel a sense of shame, or at the very least, a desire to offset in future this record of barbarism."

The talk was tough, but there was still a world war going on, the outcome very much in doubt.

When it finally was sorted out, more than a year and a half later, after first the Germans and then the Japanese surrendered and sixteen million GIs came trooping home to celebrate, the outrage of 1944 was as forgotten as Captain Dyess's shocking eyewitness account. Lost in the intoxicating flush of victory was a handful of men, relatively speaking, who limped home from factories in Japan, their long, dark, anonymous days of barbaric incarceration finally over. But not so easily forgotten.

CHAPTER ONE

September 12, 1999
St. George, Utah

THE SUN WAS JUST BEGINNING to work up the energy for another routine day of torture on the Coachella Valley as I switched on the air-conditioning, backed out of my driveway, and headed north toward the freeway. Sue, my wife of twenty-eight years, and I live in Bermuda Dunes, California, a community fifteen miles east of Palm Springs. Los Angeles is another hundred miles beyond that. Las Vegas is three hundred miles in the other direction.

It was mid-September, slightly more than a hundred days to what was being labeled in universal shorthand as "Y2K," the turn of the millennium, a day that some were saying would be our last on the planet. I was not one of them.

The leather seats of my Lexus 400 cushioned our early morning departure. Our final destination was St. George, Utah, about one hundred miles beyond Las Vegas. My objective was what in my business is called client development.

I am a lawyer by trade, specifically a personal injury lawyer—PI for short. "One of the best lawyers in the Coachella Valley," according to an article published in 1995 in *Palm Springs Life* entitled "Desert Dream Team" by Denys Arcuri. After talking to members of the legal profession Arcuri wrote, "The word from his collegues is if you need a personal injury attorney, Parkinson is absolutely the best in the desert. You may see him on television, but with his reputation he hardly needs it." Partly that was because of several significant settlements and jury verdicts I had secured for grateful, if permanently disabled, clients. But mostly it was because for the past twenty-four years I had been indefatigable—I don't think anyone who knows me would argue this point—in my pursuit of truth, justice, and 33 percent contingency fees. This wasn't the first time I had started work before dawn.

I like my job. I like the chase, the competition, and the pressure. I like just about everything about the grassroots, stick-up-for-the-victim brand of law I choose to practice. Being a trial lawyer—that's the term PI lawyers use when we're trying to impress someone—gets me out of bed in the morning.

I especially like the money. Money is how a PI lawyer keeps score, and as the millennium was coming to a close, I had played the game long enough to affirm, by any objective measure, that I could keep score pretty well. I would turn fifty in less than two months, our house was practically paid off, and our four children were in high school, at college, or married with a career.

My suite of offices, located in a business park ten minutes from my house in the town of Palm Desert, stands as a kind of tribute to the litigious age and my energetic participation therein: a one-man firm with five rooms that includes my personal corner office; an office for Lupe, my trusty, longtime personal secretary; an office for Ann, my equally trusty bookkeeper; a boardroom, complete with videotaping equipment to document injuries and depositions; and a storeroom stocked with supplies, files, and legal pads—the tools of the trade.

Overhead for this self-contained PI operation including salaries for the staff, rent for the building, gas for my Lexus, and a truly prodigious cell phone bill, was into six figures a year, and lately, that had been no worry, no worry at all. This was not only due to my aggressive pursuit of a full caseload, but also because as luck, fate, and fortuitous timing had it, I had recently found myself on the receiving end of the granddaddy of all personal injury settlements—the 1998 suit against America's tobacco companies. My tobacco fees would soon be coming in.

I was not a lead attorney in the various lawsuits that ended with a $200 billion settlement against Phillip Morris, RJR, and a number of other tobacco companies for misleading the public about the known dangers of tobacco. Far from it. I actually joined the case rather late in the game. But though my contributions were not extensive and my cut was proportionately small, even my share of the $200 billion was hardly insignificant.

Such were my financial and professional circumstances that morning as we drove out of California. Sue, who had been lured into the trip with the promise of dinner and a night at the St. George Sheraton, dozed in the passenger's seat. The next day we would turn around and drive the six hours back to our home in the desert. That was the plan.

My business purpose was to make the acquaintance of a group of World War II veterans who belonged to the 20th Pursuit Squadron, 24th Pursuit Group, the United States Army Air Corps. They had been stationed in the Philippine Islands when the war broke out in December 1941. The 20th Pursuit men were holding their annual reunion in St. George. For the past few years they had been getting together once a year in the home state of one of the members. The year before had been Texas. Next year would be Nevada. This year was Utah, where a number of 20th Pursuit vets resided.

I had been asked to take a few minutes and address the group during the business-meeting portion of their reunion, which was scheduled to begin at 2:30 that afternoon. I had carefully rehearsed my speech. The war, and their part in it, was long in the past, but as an attorney-at-law, I was going to lay out for them the legal reasons why they might choose to enlist again—not as airplane mechanics, clerks, and cooks, but as plaintiffs in a lawsuit aimed at Japanese companies that used prisoners of war as slave laborers from 1942 through 1945. Almost all surviving members of the 20th Pursuit Squadron had been taken captive by the Japanese when the Bataan peninsula in the Philippines was surrendered en masse in April 1942. After the surrender many of them had worked for two or more years for Japanese companies, mining coal and copper, working blast furnaces at steel mills, unloading ships, and performing dozens of other tasks, and they had never been paid for their work. These men were due their back wages plus almost sixty years of accrued interest, and they could ask for that in a court of law.

It was Big Tobacco that provided the entrée for me into the Japanese Prisoner of War (JPOW) case. Dave Casey Jr., a Big Tobacco attorney from San Diego and a longtime associate of mine, had brought up the JPOW case in the context of a high-powered firm he was in the process of forming. The idea, Casey explained, was to link PI lawyers at strategic locations across America. This mega-firm would have enough depth of talent, resources, and financing to be able to take on cases of national scope too big or too multifaceted for any single firm or individual attorney to handle.

In bringing a number of trial lawyers together, the tobacco case had revealed the value, as well as the potential, for this kind of coordinated national effort. By banding together, PI lawyers could realistically take on the big boys, be it Phillip Morris or, as the JPOW case developed, some of Japan's—and the world's—wealthiest corporations, such as Mitsubishi, Mitsui, Kawasaki, Ishihara Sangyo, and Nippon Steel. Since the end of the war these Japanese companies, and others like them, had raced to tremendous economic prosperity, ignoring a wartime legacy of U.S. soldiers working in their plants, mines, and shipyards with only abuse and starvation diets as reward.

That postwar prosperity brought with it deep corporate pockets that could afford expert legal representation. But if Mitsubishi, Mitsui, and others trotted their $500-an-hour attorneys—most of them American lawyers working for American law firms—into court to argue why they should not have to pay the back wages, Casey and his associates planned to respond with attorneys backed by the resources of established law firms all across the country.

The big difference between the two sides was that the mega-firm attorneys would not be working at an hourly rate. We would be working on the contingency fee basis familiar to PI attorneys. We would be paid only if we won the case, and then only out of the profits. In a typical PI case that pay amounts to a third of the verdict. In the JPOW case, out of respect for the war veterans, and in anticipation of a number that could be Tobacco-esque in size, the mega-firm agreed to reduce the contingency fee to 28 percent.

The beauty of this arrangement for our clients—and this was the message I intended to get across loud and clear to the men of the 20th Pursuit Squadron—was the absence of any financial risk to them as plaintiffs. The lawsuit would cost them nothing. All they had to do was sign up and then go back to playing golf or gardening or spoiling their grandkids. The mega-firm was a way for eighty-year-old soldiers living on pensions and often not much else to take on companies such as Mitsubishi, a worldwide conglomerate with annual revenues of $115 billion. Under this arrangement, both sides could afford to go to court. Even if a World War II veteran could afford a lawyer's hourly fee, the mega-firm essentially offered dozens of lawyers, all working for him at no cost.

As soon as I heard from Dave Casey about the mega-firm and the JPOW case, I wanted to be involved. It was exactly the kind of high-profile case I longed for—a dream come true for a "storefront lawyer" like me. Every PI dreams of David taking down Goliath; it is the nature of the business. But more than offering an opportunity to take aim at some very large targets, it was a case that would allow me to continue working with the caliber of lawyers I had worked with, if briefly, during the tobacco battles. I had found that association invigorating and stimulating. Plus, it was good for my ego. I wanted more.

The easiest way for me to get into the case was to find clients, which was my first challenge. Signing up clients for a PI lawsuit is not as easy as one might think. Lawyers are not allowed to solicit a client directly to a case. We may advertise our services, we may hand out our business cards, and we may let it be known we are available, but it is against the lawyers' code of ethics to recruit clients to a specific case. The client must come to you.

I started working the JPOW case by talking about it among my attorney friends and other contacts in the legal world—a tried and proven method of getting prospective clients to recruit *you*. My first break came when I brought up the case while talking with a group of lawyers and judges one summer afternoon outside the Riverside County Courthouse in Indio. One of our local judges mentioned to me that a colleague's father had been on the Bataan Death March. The man had died, he said, but his family might be interested in the lawsuit. "Have them call me," I said.

Within a few days, a woman named Olga Bjork, the veteran's widow, phoned my office from her home in Oxnard, California. Yes, she said, her husband was on the Bataan Death March, and yes, she wanted to join the lawsuit. Just like that, I was in. When Mrs. Bjork joined the JPOW case on behalf of her deceased husband, I joined it as well.

It was not long before Mrs. Olga Bjork discovered just how serious I was about pursuing the war debts. Within days of our initial phone conversation I arranged for her to come to the Coachella Valley to speak to the media at a press conference my staff had organized. The World War II widow teared up as she talked about her late husband's sacrifices for his country. She described the suffering he had endured as a prisoner and as a slave made to work for private Japanese companies.

Media reports followed that night on both of the area television stations, while the next morning's *Desert Sun* hit porches and newsstands with front-page coverage. Even though I had organized the media event for the express purpose of generating public interest and support, I have to admit I was surprised at the intense reaction Mrs. Bjork's story generated. The subject matter obviously struck an emotional nerve. During the press conference, one elderly woman—who was not a World War II veteran herself—had stood up to speak and the media had jockeyed for better positions to capture her on film. What would be the media response, I could only wonder, if a bona fide World War II *survivor* were standing in front of the cameras?

This was clearly the kind of PI claim that could not only generate considerable public interest, but could also easily win public approval. Who could begrudge a group of World War II veterans, now grandfathers and great-grandfathers, asking for justice? And they had won the war!

Best of all, it was a case that, from everything I was hearing, we could win. That is what the lawyers who had studied the background and the war treaties were saying. The mega-firm had done its legal homework; it was not about to bring a flagship case it did not think was winnable.

All of these issues spoke to the practical side of the matter: the payday. The financial possibilities were not endless, but they were up there. A judgment or settlement that took into account the back wages owed, a half-century of inflation, *and* pain and suffering could be in the billions. A judgment could be in the Big Tobacco neighborhood. And this time, James W. Parkinson, Esq., was in on the ground floor.

As we covered the miles to St. George, passing the hardpan, high desert California towns of Victorville and Barstow, and the world's tallest thermometer in Baker, I explained the ins and outs of the case to Sue. She was my captive audience, and as always, I talked to her to help articulate my position.

I went over the presentation I planned to give to the men of the 20th Pursuit Squadron, all of them senior citizens in their late 70s and early 80s. There was no need to make the case sound complicated or to exaggerate anything to help me justify my existence. These men had been wronged. They had been employed and they had not been paid, and they deserved justice. That was the long and short of it, and I wanted to keep it simple. The fact that the injury took place a half century ago only made the need for restitution that much greater. There was no statute of limitations on doing the right thing.

I told Sue how ironic I thought it was that tobacco was again playing a part in these men's quest for liberation. I had learned that tobacco was a rare and much-sought-after commodity in the prison camps. Cigarette rations were much more meager than rice rations, which were meager enough, and men who smoked would often barter even their small portions of rice and other food for cigarettes. The result was that soldiers who did not smoke wound up with more rice to eat. It was never much, but a handful of rice could keep you alive and a handful of cigarettes could not. Some prisoners of war did not make it to August 1945, when Japan surrendered to the United States, because of their desire for cigarettes.

"Don't you find it ironic," I said to Sue. "These men are alive today in part because tobacco is addictive, and now they're in a position to sue the companies that used them as slaves largely because of a lawsuit filed to prove tobacco is addictive?"

"Hell," I added, "These guys could have told them that sixty years ago."

We arrived in St. George, a city of about fifty thousand located just inside Utah's southern border, a little before noon. We checked into the Sheraton, and with my appointment still two and a half hours away, went out for a leisurely lunch. I then dropped Sue back at the hotel and prepared to leave for work.

The vets had given me twenty minutes on their program—they had been explicit about the time—and the motel where they were holding their meeting was across the street from the Sheraton. "I'll be back by four," I said to Sue as I left the room.

My contact with the 20th Pursuit Squadron—indeed, the only reason I even knew the squadron existed—was eighty-year-old Spec. Sgt. Harold Poole (Ret.), a postal worker from Salt Lake City. Harold was the father-in-law of a law school classmate and lifelong friend of mine, Paul Warner, who I usually call by his last name. Warner had survived law school and time as a judge advocate general, or JAG, in the navy to become appointed United States Attorney for the District of Utah.

The week before the trip to St. George, Warner and I had attended a Board of Visitors meeting at the Brigham Young University law school, our alma mater, and Harold's name had come up.

"So, Parky, what are you up to now that you've sucked tobacco dry?" Warner asked me during a break.

Ignoring the needle, I told him about the JPOW case. I was just getting started when he grabbed my arm.

"Stop! Listen to me," he said. "My father-in-law was a prisoner of war of the Japanese. They abused him for three and a half years. You need him in your case. He *is* your case."

"What's his name?" I asked.

"Harold Poole," Warner answered. "Poole with an *e*."

"Have him call me."

The call for "Mr. Parkinson" came the following day when I was back in my office in Palm Desert. Lupe answered the phone. "May I tell him who's calling?" she asked. "Harold Poole," came the reply. "Paul Warner asked me to call."

Eager at the prospect of signing on a genuine veteran, I jumped on the line. I already knew what I wanted to say. As soon as Harold Poole explained who he was, I cut in and told him I would like to catch a plane to Salt Lake City so I could meet him at his home there, explain the case to him, and if he had any interest, sign him up. But Harold had a better idea. He said all the fellows from his World War II outfit were getting together for a reunion the next weekend in St. George. He had already talked to a number of them, and they had expressed an interest in what I was doing. Could I talk to all of them there?

You do not have to ask a lawyer such a thing twice.

Harold Poole was staying at the Comfort Inn in St. George, a clean, comfortable, $39-a-night motel located across Bluff Street from the Sheraton.

I knocked on the door of Harold's motel room to introduce myself in advance of the 2:30 meeting. I was greeted by a trim, spry man, about five feet eight. He was wearing glasses and a hearing aid and still had most of his hair, all of it white.

"Hello, I'm Harold," he said, extending his hand after I introduced myself, "Nice to meet you."

With Harold leading the way, we walked through the lobby to the motel's conference room, where chairs had already been arranged for the meeting. We were not the first to arrive. Another 20th Pursuit Squadron veteran was already there and involved in a loud discussion with three women who had read in the local newspaper about the reunion of World War II soldiers. They were insisting that they had a right to sit in on the meeting. One of the women said she had a brother who had died on the Bataan Death March, the infamous forced march the men of the 20th Pursuit endured after they surrendered in the Philippines.

The war veteran essentially told the woman that it did not matter if she had been on the Bataan Death March herself, if she was not 20th Pursuit Squadron, she was not invited to this meeting. Squadron members and wives only. Period. No exceptions. As I watched this exchange I had to resist the urge to jump into the middle of it. It is my nature to wade into fights—other people's usually—sort them out, and settle them if possible. I am used to it. It is how I make my living. But something told me that I did not belong in this debate. I stood there with Harold and said nothing, which was harder for me to do than anyone might have guessed.

When the women left, I watched as Harold followed them into the lobby and intercepted them. He patted them on the arm and talked to them in an obvious attempt to make them feel better about what had just happened. The older man did this unobtrusively, drawing no attention to his peacemaking. Then he came back into the room and, as more members of the outfit began to arrive, got into a friendly conversation with the man who had asked the women to leave. The incident was over almost before it began.

The men walking into the room were all of a similar vintage, although some were in better shape than others. One man carried an oxygen canister so he could breathe. Others kept a firm grip on walking sticks or canes. Most wore hearing aids. Several were accompanied by their spouses. Of the twenty-five 20th Pursuit Squadron members still living, thirteen were present.

I was the first item on the agenda. Harold stood up to introduce me.

"You all know that my son-in-law, Paul Warner, is the U.S. Attorney for Utah," he said, his tone suggesting a familiarity among the group that went beyond a once-a-year get together. "Paul and Jim here are good friends. Paul said Jim is a very good lawyer." Then he sat down, and the floor was all mine.

I was offering these men a good deal, and I knew it. My challenge in the next twenty minutes was to make sure they knew it, too. After outlining the case, I stressed that they would be required to put up nothing in the way of money and very little, if any, in the way of time. A few might be called upon to testify in court or even in Congress, and they would need to provide details of their wartime slave labor. But beyond that, all they would need to provide were their addresses and phone numbers. The mega-firm would go after their back wages, plus interest, with dispatch. Any monetary compensation they got—and it could be substantial—could be used however they wanted: to help with medical needs, to help put grandkids through school, or to buy a brand-new Cadillac.

I was quick to add that the money was secondary. Any financial consideration would be nice, and no one was likely to turn it down. But no matter how high the amount, it could not come close to compensating them for the pain and suffering they had endured at the hands of the enemy, or for the pain and suffering of the men who had not made it. The veterans needed to know that their lawyers understood that. The highest purpose of this lawsuit would be to elicit an apology from the Japanese companies for their wrongdoings. In that way, this case could serve as a precedent to stop anything similar from ever happening again.

It was not the first time these men had heard such rhetoric. Many Pacific Theatre veterans had entertained the thought of a lawsuit a time or two; some had even thrown a few dollars at attorneys over the years, but neither the dollars nor the attorneys were still around. It had been nearly sixty years since they had been forced to work for Japanese companies, laboring in conditions that would send hardened criminals at San Quentin into revolt. They had never received a penny in wages or a hint of an apology in all that time. If the men of the 20th Pursuit Squadron were skeptical, they had their good reasons.

Still, they had never heard anything quite like what they were hearing from me—a national law firm was willing to work for them for nothing.

Their curiosity piqued, the men and their wives started asking questions, followed by more questions. Shortly after the end of twenty minutes, I turned to Gene Jacobsen, who was running the meeting, and said, "I guess my time's up." He told me to keep talking until they said to stop. Twenty minutes turned into an hour, and then another hour.

What became apparent to me was that even though it was nearly six decades later, the men of the 20th Pursuit Squadron were still looking for justice. Not money, justice. Their side had won the war, but they had never had their day of reckoning.

While collecting my thoughts after one of the most extraordinary meetings I had experienced in nearly three decades in the business, I walked with Harold to his motel room. The men and the meeting had touched me deeply, and not just from a legal standpoint. PI cases, attended as they are by pain and suffering, are by definition emotional, but I had just been witness to a depth of emotion I realized I could not begin to comprehend.

"Would you like to come in for a minute?" Harold asked.

We sat in two chairs around a small table. "You were very impressive with the men," Harold said. "I'm sure, based on your presentation, they will all sign up" (a prediction that would prove to be accurate; not only would every man in attendance that afternoon sign on to the JPOW case, but several of their friends would join as well).

As we talked, I looked around Harold's room. His bed looked untouched. Lying on top of the bed, his suitcase revealed a place for everything and everything in its place. On the sink, toiletries belonging to a man who once slept on the ground in a Japanese prison camp were laid out neatly on top of a washcloth. The whole scene suggested economy and orderliness. I could imagine the motel maids walking in and wondering if anyone had actually stayed here.

We talked for hours. I learned that Harold had been a mail carrier for thirty years and retired from that position fifteen years ago. He had been married twice, and both wives had passed on. He met and married his first wife, Kathleen, not long after the war. She died of cancer at the age of fifty, and even now, I could sense the pain of that loss as Harold spoke of her. Harold and Kathleen had a daughter named Linda—Paul Warner's wife—and a son named Stanley, and now there were nine grandchildren. Harold's second wife, Jeannette, to whom he had been married for eleven years, had died just three years ago. "Two wives and outlived them both, and both younger than me," said Harold, shaking his head. He explained that with the wives gone and the kids grown, he had more time for his hobbies. At one time he hunted and fished a lot, but now he tended more toward taxidermy, woodworking, and gardening. He said he also made as much time as he could for church work and to help his neighbors where and when he could. Harold, I noticed, said none of this to draw attention to himself or with any degree of bragging. The information surfaced on its own, much of it through my questions.

Eventually, our talk turned to the war. Harold told me he had spent three and a half years in Japanese captivity, which began with the ignominious Bataan Death March that had killed fifteen thousand men. Starvation prison-camp rations dropped him from his "fighting weight" of 180 pounds to a low of 97 pounds. He lived in intense heat in the Philippines and in brutal cold during two winters in Japan, where he was "employed" by a steel mill and a shipyard. He was beaten with clubs, spat on, branded a coward, fed propaganda, and kept with hundreds of other prisoners in the dark hold of a freighter ship when he was sent to Japan. He watched fellow soldiers die with agonizing regularity and had almost died himself from malaria and pneumonia, besides contending with a plethora of other diseases, including beriberi, dysentery, and intestinal worms.

I tried to imagine what he had gone through: three and a half years of prolonged torture and terror, away from any news of home, never knowing if his captivity would end. I asked him how he was able to withstand the repeated physical and mental abuse. That is when he told me about his most prized possession as a prisoner: a pocket-sized GI Bible he found in the jungle not long after he was taken captive. He hung on to it and read it constantly the entire time he was a prisoner of war. He said the Japanese were always taking it from him, and every time they did he was sure that was the last he would see of it, but it was always returned.

Harold said finding the Bible was only one of the miracles that came from God that he credited with enabling him to make it through. Knowing we were of the same faith, he looked at me conspiratorially. "You know," he said.

But I did not know.

It was getting dark when I finally left Harold's room and returned to the Sheraton.

"I will not be able to sleep after what just happened," I told Sue as I walked into our suite. "Let's go."

"Go where?" asked Sue.

"Home," I said. "Let's go home. While we drive, I can tell you about the men I just met and what I just heard."

The clerk at the front desk seemed more surprised than Sue at our sudden change of plans. Motels in St. George, Utah, do not often encounter guests asking for an hourly rate.

CHAPTER TWO

December 8, 1941
Clark Field, Pampanga, Philippines

RED DOTS. BRIGHT TINY CIRCLES on the bottom of airplane wings. That's what tipped off Pvt. Harold Poole of the United States Army Air Corps that World War II was about to begin.

"A bunch of us were looking up at the planes, and at first it was just sort of entertaining," Harold recalled. "One of the guys, thinking they were ours, said, 'Look, the navy's showing off.' That's when I saw the red dots, and I said, 'That ain't navy.' Right after that the bombs started to drop."

We were sitting on a comfortable sofa in the living room of Harold's home, surrounded by photographs of his grandchildren. Harold had responded without hesitation or reservation to my request to hear about his experiences during the war.

"We thought we'd get a warning, but we had no radar, and the Japanese had cut the phone lines to our lookouts in the hills. All of a sudden the planes just appeared."

It was December 8, 1941, at Clark Field, an air base fifty-five miles northwest of the Philippine capital of Manila on the island of Luzon. Hundreds of eager, young, strong, well-fed men stared at the swarm of airplanes approaching their home away from home. Among them were the 225 men in Poole's outfit.

The planes were laid out wing to wing in perfect formation. It was only natural for the soldiers to think the planes had flown in from a United States Navy aircraft carrier in the waters of the nearby South China Sea.

Once the planes were overhead, their bottoms opened, and within seconds, the sky filled with black specks that rapidly grew larger as they neared the base. Soon Clark Field and everything in it was being torn apart by bombs and shrapnel.

The assumption that they were navy planes was actually correct, but they belonged to the Imperial Japanese Navy, not the United States. Their objective was to place their red dots—the Japanese national emblem, symbolic of the rising sun—directly over Clark Field and drop bombs on the warplanes parked below, thereby severely crippling the U.S. military air capability in the Pacific. From an altitude of twenty-five thousand feet, two thousand feet beyond the range of U.S. antiaircraft guns, the death-carrying Japanese bombers, like gigantic shotguns, systematically attacked the runways, hangars, barracks, cookhouse, and other structures that made up the air base. "They hit everything," said Harold. "They expended a lot of ordnance on things that didn't count to get the things that did."

It was 1220 hours—twenty past noon.

Like most of the men on the base, Harold had just finished lunch. He was making his way across the airstrip to the operations shack to resume cleaning, repairing, and maintaining the guns mounted in the pursuit—or fighter—airplanes that belonged to the 20th Pursuit Squadron. He was an armament man, trained to load and keep in proper working order the weapons in the P-26, P-35, P-36, and the brand-new P-40 planes that made up the U.S. Army fighter plane arsenal in the Philippine Islands. The P planes—*P* for "pursuit"—were scattered about the base, in hangars and along runways. Most of them were being refueled after spending the morning looking in vain for signs of the enemy. Alongside the sleek fighter planes were dozens of B-10, B-17, and B-18 planes—*B* for "bomber."

For months P and B planes had been arriving in increasing numbers from the States; just days earlier, another shipment of the coveted new P-40s, known as "Tomahawks," had arrived in crates, ready for assembly. The month before, a supply of B-17s arrived at the dock in Manila. Capable of cruising at over two hundred miles per hour at altitudes of thirty thousand feet while carrying four thousand pounds of bombs, these "Flying Fortresses" were a fighting man's dream.

By the start of December, in answer to rumblings of unrest throughout Asia, more than three hundred U.S. warplanes had been assembled in the Philippines. When airborne, this collection of bombers and fighters represented a respectable, if not yet formidable, Far East Air Force.

But at that moment, they were not airborne.

Harold felt hypnotized by the sheer spectacle of Japanese bombers flying over the tops of the Zambales Mountains with nothing but blue sky to stop them. "They were packed in nine tight Vs of three planes each, and they came in two waves, fifty-four in all," he told me. Harold waited until he had finished counting the planes before he looked for cover, and since shrapnel was already spraying the far end of the field, he looked quickly. "It was every man for himself. We all had to find some cover and get under it fast. The bombs going off, coming nearer and nearer, made me think of a giant walking toward me."

He sprinted for a foxhole just yards away, dove in, and held his head. Looking from side to side, he discovered he was alone, accompanied only by a machine gun mounted on a steel pole in the center of the hole. The gun was covered with dirt. Whoever had been manning the weapon, if anyone at all, had left for better shelter or been blown to bits. There was no indication of either. What he did know was that the machine gun might come in handy, because the bombers were already departing Clark Field, and on their heels were dive-bombers, the Japanese fighter planes.

"The dive-bombers came under cover of the billowing smoke from our burning gas and planes and buildings," said Harold. "Suddenly, there they were. The sky was full of them."

There were thirty-four fighters in the first wave, followed by a second wave of fifty-one. It is the job of fighter planes to protect the slower, higher-flying bombers by engaging enemy fighter planes in chase, or better yet, by strafing the target area and preventing enemy fighter planes from taking off in pursuit. Dive-bombers, as the name suggests, come in low, sometimes within mere feet of the ground, their guns firing bullets at several rounds per second.

Harold crouched in the three-feet-deep foxhole, wanting it to be deeper. "I wished I was a mouse," he said, "or something smaller." He could see that a few undamaged P-40s were struggling down the pock-marked, smoke-filled runway in an attempt to take off. He could also see that the incoming Japanese fighter planes were on course to stop them.

In another setting, the Japanese fighter planes would have been quite a show. Most of them were the new Type O fighters, or Zeros, a nickname derived from the year the Mitsubishi Corporation produced them: 1940 in the Christian year and 2,600 in the Japanese year. The plane had made its debut the year before in Japan's long-running war with the Chinese, giving the Japanese a significant edge in the skies. Word quickly spread in military circles of these light, agile planes. Maybe the American P-40—America's newest fighter plane, with a pair of .50-caliber machine guns in the nose, four .30-caliber guns in the wings and a maximum speed of nearly four hundred miles per hour—had more overall strength and firepower, but the P-40 could not dart in and out of the skies like the Zero.

Harold was getting a firsthand demonstration of the Zero's agility. One fighter, in particular, had his undivided attention as it dove in from the north, on a course directly in line with his bunker.

Instinctively, he grabbed the machine gun beside him, aimed at the incoming plane, pulled the trigger . . . and nothing happened. The gun was jammed, clogged by dirt or shrapnel, or maybe it was just bad luck. An old .30-caliber air-cooled Lewis machine gun, a World War I relic, it was not the most dependable of guns under any conditions. The Lewis was not a pursuit plane gun; it was an infantry weapon, meant to stay on the ground, so Harold had never personally shot one, or for that matter, cleaned one. But as a certified armament man, with the superior air-mechanic rating he had earned just weeks earlier to prove it, if Harold Poole knew anything, he knew guns. In his civilian days he liked nothing better than to hunt in the hills and fields and duck blinds back home. Until he came to the Philippines, he had never missed a Utah deer hunt, or his deer.

Harold's love affair with guns was contrary to his mother's wishes. He was born on December 20, 1918, barely a month after the conclusion of World War I, the war to end all wars. Shortly after Nina Poole delivered her first and only son she had declared with conviction, "He will never own a gun." And Harold had not owned a gun until he was sixteen. Ever since, he had rarely been without one, including, thank goodness, now.

Somehow the first Zero missed him, diverted perhaps by a bigger target. Or maybe it was just bad shooting. Harold could not tell in the chaos of bullets striking around his foxhole. Moments earlier, during the bombing raid, a fifty-five-gallon drum of gasoline had taken a direct hit near where he crouched, sending dirt, shrapnel, and petrol around him like a shower, and partially filling up the foxhole. Everywhere Harold looked, men were running and screaming, bombs were bursting, shrapnel was flying, gasoline tanks were exploding, fires were burning. "It was awful," he said. "I could see the bodies and limbs of my buddies strewn everywhere." Most of the squadron's pilots who were in their planes would be hit before they had a chance to take off. Just three of the outfit's P-40s managed to take off. The others were badly damaged or outright destroyed. War had arrived quickly at Clark Field, and death with it.

Harold forced himself to turn his attention from the overall carnage and focus on a more immediate problem, the jammed machine gun. With practiced fingers he took the Lewis off its mount, laid it across his lap, took it apart, and cleaned it with the rag he always kept in his back pocket. He got the relic back together just in time to see another Japanese Zero strafing the tarmac a hundred feet up and angling straight for him.

He put his hand on the trigger again and sighted in on the enemy fighter. He let his instincts take over, imagining he was in a duck blind back home. "I hunted ducks a lot," he said, "and I knew you had to lead them. Sometimes I would aim at the first one and the last one would fall. I know that when they're moving, you have to shoot in front." He applied the principle with the fighter plane, trying to determine the plane's speed and aiming ahead of it. He then squeezed the trigger on the Lewis, and as he would tell it later that night when the troops huddled in foxholes on the higher ground of adjoining Fort Stotsenburg, "This time she spoke beautifully."

The drum atop the gun was fully loaded with ninety-seven rounds of bullets. Intent on using every last one as fast as possible, Harold began firing. He had no tracer bullets—illuminating ammunition that shows the arc of shots—no gun sight, and no idea if the inch-long .30-caliber ammo could even stop a fighter plane. Harold's hunter instincts told him that a bullet as small as a .30—not much bigger around than his index finger—would have to hit a strategic spot to do much damage; he needed to hit this duck right between the eyes. He stayed on the enemy plane as it came at him, its guns blazing. Harold tilted on his back and kept firing as the Zero flew directly overhead. That was when he saw the flames. The plane was on fire and losing altitude as it passed his foxhole. Observers later verified that the Zero crashed in the jungle beyond the south end of Clark Field. In the face of overwhelming odds, cowed and seriously outgunned, an arms mechanic lying on his back scored what was in all likelihood the first enemy kill in the Philippines.

The circumstances that conspired to turn Pvt. Harold Poole and a World War I–era machine gun into an antiaircraft weapon underscored the frustrations that accompanied America's entrance into World War II. When the Japanese attacked the Philippines, more than nine hours had already passed since the Japanese attack at Pearl Harbor, Hawaii.

The surprise air strike at Pearl Harbor began at 7:55 AM Honolulu time, on Sunday, December 7, 1941. In the Philippines, five thousand nautical miles across the international dateline from Pearl Harbor, it was 2:55 AM on *Monday* morning, December 8.

News traveled more slowly in 1941. Neither CNN nor the Internet existed yet to report the Pearl Harbor attack as it happened. But word spread fast enough, especially at the top level. In the penthouse of the Manila Hotel, where Gen. Douglas MacArthur maintained opulent digs as commander in chief of the combined U.S.–Philippine armed forces, the general knew about the massacre at Pearl Harbor less than a half hour after it began. So, too, at the port of Cavite on the shores of Manila Bay, where Adm. Thomas Hart commanded a small U.S. Navy garrison, and at Nielson Field on the outskirts of Manila City, where Maj. Gen. Lewis Brereton commanded the U.S. Army Air Corps, the word of the Japanese attack was officially verified before three thirty in the morning.

But no alarms were sounded and no troops were awakened. Other than the commanding officers and a few radio operators who heard the broadcasts from Hawaii, no one was alerted. Private Poole and the rest of the troops at Clark Field, the islands' largest air base, remained asleep, as did those at all other battle stations in the Philippines.

Only when the men stumbled out of their bunks nearly three hours later, expecting a routine Monday, did they hear the stunning news. And though Pearl Harbor quickly became *the* topic of the morning, talk was essentially all anyone was doing: Were the reports really true? Did this mean America was now at war? Would Clark Field be next? There was little preparation made to defend against attack and none to go on the offense. The soldiers were fed breakfast and sent to their workstations. At Clark, the base was officially put on full alert, as was the case at military installations throughout the country, but as the men went through their normal routines, most of them had no idea what full alert meant.

The fifteen million citizens of the Philippine Islands, however, suspended their usual activities to wait and see what would happen next.

Much of the population in and around Manila first heard the news when radio announcer Don Bell, known to locals as the "Walter Winchell of the Philippines," shouted into his microphone just as the city was stirring: "Those dirty little bastards have struck Pearl Harbor! Reports remain sketchy, but there is no doubt. Oh, God! The yellow-bellied Japs have hit our ships at anchor!"

Schools were ordered closed and most businesses either did not open their doors or neglected to do any work as Manila and the rest of the country settled into a nervous quiet. The Japanese had already launched an attack five thousand miles to the east. Were there not more ships at anchor here that they might be interested in targeting?

Bell's use of the possessive pronoun "our" was not merely the product of excitable emotion spilling out of an American expatriate far from home. The Philippine Islands in 1941 were "home" to the United States of America every bit as much as the Hawaiian Islands. Like Hawaii at the time, the Philippines was an American territory, and it had been since 1898 when Commo. George Dewey commanded a U.S. naval fleet that sailed from Hong Kong into Manila Bay and defeated the Spanish fleet stationed there in a single afternoon. The battle was part of the short-lived Spanish-American War, which began with a dispute over Cuba, half a world and an ocean away. America was determined to defeat Spain, which by default included the colonies in its aging and far-flung empire. The Philippines, long under Spanish rule, fell along with Guam and Puerto Rico (although Cuba, ironically, did not), and when a treaty was signed in Paris later in the year, the United States gained possession of the three island nations it conquered in exchange for peace and $20 million in American greenbacks.

For more than three centuries Spain had controlled the Philippines, dating back to the day in 1521 when Ferdinand Magellan "discovered" the archipelago and named the collection "Saint Lazarus Islands." Neither the name, nor Magellan, who was killed by the locals, survived, and it remained for another conquistador, Ruy Lopez de Villalobos, to give the place the name that stuck, "Las Islas Filipinas," in honor of Prince Philip II, future king of Spain.

Spain's vision for its new and distant property was heavy on saving souls—Catholic priests and monks soon arrived by the galleon full—and light on details. Most taxation and other government-type functions were handled through Mexico, reducing the Philippines to the status of a colony ruled by another colony. The islands of Philip (who never personally set foot on any of them) were not officially counted until Spain vacated the premises entirely, and an American survey in 1939 estimated the number of islands, islets, atolls, and bare specks of land to be 7,107. Of these, about 2,700 were big enough to be named, and about 2,000 were inhabited, with 94 percent of the population located on just 11 of the islands, and the majority of that on the northernmost large island in the chain, Luzon.

America's sudden military arrival in 1898, it turned out, collided with a two-year-old native rebellion ongoing against Spain. Rather than laying down their arms as the Spaniards fled, the Filipino rebels shifted their rifle sights on the newest occupier and continued to fight for their independence, giving way to the Philippine-American war, which lasted in one form or another until 1913. It was during this period that a succession of U.S. Presidents—first William McKinley, then Theodore Roosevelt, then William Howard Taft, and finally Woodrow Wilson—sorted out an arrangement that would grant independence to the Philippines but only after the natives had time to organize a government, and an army, capable of withstanding any future would-be invaders.

After three initial years of military rule, in 1901 President McKinley sent from Washington a governor-general, William Howard Taft (the future U.S. President), to maintain sovereignty and begin the transition to local rule. By 1936, a commonwealth government was established, with a native president, congress, and constitution that local legislators patterned after the U.S. Constitution. After a ten-year breaking-in period, it was agreed that the United States would officially turn over all power. The date for Philippine Independence Day was set for July 4, 1946. Exactly 170 years after America's first Independence Day, the Philippines would be its own independent republic.

But in December of 1941, with the landmark Fourth of July four and a half years away, the Philippine Islands and the United States of America were still very much joined at the hip: Francis Sayre was the American governor-general; native Filipino Manuel Quezon had become the president of the Philippine Commonwealth in its first presidential election, held in November of 1935; and Gen. Douglas MacArthur, recently retired from the U.S. Army, served as the head of the combined American-Filipino military.

When General MacArthur was awakened with the news that Pearl Harbor had been attacked, he was reported to have exclaimed in disbelief, "Pearl Harbor! It should be our strongest point." He then asked his wife, Ann, to bring him his Bible, and he sat in his favorite chair and read verses of scripture before dressing. He then made his way through the predawn darkness the short distance to military headquarters in the old fortified section of Manila known as Intramuras. Behind thick rock walls that had been erected long before by the Spanish as a hedge, ironically enough, against invasion, MacArthur joined other military officers similarly rousted from sleep. All eyes were on him.

In 1941 MacArthur was already a figure of somewhat mythical proportions in the islands, a man who had spent much of his life returning to a place far from the privilege of his American boyhood. He had first come to the Philippines in 1903 as a twenty-two-year-old West Point graduate to serve as a construction officer under his father, Gen. Arthur MacArthur, the first commander in chief of U.S. military in the Philippines after the United States took over in 1898. Between stateside appointments and World War I duty in Europe, MacArthur returned to the islands repeatedly. In 1921 he was appointed U.S. Army commander of the district of Manila; in 1928 he followed in his father's footsteps and was named commander of all troops in the country; and in 1935, after retiring following a term as U.S. Army chief of staff in Washington, he returned yet again, as President Quezon's personal choice for chief military adviser to the Commonwealth. Quezon considered MacArthur just the man to develop a freestanding citizen army for the soon-to-be-independent country. MacArthur and the Philippines were halfway to these goals in July of 1941 when President Roosevelt, alarmed by increasing threatening actions and rhetoric of the neighboring Japanese, combined all military in the region into the United States Armed Forces of the Far East (USAFFE) and named sixty-one-year-old Douglas MacArthur commander in chief.

MacArthur's incredulity that the Japanese would attack Pearl Harbor followed him that fateful muggy morning to USAFFE headquarters offices on Victoria Street. Although he had heard news of the attack from verifiable sources, he still had a hard time grasping that it was true, chiefly because he himself had said it was not possible. Based on what he knew of Japanese military capability, he did not think Japan could possibly be ready to attack America anywhere, especially not at a place as distant and well fortified as Hawaii. The general had been quite public with his projection for a Japanese offensive in the Philippines, which was much closer to Tokyo than Pearl Harbor, to occur no earlier than the following April, if ever. Just two days earlier, in a December 6 meeting with Admiral Hart of the U.S. Asiatic Fleet and Vice Admiral Phillips of the British Royal

Navy, he had boasted of the problems the Philippines posed for Japan or any other invader: "The inability of the enemy to bring not only air but mechanized elements leaves me with a sense of complete security."

But the Japanese had attacked a U.S. military installation in Hawaii, nearly four thousand miles from Tokyo—and with enormous success, if the reports were to be believed. At five o'clock in the morning, with the light of dawn approaching, Gen. Douglas MacArthur faced one question: what did Japan's attack on Pearl Harbor mean for the Philippines, just fifteen hundred miles from Tokyo and less than five hundred miles from Japanese army and navy bases on the Japanese-owned island of Formosa?

That the Japanese were in a warring mood was no surprise. Their ongoing conflict with China, with Japan the clear aggressor, had been escalating for some time and for the past several months Japan had been increasing its military presence at strategic locations throughout the region. What made Japan's posturing all the more unsettling was who its friends were. In September of 1940 the Japanese signed an alliance with the governments of Germany and Italy, the instigators of Europe's full-scale war. The formation of this Axis put the world, especially the United States of America, on alert. Indeed, it was what conspired to bring Poole and the men of the 20th Pursuit Squadron, along with hundreds of other servicemen, to the Philippines in the first place. Japan needed to be watched, and closely.

In November of 1940, barely two months after Japan's signing of the Tripartite Pact with the Germans and Italians, the 20th Pursuit Squadron, along with the 17th Pursuit Squadron, had been transferred to Manila from its home base in Hamilton, California. The arrival of these two Army Air Corps squadrons and other military outfits signaled the start of increasing, if still somewhat limited, attention to the defense of the western Pacific.

When the stateside pursuit squadrons arrived, the U.S. Army's air presence in the Philippines consisted only of a small collection of aging B-10 bombers and P-26 fighters, planes long since rendered obsolete and dumped in the Philippines because no one else wanted them. But new men meant new planes. A shipment of fifty-seven P-35s originally intended for export to Sweden (until Nazi Germany swept through Europe) came with the 20th and 17th Squadrons, complete with Swedish crowns on their wings and dashboards. The P-35s were a start, but what MacArthur and USAFFE really wanted were the new P-40 Tomahawks.

By March of 1941, a shipment of thirty-one of these planes arrived and two months later thirty-five B-17s—the coveted Flying Fortress bombers—joined them.

The pace and intensity of the American military buildup in the Philippines, both in manpower and warplanes, picked up substantially in late July of 1941, spurred by Japan's audacity to establish air and naval bases in the French colony of Indochina, the country south of China and east of Thailand that would later become Vietnam.

On the surface, setting up the bases was a nonovert act, as Japan had dutifully walked through the diplomatic paces of first asking the French government for permission to bring Japanese men, planes, tanks, bombers, and destroyers into Indochina. But since France at that time was under German control, the puppet French government in Vichy was powerless to say anything to Tokyo but *oui*. Suddenly, Japanese fighting men and machines were in downtown Saigon, in the heart of Southeast Asia, a strategic vantage point that put them within striking range of all the capitals of the region. It was like moving a part of Tokyo twenty-five hundred miles southwest.

For the Dutch in the Dutch East Indies, for the British in Singapore, Malaya, and Hong Kong, for the Americans in the Philippines, Guam, Wake Island, and Guadalcanal, and for the native populations in China, Thailand, Borneo, India, and elsewhere in Asia, the Japanese had overnight become a neighborhood problem. Even New Zealand and Australia, located farther south, could not rest easy.

America, Holland, and Britain answered the perceived Indochina threat quickly, freezing all Japanese assets in their respective countries and embargoing the export of war materials to Japan, including steel and oil. Turning off the oil was no small sanction. Instantly, 90 percent of Japan's oil supply was cut off.

The Dutch and the British were hard-pressed to augment their economic sanctions with much in the way of military manpower. Both had more than they could handle with Hitler's Third Reich, not to mention Mussolini and the Italians. But America, not yet at war with anybody, had more military options, and responded, in addition to MacArthur's appointment as commander and the establishment of USAFFE, by increasing troop buildup. Throughout the summer and fall, more men, weapons, aircraft, and naval reinforcements were sent across the Pacific. By the beginning of December 1941, there were nearly thirty-two thousand professional military fighting men in the Philippine Islands. This number included more than nineteen thousand U.S. military and more than twelve thousand members of the Philippine Scouts. Another eighty thousand Filipinos in the part-time civilian army were in various stages of basic training.

New equipment included 108 M3 tanks and hundreds of new rifles for the Army—not nearly enough for every soldier, most of whom still carried World War I–vintage firearms, but at least a start. In addition, at Cavite the U.S. Navy had one heavy cruiser, thirteen destroyers, and seventeen submarines in its burgeoning fleet.

But by far the most impressive buildup was the rapidly developing Far East Air Force. The aging fleet was quickly becoming modernized and growing daily, with 107 P-40s and 35 B-17s joining more than a hundred older aircraft, and more planes on the way. With nearly three hundred operational warplanes—about fifty more than Pearl Harbor—the Philippines had the largest accumulation of air power outside the United States and was the strongest deterrent to war in the western Pacific.

Although America knew what it was doing to arm the Pacific, it knew little of what the Japanese were planning. The campaign known in Japan's military circles as X-day began shortly after midnight, Tokyo time, on December 8, 1941. The bombing of Pearl Harbor—the only target on the other side of the international dateline—was not the only strike. In a coordinated, simultaneous offensive that had been in the planning stages for months and had been given a definite go since December 1, the Japanese struck first in Malaya in the southeast tip of Asia at 1:40 AM, Tokyo time. Less than an hour later, Pearl Harbor was hit, followed by strikes on Thailand, Singapore, Guam, Hong Kong, and Wake Island. Before breakfast time in Tokyo, Japan had attacked a Pacific perimeter seven thousand miles in length.

But while the "Rising Sun" X-day early morning attacks went off like clockwork everywhere else, there was a problem in the Philippines.

Like every other target, the Philippines was scheduled to be hit at first light. Hundreds of heavy bombers and fighter planes belonging to the Japanese navy were to leave their bases in Formosa at four o'clock in the morning, two hours before sunrise, enabling them to arrive over their various assigned military targets on Luzon Island in the Philippines at dawn. But at three o'clock in the morning—just as Pearl Harbor was being pulverized on the other side of the ocean—a heavy fog rolled in and covered the western coast of Formosa. The Japanese were powerless to move out, their planes stuck as if riveted to the ground. Only a few bombers belonging to the Japanese army on the eastern side of Formosa, where there was no fog, were able to lift off on schedule. These were smaller and slower short-range bombers, however, capable of carrying only enough fuel to make it to the northern part of Luzon. The planes successfully dropped bombs on the city of Baguio—the Philippine summer capital—and at other minor military targets nearby just after nine o'clock in the morning before returning to base.

The hors d'oeuvres had been delivered, but the main course sat moored on the runways of the western Formosan air base of Tainin. It was more than six hours before the fog lifted, and then an accident on the runway caused further delay. It was not until 10:45 AM that the Japanese warplanes—the final component of X-day—were finally able to roar off to the south, in the direction of Clark Field. They were almost seven hours late.

The Japanese spent a nervous morning in Formosa, fully expecting American bombs to slice through the fog and shatter the silence at any moment. But the American attack never came.

There were those in the Philippines who lobbied hard for such an offensive. As early as five o'clock in the morning, an hour before sunrise, Maj. Gen. Lewis Brereton, head of the Far East Air Force, had sent word to Intramuras asking MacArthur for permission to arm the B-17s at Clark Field and attack the Japanese bases in Formosa. For nearly four hours Brereton's pilots stood on the tarmac at Clark Field waiting outside their cockpits. Finally, at nine o'clock, word came from MacArthur that the B-17s could fly to Formosa, but without bombs. They were allowed to conduct reconnaissance flights only; no shots were to be fired. MacArthur based his decision on communications received earlier from Washington specifying that, should fighting begin, Japan or Germany would be the one to "commit the first overt act." Upon hearing this explanation, Brereton, his pilots, and others begged the obvious questions: Hadn't Japan already fired thousands of first shots at Pearl Harbor? Didn't that constitute an overt act? But MacArthur held firm.

When scattered reports about the Japanese strikes in and around Baguio filtered in about the same time as MacArthur's negative response to an armed offensive, the B-17s and a majority of the P-40s at Clark Field were sent armed and airborne in search of the enemy. But Baguio was to the north and the planes searched to the south, in the direction of Manila City and Manila Bay, and to the west in the direction of the Iba airstrip on the coast. No Japanese warplanes were seen and the bombers and fighters landed back at Clark after more than two hours of patrol, parking their aircraft for refueling while the pilots joined members of the ground crew already in line for chow.

When the planes with the red dots finally arrived just after noon, the entire U.S. air fleet sat anchored to the earth, the stationary planes glittering harmlessly, like sitting ducks, in the sunlight.

If the United States military had made a proactive strike and hit the Japanese planes on the ground in Formosa, what then? If MacArthur had done something, if only to alert the men at Clark and Iba to hide their planes in the jungle and take cover, or ordered them to fly every plane in the Far East Air Force to safety in the southern islands, how different might the course of war been, not just for the Pacific but for World War II as a whole?

Why did MacArthur not act? Why was a man whose entire life was military planning and strategy incapable of action?

As the author/historian William Manchester points out in his book, *American Caesar*, Douglas MacArthur was far from the only commander to freeze up at the moment of truth:

> The key to the riddle (of inaction) is the General himself. And we shall never solve it, because, although those who were around him would recall afterward that he looked gray, ill and exhausted, we know little about his actions and nothing of his thoughts that terrible morning. He was the commanding officer, and therefore he was answerable for what happened. Assigning responsibility does not clarify the events, however. He was a gifted leader, and his failure in this emergency is bewildering. His critics have cited the catastrophe as evidence that he was flawed. They are right; he was. But he was in excellent company. Napoleon lost at Waterloo because he was catatonic that morning. Douglas S. Freeman notes that Washington was "in a daze" at the Battle of Brandywine. During the crucial engagement at White Oak Swamp, Burke Davis writes, Stonewall Jackson "sat stolidly on his log, his cap far down on his nose, eyes shut . . . the day was to be known as the low

> point in Jackson's military career, though no one was to be able to present a thorough and authentic explanation of the general's behavior during these hours." Like Bonaparte and Washington, Old Jack was unable to issue orders or even to understand the reports brought to him. That, or something like it, seems to have happened to MacArthur on December 8, 1941.

Meanwhile, as the commander in chief sat at USAFFE headquarters frozen in inaction, fifty-five miles away at Clark Field, Private Poole dove into that foxhole, fieldstripped the Lewis, and started firing.

That night in the hills above Fort Stotsenburg the shocked men of the 20th Pursuit Squadron hid in the trees and nervously took inventory. Twenty-two members of their outfit, including seven of their pilots, were dead, accounting for nearly half of the fifty-five men at Clark and more than a fourth of the eighty men who died that day in the Philippines. Many more men in the outfit were wounded, and many of the warplanes they had fussed over for a year sat in ruins. The B-17s lost 18 of 35, and 55 of 107 P-40s had been destroyed beyond repair, along with another 30–35 miscellaneous aircraft. Overall, at least a hundred warplanes were destroyed in the Philippines, and dozens more were damaged. In less than an hour, the Far East Air Force had been reduced by more than half.

Add in the day's losses at Pearl Harbor—188 destroyed planes, 3 sunk battleships, another 16 seriously damaged navy vessels, and 2,280 men dead—and it amounted to a military disaster of unprecedented proportion for the United States of America. And while Pearl Harbor's casualties were far greater, and "Remember Pearl Harbor!" would become the rallying cry America would take into its war against Japan and the Axis powers, the Other Pearl Harbor in the Philippines, obscured by the black smoke of the Hawaii attack and all but ignored back home, would prove in the long run to be far more costly and deadly. War would not return to Hawaii. Its first day there would be its last day. But in the Philippines, December 8 was just the beginning. For three and a half more years, World War II would rip apart the country and account, on both sides of the fighting, for more than two hundred thousand civilian and military deaths.

The first day was almost entirely in favor of the Japanese. There were few American triumphs. The three Clark Field P-40s that managed to get into the air accounted for five enemy hits, while on the ground, there had been at least one hit and possibly two. Private Poole's was the lone verifiable hit from a foxhole.

War had begun. There would be little time for reflection as the men of the 20th Pursuit Squadron, along with the rest of the nearly one hundred thousand fighting men defending the Philippines, hurried to regroup.

It would not be until more than three months passed and the massive combined U.S.–Filipino military force had moved into the Bataan Peninsula that the machine of war would pause long enough to recognize Private Poole for his actions on the first chaotic day of the war.

On March 15, 1942, an army clerk sitting behind a desk at a makeshift air base in a jungle clearing at the edge of Manila Bay rolled into his typewriter a blank citation granting approval for the Silver Star. What he wrote would make its way to the Pentagon in Washington for official certification. Under orders from Brig. Gen. Hal George, the clerk typed:

> *For gallantry in action at Clark Field, Fort Stotsenburg, Pampanga, Philippine Islands, on December 8, 1941. During intense ground straffing* [sic] *by enemy airplanes, Private Poole manned a machine gun position and maintained a constant fire on low-flying airplanes. One enemy airplane is known to have been destroyed by this intrepid man.*

CHAPTER THREE

December 7, 1999
Los Angeles, California

ON A TRADEMARK SMOGGY LOS ANGELES DAY, exactly fifty-eight years after the attacks on the Philippines and Pearl Harbor, Harold Poole and V. O. "Johnny" Johnson, a mate of his from the 20th Pursuit Squadron, stood on the steps of the courthouse, rocking back and forth on the balls of their feet, waiting for something to happen.

Motorists zipped by on the adjacent freeways, as oblivious to the two men as to the war the veterans once fought in. Japan and the United States had become allies, their differences long since patched up. As many Japanese cars were now on the streets as American cars, maybe more.

I had invited Harold and Johnny to LA with the intent of putting the last Pearl Harbor Day (and Clark Field Day) of the twentieth century to good use. In the three months since we had first met, the JPOW case had gained momentum, but it needed more. The idea was to file their lawsuits in a California Superior Court and then hold a press conference with both men so the public could put faces to the case.

By themselves, two old veterans would have been a tough sell in a competitive news town like LA. But I had arranged for Harold and Johnny to have company. Orrin Hatch, the United States senator from Utah who had recently announced his candidacy for the Republican presidential nomination, would join them. By appearing with Harold and Johnny, two constituents from back home, the senator's presidential campaign would receive exposure, as would our case.

But Hatch was running late. The night before, he had been involved in a nationally televised campaign debate in Arizona and was flying in on a morning flight. We thought we had allowed plenty of time for him to make it to our press conference, which was scheduled for noon. The Los Angeles traffic, however, had not been factored in. By 11:30, everyone was getting nervous. Running low on options, I turned to Harold, "Pray for the senator to show up, please. We really need him here."

Harold and Johnny had flown from Utah the day before, and we had put them up overnight at the Intercontinental Hotel. After the men got settled, we met in their room to talk about the next day's press conference. Both men had been at Clark Field the day the Japanese attacked. Both were taken captive when Bataan fell and both spent the duration of the war, nearly three and a half years, as prisoners of the Japanese, though they never saw each other while they were prisoners.

While discussing what kinds of questions they might expect from the media the next day, the conversation naturally turned to the war. I watched the years melt away as Johnny mentally and verbally opened old wounds and began to weep. "Remember the time they shot the captain?" he asked. "Remember the worms? Remember how hard it was to get a drink?" Harold nodded to these questions and many more as Johnny continued. Harold's eyes were moist too, I noticed, but he managed to keep his emotions in check.

When these soldiers talked, they did not boast or lecture or judge. They conversed with a quiet self-assurance and what was clearly a mutual understanding. It seemed that the suffering they had endured long ago had made them stronger, not weaker. They were not more cynical and less tolerant; they were just the opposite.

Eventually we left to go to the lobby. We were on one of the upper floors of the hotel, so naturally we walked toward the elevator. I avoid taking elevators whenever possible. The tight, confining space makes me anxious and nervous. But just as I was about to suggest that we walk down, I thought about what these men had endured crossing the ocean from the Philippines to Japan in the bottom of ships with no windows and almost no light. When the elevator arrived, I took a deep breath and stepped in with them.

I had first been introduced to Orrin Hatch in the mid-1970s, when he was in his first term as a United States senator and several of my classmates from Brigham Young University's Law School had gone to Washington, D.C. to work for him. Later, after I joined ATLA, the Association of Trial

Lawyers of America, I developed a personal relationship with Hatch, a former trial lawyer himself. Through the years, that relationship had grown into enough of a friendship that I felt comfortable asking for his support for the JPOW case. I knew how much the senator idolized his older brother, Jess, who was just nineteen when he was killed in a B-24 raid in Europe during World War II. A lock of Orrin's hair had turned white the day he heard his big brother died.

As the minutes ticked toward noon, all eyes turned to me. Carol Hemingway, our public relations director, did what PR people do in times of crisis. She came up with a plan B.

"You're it," she said to me.

"I'm what?" I asked.

"You're plan B. If Hatch isn't here in five minutes, you start this thing."

Just then, as if providentially, my cell phone rang. It was a Hatch staffer. The Hatch For President caravan was approaching the courthouse.

Seconds later a town car pulled up, the doors opened, and the Hatch campaign team, fresh from the previous night's TV debate, stepped out into the hazy LA sunshine. The highlight of the debate for them had come when Hatch, a four-term senator, reasoned that he had considerably more political experience than the frontrunner, George W. Bush, and suggested to Bush that he could learn the ropes by being his vice president for the next eight years. During what would prove to be an unsuccessful bid for the presidency, it was one of Hatch's finer moments, so he was caught off guard when I met him at the curb and said I was disappointed in the debate.

"I thought it went rather well," the senator said, stiffening.

"What bothered me," I said, "is that I thought you promised the vice presidency to *me*."

The senator broke into a laugh and his aides exhaled.

Wasting no time, Senator Orrin Hatch, arm in arm with Harold and Johnny, stepped to the bank of microphones. "I am here today to offer my support for Harold Poole and Johnny Johnson," he said. "They have been forced to take one last march, this time from their homes in Utah to California, in order to seek compensation for the inexcusable and illegal treatment of them as prisoners of war during World War II." The senator turned to the two veterans. "Gentlemen," he said, "you should not have to take this last march."

Looking directly into the cameras, Hatch said, "I promise to leave no stone unturned in helping to find just compensation for these brave men, for their fellow POWs, and for the estates of those who died." The senator went on to question why German companies were at that moment finalizing a schedule to compensate the forced and slave laborers they used during the war—including Jews held in captivity—and Japanese companies were not paying theirs. The soldiers not only had his full support, he said, but the support of the Senate Judiciary Committee, which he chaired. He informed the media that he had sent a letter to Secretary of State Madeleine Albright soliciting the help of the U.S. Department of State. Depending on what happened in that regard, he said he was prepared to hold senate hearings on the matter.

As for Harold Poole and Johnny Johnson, Hollywood could not have cast them better. When it was his turn to talk, Johnny teared up as if on cue, exactly as he had at the hotel when he spoke about the treatment he was forced to endure at the hands of the Japanese companies. Harold's voice was even as he spoke of the need for justice but not revenge. They were just two old vets from America's most popular war telling it like it was.

Coverage followed that evening on all of Los Angeles's major television stations, and the next morning the newspapers gave us good play. I especially liked a column written by Mike Downey of the *Los Angeles Times*:

> Two Men, Still Haunted by War, Seek Justice
>
> They came to Los Angeles in the middle of the week, Harold Poole and his old comrade in arms, V.O. "Johnny" Johnson, a couple of elderly Mormon men, in town for a day from their homes in Utah.
>
> They were stationed together with the U.S. Army Air Corps in the Philippines one terrible day in December long ago, when Japanese warplanes appeared in the sky.
>
> Bombers had already hit Hawaii. Now a second island was under attack. Thousands of scrambling allied servicemen ran for cover.
>
> Johnny Johnson was an aircraft mechanic, Harold Poole worked in munitions. In the months to come, they would be prisoners of war, brutalized and used for slave labor. They were among the nearly 20,000 put aboard transport ships with neither medical

treatment nor nourishment and taken to Japan. There they were not imprisoned but exploited by private Japanese industries under inhumane conditions.

Fifty-eight years later, they came to LA, still wishing they could forget it, but still wanting for somebody to make it right.

I left LA on a high. December 7, 1999, had certainly gone much better than December 7, 1941. Fifty-eight years later, people were not just remembering Pearl Harbor. The Other Pearl Harbor was finally getting some attention as well.

CHAPTER FOUR

Christmas Eve, 1941
Bataan Peninsula, Philippines

AS WAR BEGAN IN THE PHILIPPINES, conditions for the defenders were far from ideal. The USAFFE troops lacked weapons, barracks, informed reports about what they were doing and why they were doing it, medical supplies, mail from home, ammo, and food. Beyond that, they were surrounded by the enemy, and barely two weeks into the war they had been shoved into Bataan, a place few people, even Filipinos, knew much about.

Few of the men had even been to the Bataan Peninsula, including soldiers like Harold, who had already spent more than a year in the islands. Bataan was geographically close to Manila, easily visible to Manileños by looking westward from high points in the capital city, but it was not easy to get to, and not welcoming once you got there. Thirty miles long and twenty miles at its widest, the peninsula jutted south at the bottom of the island like the heel of a boot. It contained two of Luzon's highest mountains, Mount Natib in the north and Mount Bataan in the south, with jungles and dense rain forests bordered by rugged coastline in between. There were more monkeys than people. What little human population called Bataan home resided primarily in a string of barrios, or villages, on the eastern coastline, where the terrain leveled out at the edge of Manila Bay.

Teeming with malaria-carrying mosquitoes, poisonous snakes, jungle canopies so long and thick the sunlight never hit the ground, and high impenetrable cliffs overlooking much of the rocky coastline, Bataan was overall a foreboding place. The only way out by land was the way you came in, from the north. The sea surrounded the west, east, and south, with few safe harbors. For two thousand years, civilized man, to his credit, had mostly stayed away.

It was precisely what the army was looking for.

The troops received their orders to move out on Christmas Eve. For the sixteen days since the surprise Japanese attack they had stayed as close as possible to Clark Field and the other bases and camps in Luzon, hoping against hope for the day when they could become operational again. "We did our best," said Harold. "We'd take three or four damaged planes and make one good one." But the advantage the Japanese had seized proved formidable and hour by hour that advantage only increased. Daily, more U.S. airplanes went down, to the point that after two weeks American pilots were put under strict orders to use their planes for defensive purposes only. No more dogfights in midair. No more daylight raids. The Far East Air Force, what was left of it, could not afford any more losses.

As for the navy, it had taken its own hard lumps. With no ground or air cover for protection, most of Admiral Hart's fleet at Cavite had been wiped out by Japanese bombers, sending what was left on the run to Australia.

The only decent force left was the infantry, long on numbers—almost one hundred thousand soldiers, including nearly twenty thousand Americans and approximately eighty thousand Filipinos—but short on weapons, ammunition, and especially experience. The Philippine Scout Division, twelve thousand men strong, was as disciplined and trained as any military unit anywhere, but beyond that the native military was fledgling. Many of the Filipino soldiers were so newly conscripted that they had never fired a gun. And they could not learn now because every available bullet needed to be saved for the enemy's inevitable assault. Added to that problem was the language barrier between the Filipino trainees, who spoke only their native Tagalog or some other Filipino dialect, and their U.S. company commanders, who did not.

The first major Japanese ground offensive came on Monday, December 22, when forty-three thousand men landed on the shores at Lingayen Gulf on the northwest coast of Luzon. The Philippine Army unit MacArthur sent to resist the invasion was quickly overrun. Two days later, at Lamon Bay on the other side of the island, another seven thousand Japanese soldiers—crack troops, armed to the teeth—came ashore, again meeting little resistance. Suddenly, fifty thousand healthy, focused Japanese troops, flanked by tanks on the ground and warplanes overhead, were on the ground in the Philippines, a human vise squeezing toward Manila.

In the face of this swift and ferocious Japanese offensive, the predetermined plan of the USAFFE to make a stand and fight the enemy head-on had to be scrapped. Instead, MacArthur reverted to a defensive military strategy plotted years before by Washington called War Plan Orange 3. In the event of an all-out overt offensive against the Philippines, WPO-3, as it was known, called for a retreat of all military equipment, supplies, and manpower to the cover of the uninviting jungles west of Manila, where they would take a defensive position and hold out until help arrived.

In other words, hightail it to Bataan and keep your head down.

In addition to the natural box canyon hideout Bataan offered, there was one other key component to the strategy behind WPO-3: Corregidor Island.

Corregidor is a two-mile by four-mile block of land made up mostly of rock. The island sits at the entrance to Manila Bay some twenty-six miles southwest of Manila City and two miles off the southern coast of the Bataan Peninsula. Like a cork, the island, known as The Rock, lies in the path of anything arriving or leaving the bay.

For centuries, occupiers of the Philippines had recognized the defensive value of Corregidor's location. This included America. Since taking over occupation at the turn of the century, the United States had heavily fortified Corregidor. Huge guns with barrels as long as telephone poles and capable of firing shells a foot in diameter seventeen miles in any direction were mounted on the island's highest points. Several sturdy cement barracks, the largest nearly a half mile long, stood near the guns to house the troops who manned them. As the coup de grace, a tunnel 835 feet long, with twenty-four angling laterals, was burrowed into the solid rock during a U.S.-led construction effort that lasted from 1922 through 1932. Inside was a thousand-bed hospital and rooms for military headquarters and supplies. The Malinta Tunnel, as it was known, provided sanctuary for tens of thousands of humans from any outside attack. The bomb was yet to be built that could penetrate eighty feet of solid rock.

In the face of Corregidor's guns, the Japanese would not be able to move their warships in and out of Manila Bay, or safely fly their warplanes overhead. No matter how many men they marched into Manila, until they occupied The Rock, they could not truly occupy the Philippines.

General MacArthur, President Quezon, and the majority of the ranking military and commonwealth leaders had relocated to The Rock to set up their headquarters. The only way for the Japanese to get to the island was to go through Bataan.

Thus the stage was set for nearly two hundred thousand men (the size of Japan's army would roughly match that of the USAFFE) to fight over a godforsaken jungle nobody wanted.

Along with virtually all of the troops still in Luzon, Harold Poole and the rest of the men of the 20th Pursuit Squadron shoved out from Clark Field as darkness fell on Christmas Eve, 1941. The war cared little about Christmas, and the Japanese cared even less. The Japanese troops that had landed at Lingayen Gulf were aimed straight for Clark Field and by all reports were not dawdling. Orders to move out had been delivered that morning as the men awoke in their camouflaged campsites in the hills above Fort Stotsenburg. They were to spend the day salvaging materials and scavenging supplies from Clark Field, and at sundown, they would be off. Harold was told he would have time to return and collect his personal belongings from his campsite, but as the day grew shorter and the enemy came nearer, plans changed. When the trucks loaded up at Clark Field in the early evening they turned due south for Bataan.

"They said, 'Come on, climb in. We're going,' and that was that. I went to Bataan with nothing except the clothes on my back."

On a night with no moon, the soldiers of the 20th Pursuit Squadron joined a caravan converging on Bataan from the north, east, and west. In all, about 80,000 men were in retreat to Bataan—12,500 Americans and 67,500 Filipinos—with another 18,000 men moving onto Corregidor.

Their destination was the harbor town of Mariveles on the southern tip of the peninsula directly across from Corregidor, about fifty miles south from Clark Field. They rode along National Road in the darkness and quiet, with no lights to guide them (or the Japanese). They stopped rarely and then only briefly, clinging to the cover of darkness. But there was one bright spot that Harold, for one, would never forget. As the caravan rounded a corner near the end of its journey, a tree to the side of the road was lit up with what appeared to be Christmas lights. Only on closer inspection did the men realize they were looking at hundreds if not thousands of fireflies, their welcoming committee to Bataan.

"I had never seen so many fireflies in one place. That tree gave us faith and hope for the future."

Faith and hope would prove to be important commodities in a place where there was little else to pass around. War Plan Orange-3 called for enough supplies—food, medicine, clothing, fuel, and ammunition—to be cached ahead of the retreat to sustain a six-month siege. Recognizing the need to be self-sustaining in a place of such limited resources was an essential part of the plan. The very virtues that made Bataan an ideal place for a siege made it a supply sergeant's nightmare.

But in the Army's haste to leave the Luzon mainland, the trucks were loaded mostly with men, not supplies. Abandoning Harold Poole's personal items—including his eyeglasses, extra clothes, letters from home, and his father's pocket watch, which was a prized family keepsake—paled alongside what else was left behind. Vast stockpiles of rice and other food rations and medical supplies were ignored. The quartermasters had hauled in what they could as fast as they could. But the suddenness of the Japanese assault, the quick change in strategy from offense to defense, the narrow roads that congested quickly, the lack of trucks and manpower to move the supplies, and poor planning throughout left enough rice and C-rations to feed an army—not only at Fort Stotsenburg, but at numerous other sites in and around Manila and southern Luzon.

To add to the problem, almost double the number of troops anticipated by WPO-3 arrived on the peninsula, along with some twenty thousand unexpected refugees, who followed them there. By Christmas Day, more than a hundred thousand people had arrived on Bataan, and even though they were mere miles from Clark Field and Fort Stotsenburg, they might as well have moved to the moon. They could not go back if they wanted. They had blown up the bridges behind them.

As they set up their camps and bases, the soldiers quickly sized up their situation. They had no mail call, no telephones, no radio contact with the outside world, and no days off. They slept on the ground, showered in cold water, and on January 2, after they had been in Bataan barely a week, MacArthur ordered rations cut in half. Fighting men used to nearly four thousand calories a day would have to get by on less than two thousand calories.

It would not last long, they were told. The reduction was merely a precaution to make sure they had enough rations until reinforcements and supplies arrived. "The prearranged plan was to hold on until the Pacific Fleet could come and relieve us," said Harold. "We were assured that ships and planes were coming to help."

Harold's outfit got started right away clearing flat land near the bay in Mariveles for an airstrip to park their remaining P-40s. Following orders, they dutifully built revetments exactly 105 feet wide to accommodate the wingspan of the B-17s they were promised were on the way.

Meanwhile, the enemy kept pressing onward. On January 9, the Japanese infantry made their first assault on Bataan, attacking the ground around the eastern coastline. The next day they attacked the west coast. They already had Manila. Bataan and Corregidor were all that were left.

From his headquarters on Corregidor, MacArthur urged the men on Bataan to stay strong. The strategy was not to win the Philippines, he said, it was not to lose the Philippines. On January 10, the day after the first Japanese attack, MacArthur made his one and only visit to Bataan. Five days later, he sent this communique from Corregidor, which was distributed among all the troops:

> Help is on the way; thousands of troops and hundreds of planes are being dispatched. The exact time of arrival of reinforcements is unknown as they will have to fight their way through Japanese attempts against them. It is imperative that our troops hold until these reinforcements arrive. No further retreat is possible. We have more troops in Bataan than the Japanese have thrown against us; our supplies are ample; a determined defense will defeat the enemy's attack. It is a question now of courage and determination. Men who run will merely be destroyed, but men who fight will save themselves and their country. I call upon every soldier in Bataan to fight in his assigned position, resisting every attack. This is the only road to salvation. If we fight, we will win; if we retreat, we shall be destroyed.

But day after long day the promised ships, planes, and men did not arrive, the Japanese kept advancing the fight, and MacArthur—whom the men began to refer to as "Dugout Doug" for his avoidance of the front lines—did not return to Bataan. The general stayed on Corregidor, where the troops were still on full rations, and had his personal press attaché send press releases to newspapers in the States. Hundreds of these reports made their way to America, an average of more than one a day the entire time MacArthur was on Corregidor. Each one was a variation on a theme that characterized MacArthur as a one-man defender of truth, making America's heroic stand on a lonely tropical island far away. To the folks back home, MacArthur himself was standing up to the Japanese, staring them down on Bataan.

The world bought what MacArthur was selling. Diplomats and dignitaries, among them the King of England, sent telegrams and letters of support, praising the courage of MacArthur and his fearless defense of Bataan. Military leaders in Europe and other battlefields of World War II joined in with their congratulations and encouragement. Editorial writers in newspapers back home sang the commander's praises and brought up the possibility of MacArthur running for president in 1944.

Meanwhile, on the real Bataan, the fighting men of the Philippines were living on rice and rumors, and running low on both.

Assessing their collective plight, a United Press International war correspondent-turned-poet named Frank Hewlett sat down one day in a jungle clearing and wrote a verse about the situation that rang so true to the men that it became their anthem:

Oh, we are the battling bastards of Bataan,
No mother, no father, no Uncle Sam
No aunts, no uncles, no nephews, no nieces,
No ammunition nor artillery pieces,
And nobody gives a damn!

Among these battling bastards was twenty-three-year-old Harold Poole, whose parents sang in the Mormon Tabernacle Choir and whose five sisters dutifully kept writing letters to their brother that never got delivered.

He was the family's only boy. Katherine and Margaret were older than he, and Vivian, Afton, and Ethel Marjean ("Patsy") were younger. The entire family had seen Harold off at the Union Pacific train station after he joined up at the end of the summer of 1940.

They would miss him madly, his sisters told him, but they would not miss his lizards and snakes, which he had a habit of bringing to his room when he returned from his regular excursions into the foothills and canyons above their home. Harold liked to stuff the snakes after he killed them, and thus began his lifelong interest in taxidermy.

When he went off to the army his sisters were sure their mother, who shared their dislike of snakes and other wild creatures, would do some quick housecleaning and get rid of the dried snakes Harold used as room décor. But with her son in the thick of a world war halfway around the world, Nina Poole felt the need to leave his room exactly as he had left it.

The Pooles lived in a framed wood house in the avenues section of Salt Lake City, three blocks from the Mormon temple and the heart of downtown. Another half-dozen blocks in the opposite direction was the solitude of City Creek Canyon and beyond that the expanse of the Wasatch Range of the Rocky Mountains, where Harold spent a good share of his growing-up years.

A midwife delivered Harold in a farmhouse in 1918, five days before Christmas, in the town of Woods Cross, next door to Salt Lake City. His father was so elated at finally getting a son that he ran toward his in-laws' house on the other side of the orchard, shouting, "I've got a boy! I've got a boy!" Then, as Harold would say, "He filled the house full of girls trying to get another one."

Stanley Scottern Poole, Harold's father, was born in Nottingham, England, and emigrated to the United States in 1912, accompanying the Mormon missionary, Hugh Wood, who assisted in his conversion to Mormonism. English converts and immigrants were the norm at the turn of the century in Salt Lake City, and hundreds of them arrived each year.

Hugh introduced Stanley to his sister, Penninah, whom everyone called "Nina" and whom Hugh had bragged about incessantly on the trip across the Atlantic. At first Nina Wood was not taken by the stiff-mannered Englishman and wanted nothing to do with him. But the romance eventually warmed and, as Harold put it, "He said wilt thou and she wilted."

Everyone who knew Harold and his parents agreed the son was a combination of Stanley and Nina—except for the musical part. Whereas both parents were thirty-year regulars in the Mormon Tabernacle Choir, Harold either could not or would not carry a tune.

From Stanley, an accountant by trade but an avid sportsman who exchanged soccer and rowing for tennis and handball when he got to the States, came an active, healthy lifestyle and also a good dose of discipline.

Stanley's family had a tradition that children at mealtimes ate everything on their plate. If they failed to do so, nothing was said, but when the next mealtime arrived, the unfinished portion would still be there.

From Nina, Harold got what he called his get-along genes. His mother "never wanted to stir up the mud in the pond" and Harold was similar: an easygoing boy who turned into an easygoing man. No one could remember Penninah Poole ever having an enemy. She was a peacemaker, and so, unless you happened to be a snake or some other varmint, was her son.

Their religion was central to the Pooles. Stanley was as staunch as new converts get and Nina's Latter-day Saints roots stretched virtually to the Church's very beginnings, when a group of believers that included Harold's maternal great grandfather left Illinois in 1847 on a thirteen-hundred–mile pioneer trek that would end with the settling of Mormon headquarters in Salt Lake City. Living in the shadow of that headquarters, the Pooles prayed every day, morning, and night; read their scriptures in the Bible and the Book of Mormon; paid a 10 percent tithe to the Church; and when things got rough, tended to turn things over to the Lord. During Harold's formative years, which coincided with the Great Depression, they turned a lot of things over to the Lord, and things seemed to turn out just fine.

Mormonism, and hence the Pooles, adopted a no-nonsense look at life that demanded steering clear of, among a myriad of other things, drinking, smoking, and out-of-marriage sex. Mormonism also encouraged turning the other cheek and forgiving others their trespasses, two tenets that would be helpful for Harold in a wartime experience that would stretch both to their limits.

Harold was twenty years old, owned a 1932 Chevrolet, and had a steady job as a dynamite maker at the Hercules Powder Company when Germany invaded Poland in September of 1939. Adolf Hitler's Third Reich had not stopped there. The spring and summer of 1940 was busy and bloody in Europe. The shots heard 'round the world were fired on May 10 when Hitler's troops simultaneously attacked Holland, Belgium, Luxembourg, and France. Holland lasted five days, and the rest not much longer. With faster tanks, more troops, swifter submarines, and a new breed of airplane called Messerschmitts, Germany was changing the face of modern warfare.

At the end of June, with German swastikas flying from flagpoles in Paris and British troops making their escape from France across the English Channel at Dunkirk, British Prime Minister Winston Churchill declared from the House of Commons, "We shall fight on the beaches, we shall fight on the landing grounds, we shall fight in the fields and in the streets, we shall fight in the hills; we shall never surrender . . ."

Half a world away Harold Poole, along with millions of other young American men, started thinking seriously about when the United States of America would have to fight.

America was not yet officially at war with anyone, but Americans were paying close attention. Every day millions of immigrants not long removed from Poland, Czechoslovakia, Norway, Finland, Denmark, Holland, France, and other countries that had recently fallen under German rule watched with increasing horror at what was going on "back home."

The crusade of the America First movement to keep the United States out of "Europe's fight" was losing steam with the passing of every battlefield life and every trampled border. Hitler was only getting stronger, allying first with Mussolini and the Italians and then, at the close of September, with Emperor Hirohito and the Japanese. The members of the Axis powers made no secret of their common goal: to rule the world. As summer turned toward fall in 1940, it appeared they just might.

In the White House, Roosevelt was giving as much aid as possible to the British without officially entering the war. There was already a draft in America for anyone twenty-one and over, and all able-bodied young men were inhaling, waiting for the draft board to call, twenty-one-year-old Harold Poole among them.

He decided to make it his decision, not theirs. He wanted to serve his country and he would rather join than be drafted. That way he could choose the branch of service and type of training he preferred, and he preferred the air force.

It was not officially the air force back then. Barely thirteen years from Lindbergh's solo flight across the Atlantic and only thirty-seven years since the Wright brothers became the first humans to fly, the airplane was still very much a work in progress. There was no separate distinction yet for airplanes in America's armed forces. Most of the military flying came under the auspices of the United States Army, known officially as the United States Army Air Corps, and it was that subbranch of the service that Harold Poole signed onto of his own free will on August 30, 1940.

Harold fancied airplanes, so the Air Corps was an easy choice. He had already taken a few flying lessons, although at $5 a lesson the instruction had not lasted long during the Depression. This was a way to be around airplanes, maybe even occasionally get to fly one.

And if he couldn't fly the planes, he could arm them. He told the U.S. Army he wanted to be an armament man in the Air Corps, and he was told that was exactly what he would be. He was assigned to the 20th Pursuit Squadron in the United States Army Air Corps, 24th Pursuit Group, and told to report immediately to Hamilton Field, California.

"I'm going to California," Harold told his mother. "I'll probably sit at a desk the whole time."

Sixteen months later, as he sat in the jungles of Bataan, the one consolation for Harold was that he had at least been right about the war. America's entry had been imminent, just as he had predicted. If he had not volunteered he would have been drafted, as sure as the Philippine sun was hot.

He tried to blot out the fact that getting drafted might not have landed him in this no-man's-land on the other side of the world. As a draftee, he might well be riding a desk at some stateside base.

He also tried not to dwell on what he had told his family at the railroad station the day he left Salt Lake City for California. "Don't worry," he had said. "This is September. I'll get a furlough and come see you at Christmas."

At least he had not specified the year.

Bataan meant safety—for now—but it was a maddening way to fight a war. The Japanese had most of the ground and with it most of the advantage, especially now that the Americans posed no real air threat. The U.S. fighter planes that managed to survive the month of December—a grand total of seven—had to be hidden in the jungle all day, only to be taken out for quick strikes, usually at night. What was left of the heavy bombers had already flown to Australia.

Harold stayed in close proximity to the fighter planes. Shortly after the troops had settled into Bataan, he was promoted to the rank of corporal and ordered to leave his squadron at Mariveles and join the staff of Gen. Hal George, commander of what was left of the Far East Air Force. The general's headquarters was at Bataan Field, an airstrip located at the edge of Manila Bay about fifteen miles northeast of Mariveles. The airstrip became a favorite target for Japanese warplanes making their way to and from Corregidor and was constantly under attack. General George did not want men who would cut and run at the first sign of trouble. "I want that man who shot down the Zero," he had said to the 20th Pursuit Squadron commander.

Keeping the seven surviving P-40s in working order was an around-the-clock job, which gave Harold plenty of waking time to think about food and getting shot. There was little opportunity for the former and plenty for the latter. "Every time the Japs were returning from bombing Corregidor, they would unload any bombs they had left. They hit us at least once and sometimes two and three times a day, which we began to get used to," said Harold.

If the troops on Bataan weren't going anywhere, they still were not easy to hit. As WPO-3 theorized, taking Bataan was not easy. Anxious to secure the Philippines and move on, the Japanese turned to psychological tactics to try to speed up the process. Along with thousands of bombs, tens of thousands of leaflets were dropped over the peninsula. One showed a photo of a beautiful woman with "Don't Wait to Die" printed across the top of the page and a poem:

> Before the terror comes, let me walk beside you in a garden deep
> in petaled sleep . . . Let me, while there is still a time and place.
> Feel soft against me and rest . . .
> rest your warm hand on my breast . . .

Another was covered with a picture of food and drink and a caption below that simply read: "What Are You Fighting For?"

The men could handle the beautiful woman, but the pictures of the food hit below the belt.

Day after day of half rations had a sustained, debilitating effect. It got to the point that eating, or searching for something to eat, became the men's only real pastime. No effort was too great if it offered the prospect of food, as the men of the squadron demonstrated one hot February afternoon when they dragged a damaged navy boat-plane out of the bay, hid it in the jungle, and repaired it with an urgency in inverse proportion to everyone's lack of energy.

"It had cargo space in it, so we worked on it day and night and then some of our pilots flew it down to one of the southern islands that had not yet been invaded and brought back medicine, food, and candy. It made several trips and became known as the Candy Clipper."

It was impossible to overvalue food. Money meant nothing, food meant everything. By late February, American candy bars were selling for $30 apiece, cigarettes for as high as $200 a pack, a healthy carabao went for as much as $2,000 cash. All the while supplies, weight, health, and morale steadily declined. The army was officially out of quinine, the antidote for malaria, which Bataan's mosquitoes carried in abundance, and other medical supplies were just as nonexistent. The field hospitals were overflowing with more than twenty thousand patients, both Filipino and American, the majority suffering from malaria or fatigue, and often both.

It only got worse. On March 2, MacArthur cut the food rations again, to three-eighths of a full ration. Soldiers in the heat of battle were now getting barely more than a thousand calories a day. Later in the month rations would be cut in half yet again. Meals were down to two a day, each consisting of rice, a slice of bread, and a small piece of fish. The situation was desperate. Men who had never fished in their lives threw nets or bare hooks into Manila Bay. They carved up cavalry horses that died on their feet. Some might have been nudged to their demise—in the end, all 250 U.S. cavalry horses were eaten, along with the entire military inventory of 48 mules. They boiled iguana, lizards, monkeys, wild pigs, pythons, and bugs that were big enough to eat, and scoured the jungle for mangos, papayas, coconuts, and bananas.

Every time an enemy plane flew over spraying bullets, the men crawled out as soon as it had passed and scoured the countryside with the hope that a carabao had been killed.

"A lot of the guys got dysentery because they were eating anything they could find," said Harold. "One time a bomb hit our camp and killed a horse. That was a nice, tasty dish."

Morale deteriorated, and then began to disappear entirely. Many soldiers feared that no reinforcements were on the way, and no food either.

The nadir arrived on a dark night in mid-March. The Far East Air Force was down to two planes and Bataan Field, for the most part, had gone out of business. Harold had been sent back to his outfit at the tip of Bataan in Mariveles, directly across from Corregidor Island. He was with the enlisted men when word spread through the camp that General George, their leader, was down at the water.

All eyes were on the Mariveles dock as the sun disappeared over the far side of Manila Bay and blackness covered the sea. That is when, from Corregidor, came the distinctive sound of a PT boat. When it arrived the boat was quickly secured as General George, two other generals, and a colonel stepped in. Each officer was carrying a small bag containing his personal possessions. The officers were leaving Bataan and the Philippines altogether. Another eleven officers, including MacArthur, were waiting at Corregidor, where four PT boats would escort them, under disguise of night, toward the southern island of Mindanao. From there the officers, along with several of their clerks, a doctor, and MacArthur's wife and young son, would be airlifted to an air base near Darwin, Australia.

Their orders had come directly from Washington. President Roosevelt wanted the high-ranking officers in the Philippines to flee to Australia, where they could organize a counteroffensive for the Pacific.

From the incline above the harbor, hundreds of rail-thin soldiers watched as the PT boat pulled away from the dock, taking General George and the others quickly from their sight. No one spoke. No one could think of anything to say.

"I'll tell you, that leaves you with a real empty feeling in your stomach," Harold told me as he recalled the incident. "Watching your leaders leave, and you're still there, standing on the shore as they disappear."

A week later, MacArthur was safely in Australia, where he stopped at a railroad station in Adelaide to address the press. It was there, on March 20, that he delivered his "I shall return" promise. It would become one of the most famous and oft-quoted phrases of the war, ranking up there with Churchill's speeches. And MacArthur would indeed return to the Philippines, thirty-one months later, armed with two hundred thousand troops. But that would be much too late for the troops he left behind.

They were hot, tired, hungry, deserted, and ready to be finished off. But for some inexplicable reason the U.S. forces on Bataan could not fathom, the Japanese had not mounted a serious offensive since mid-February. They had kept up the air harassment and tank volleys, and their propaganda leaflets kept falling from the sky, but the Japanese front line stayed immobile.

The truth was, Bataan had taken its toll on the Japanese as well. Even at full rations, the conditions were brutal. Thousands of Japanese Imperial Army troops had contracted malaria and other jungle diseases and were sent to hospitals back in Japan. Awaiting much-needed reinforcements, replacements, and quinine, the Japanese rested while the American defenders only got hungrier and weaker.

During this lull Harold got one more shot at a Japanese fighter plane. He was back in Mariveles when a gunnery crew asked him to watch their machine gun while they looked for food. While they were away, two enemy dive-bombers appeared, sighting in on a dry dock in the bay. Harold put his sights on the first plane. Unlike the first day of the war, this time he had control of a serious machine gun, a .50-caliber marine water-cooled unit with bullets six times as long and fifty times as powerful as the old .30-caliber Lewis at Clark Field. When Harold squeezed the trigger, the gun worked—another difference. Every fifth bullet was a colored tracer, enabling him to see the trajectory and direction of his shots, so he was able to watch as he scored a direct hit on the enemy plane. Seconds later it plunged into the bay, shot by several other .50s as well.

"I could see my tracers going into it before it crashed," said Harold. "The gun crew was quite perturbed when they returned and found they had missed all the action."

But such occasions of triumph were few and far between, as March neared its end and ushered in the beginning of the brutally hot Philippine summer, when temperatures and humidity regularly rise into the high nineties.

Impatient to take the Philippines and free its army for assignment to other fronts, Tokyo ordered an all-out offensive on Good Friday, April 3, which also happened to be a major holiday in Japan: the anniversary of the birth of Emperor Jimmu, the first ruler to sit on the imperial throne. With twenty-two thousand fresh troops in place, and Japan's Bataan veterans revived after nearly a six-week rest, the Japanese assaulted the American frontline trenches dug into Mount Samat. In preparation for the attack, the Japanese had laid out a square mile of field pieces, with 150 cannons spaced thirty yards apart. When the cannons started firing, overhead bombers flew 150 sorties.

Fighting was fierce, heavy, and completely one-sided. By Easter morning, a blood-soaked Mount Samat was in Japanese hands.

The Japanese continued to surge and squeeze, forging southward toward Mount Bataan and the hills above Mariveles. The ultimate target of Corregidor was now within range. On the Monday after Easter, the U.S.-Filipino force found itself mashed into a triangle no more than ten miles on all sides. Seventy thousand men, so close they could hear each other's anxious breathing. It was a massacre in the making.

Under these circumstances—almost out of food and trapped in a small area, with maybe one soldier in twenty physically able to put up anything approaching a decent fight—Maj. Gen. Edward P. King Jr., the superior American officer remaining on the peninsula, called his staff officers together on the night of April 8. After discussing the few remaining rations, the mounting butchery of American troops at the increasingly lopsided front lines—where the wounded were being bludgeoned and hacked to death instead of being spared and taken prisoner—King made the decision to surrender all forces under his command. To continue any longer would be tantamount to suicide.

Corregidor, under the command of Gen. Jonathan Wainwright, could hold on for as long as possible. That was Wainwright's call to make. But as far as General King was concerned, Bataan was through. On Wednesday night, April 8, despite General MacArthur's insistence—relayed from Australia—that the troops on Bataan fight to the death, and in contradiction of Wainwright's command from Corregidor that surrender was out of the question, King made the decision to formally surrender the next morning. It meant that, in a quirk of history, Bataan and some 70,000 U.S.-Filipino troops on it would surrender to the Japanese on the same date Confederate Gen. Robert E. Lee surrendered 26,765 troops to Union Gen. Ulysses S. Grant. That surrender, tendered on April 9, 1865, at Appomattox, South Carolina, effectively ended the U.S. Civil War.

As if to emphasize the beginning of the end, an earthquake and several after-shocks rippled through the Bataan Peninsula late that night. With the country in chaos and the government in exile, the precise magnitude of the quake and the exact time of its occurrence were not officially recorded, but many soldiers who felt the earth heave regarded it as a sign—of what, they were not sure. After the earthquake, a heavy rain fell until dawn.

General King resolutely left his headquarters at nine the next morning and was driven north to rendezvous with the Japanese commanders in a farmhouse near the town of Lamao. As with most everything else during the siege of Bataan, the planned logistics of the American surrender broke down. The officers dispatched by General King got lost and then, when they eventually made contact with the Japanese leaders, they were refused their request for a meeting with Gen. Masarahu Homma, commanding officer of the Imperial Army. Instead, a meeting was arranged with Maj. Gen. Kameichiro Nagano, who thought he would be meeting with Wainwright and that both Bataan and Corregidor would be surrendered.

When King finally arrived at the farmhouse a little after noon and informed Nagano and Col. Motoo Nakayama, that not only was he not General Wainwright, but also that he could surrender only Bataan, the Japanese officers became outraged. A surrender without Corregidor was no surrender at all. It ended nothing. For a time the officers sat there, a heavy stillness in the air as the fate of Bataan, and the men on it, hung in the balance. Finally, without formally accepting a surrender but accepting the troops on Bataan, Colonel Nakayama asked General King for his sword. King did not have a sword, he informed Nakayama, but he would give him his pistol.

As he placed the pistol on the desk in front of him, the largest number of troops in United States military history was surrendered.

Bataan had lasted ninety days.

CHAPTER FIVE

January 1, 2000
Palm Desert, California

THE NEW MILLENNIUM ARRIVED ON TIME and without any attendant destruction. The world did not end. Life did not cease to exist. The courthouse did not collapse, which was a good thing, because we had a major lawsuit to prepare and win.

In twenty-four years doing PI work, I thought I had seen it all. Whiplash cases, paralysis cases, dog bite cases, wrongful death suits, you name it, I had seen it or been involved in it. I had personally handled over one thousand cases, almost one per week the course of my entire career, with twenty-eight of those going to jury trial.

But I had never represented prisoners of war, I had never joined forces with a national mega-firm, and I had never had clients impact me quite like these men.

"I have a sense that everything I've done in my career has been to prepare me for what I'm doing now," I told Sue on the first day of the new century. "I don't mean to be overly dramatic, but that's how I feel."

To which Sue responded, "You are being overly dramatic."

Although I was not born until four years after the war was over, it came natural for me to connect with the men who fought World War II. I suppose that stems from my father, Richard P. Parkinson, who missed the start of the World War II but not the finish. He was in the Philippines when the Japanese were expelled and was part of the peacekeeping force during the occupation of Japan after VJ-day in 1945.

When his tour in Japan was over, Lieutenant Parkinson returned to the States, took his leave of the military, and married my mother, the former Marilyn White. They first lived in Idaho, where my oldest brother, Richard, was born. Then they moved to New Orleans, where Dad enrolled at Tulane Medical School and where I was born, on October 29, 1949. My brother Brett came along five years later and my brother David, eight years after that. Rick became a dermatologist, Brett a radiologist, David a mortician, and I became the family barrister. The Parkinson brothers can heal 'em, patch 'em, defend 'em, and bury 'em.

When I was seven, we moved to Indio, California, at the time a small desert town about ten miles and a million tumbleweeds east of the traffic signal in Palm Springs, the only stoplight in the Coachella Valley in 1957. Richard Parkinson, MD, set up a general practice that, like the rest of the area, would grow and flourish.

I was close to my father growing up, or at least as close as it was possible to get to a man who took house calls, cared for the local prison inmates, trained and competed in triathlons (ten times an Ironman in Hawaii), trekked the Himalayas, met Mother Theresa in India, ran the Bío-Bío River in Chile, and never seemed to have enough hours in the day to do everything he wanted. Growing up, I idolized my dad, and I suppose I inherited my drive from him, although I've always preferred hiking the trails in the mountains surrounding the Coachella Valley to trekking the Himalayas.

The Los Angeles Dodgers and I moved to California simultaneously. As a boy, I would lie in bed at night and listen on my transistor radio to Vin Scully broadcast their games. The power of Scully's *just right* delivery had a profound effect on me, and his broadcasts ignited a love affair with the spoken word that has never left me.

Another early love of mine was golf, a game that changed the landscape and popularity of the Coachella Valley. We lived across the street from the local golf pro, who taught my brother Rick and me the fundamentals when we were young. I practiced from sunup to sundown and became a very good golfer by the time I got to Indio High School, but even so, I missed making the varsity golf team my sophomore year by one stroke. That team turned out to be the strongest in the league, but the impact and disappointment of that early setback was profound, and, from a competitive standpoint, I tended never to take anything for granted again.

For the most part high school was very, very good to me. I was a starter on the basketball team, and appointed to the California Scholarship Federation. The Indio High yearbook of 1967 voted me "Most Likely to Succeed" and also anointed me "King of the B.S.," due to the well-attended bull sessions I led under the palm trees during lunch.

Sue and I met when we were both undergraduates at BYU, which I attended after spending two years in Argentina on a Mormon mission. We were married before I started law school, and by the time Brigham Young granted me my Juris Doctor degree, one daughter, Krista, and a son, Brett, had already been born. We left Utah in 1976 and moved to Indio, where I got my first job as a lawyer with a small PI firm. I won my first jury trial—an intersection accident—getting a $12,500 award for my client. The firm got a third of that. It was a way to make a living.

But in truth it was always more than that. Lawyering became my identity. I thrived in the profession, where talking was the name of the game and hustling was rewarded more than class rank or test scores. Like my father, I never stood still, and never seemed to have enough time for everything I wanted to do. I was never satisfied. I was constantly trying to get a bigger edge and a bigger practice. To improve my courtroom delivery, I studied with a retired high school drama teacher, Rod Basehore. I read book after book on how to speak persuasively. I became a student of the tactics of legendary plaintiffs' attorneys. To expand my list of contacts, I joined various legal groups, including the state and national trial lawyers' associations. I advertised my services on television.

I was good at what I did, I enjoyed doing it, and I felt what I did made a difference. Monetary payments to compensate for pain and suffering make society a better place. It might not be a perfect system, but life is not perfect, either. To skeptics, I like to quote Oliver Wendell Holmes, who said, "All liability law is revenge or vengeance. We've just now worked our way into giving compensation as opposed to doing some kind of harm."

The injured of the Coachella Valley beat a steady path to my door. White, black, Hispanic, young, old, rich, poor, male, female—anybody with a grievance. I listened to all their stories, but I was careful which ones I accepted as cases. "Your success isn't defined by the cases you win, it's defined by the cases you reject," became my personal PI credo.

I did not become filthy rich, but I became rich enough. We moved out of Indio and bought a house with a pool on the fairway behind the gate in

Bermuda Dunes. Sue did not have to work outside the home and was free to raise the kids. We joined the country club next door.

In so many ways, life was rewarding in the California desert. I trotted out my professional resume with pride, and as the TV ads clearly showed, without compunction. The only problem was the constant yearning for more and the imbalance it created. I tended to be so absorbed by the next quest that I rarely stopped to appreciate or enjoy where I was or what I might have accomplished. My children grew up without enough of me being in their lives.

The JPOW case helped me see my imbalance. The general perspective of the World War II veterans that all life is good and every day is important was infectious.

Beyond that I found the legal challenges invigorating. I had managed to become part of a case that was igniting a significant legal debate with worldwide implications. If wartime abuses could be heard in peacetime courts of law, the ramifications could be huge, opening a vast new legal frontier.

The debate's origins could be traced to the California Statehouse in Sacramento, where California Senate Bill 1245 was introduced by Senator Tom Hayden in the summer of 1999. SB 1245 made it legally possible for victims of slave labor abuses during World War II to file suit in a California court against a company alleged to have committed the slave labor abuse as long as said company conducted business in the state of California. The bill superseded any prior statutes of limitations against such actions and extended the filing period deadline to December 31, 2010.

The bill's specific intent was to allow civilian victims of the German Holocaust to collect damages from those companies that profited from their forced or slave labor during the war. But the bill's language covered *all* wartime slaves, not just those used by the Nazis, and not just civilians. That opened the door to anyone used as a slave laborer by the Japanese companies as well.

The Tom Hayden of Senate Bill 1245 was *that* Tom Hayden, former husband of Jane Fonda, who, like the actress, was a well-known antiwar activist of the 1960s and 1970s. To add irony to that irony, it was Bill Clinton, another well-known antiwar activist from that time, who helped pave the way for Hayden's bill. The passage of the Nazi War Crimes Disclosure Act of 1998 during the Clinton presidency established a presidential commission that succeeded in declassifying all intelligence records on World War II crimes. Besides the German records, the CIA and other intelligence organizations also turned over dossiers about Japanese war criminals and crimes. The objective was to uncover any mistreatment and atrocities, no matter where they occurred, that may have been overlooked during the Cold War.

Besides jump-starting the filing of lawsuits in U.S. federal courts against Nazi-era companies doing business in the United States, President Clinton's Disclosure Act opened the eyes of a number of state legislatures that recognized the need for laws that would allow such lawsuits—against all wartime violators—to also proceed in state courts wherever the targeted multinational companies did business.

It was amid this atmosphere that three essentially similar lawsuit-friendly bills aimed specifically at Japanese companies were introduced in the late 1990s in the state legislatures of Rhode Island, West Virginia, and Nebraska. Amid intense adverse lobbying by business groups, including Japanese lobbyists, however, the bills died.

Only in California did a wartime reparations bill that targeted the Japanese, at least obliquely, manage to survive. It was the California legislature that opened the door; it would be up to the California courts to decide if that door would remain open.

As I educated our clients about the legal possibilities, they educated me about their part in the war that had brought us together. In many ways, World War II was a lifetime ago, in others it was still as fresh as yesterday—and, I soon realized, would clearly never be over.

I remember, for instance, my shock the first time I heard Harold Poole refer to the Japanese as "Japs" and "Nips." The rest of the former JPOWs spoke the same way. The Japs this, the Nips that. It sounded crude and ill-mannered. But over time it became obvious to me that the former prisoners of the Japanese used such terminology in a war context. When speaking of the current-day Japanese, most of them did not say "Jap." They did not say, "I bought a Jap TV."

Their use of the term was in reference to the war and the people who tried to kill them, and the people they tried to kill. I remembered reading in Erich Maria Remarque's World War I epic *All Quiet on the Western Front* that the only way to effectively get one human being to kill another is to make sure that the human being who is going to do the killing does not think of the other person as a human being but as something rather less than that; as an idea, an abstraction. The enemy is reduced to a Kraut, a Commie, a Nip, a Yank. *Then* he can be shot or stabbed. It seemed to me that was what the World War II veterans were doing, even sixty years later.

The men had extraordinarily clear memories of the war. Six decades seemed to have made nary a dent in their recall. It was especially uncanny how vivid their details were of their captivity.

What did vary were their reasons for wanting to join the lawsuit. Some, although not all, wanted, more than anything, some form of vengeance for the pain and suffering they had been forced to endure and, in many cases, continued to endure. They had seen and experienced so much cruelty. They had watched their best friends die in front of their eyes, and they had personally been tortured and abused almost beyond belief. Moving beyond any of it was clearly not easy.

One veteran I signed on as a plaintiff to the lawsuit explained to me in great detail how his violent war-related nightmares made it impossible for him to sleep in the same room with his wife. When the nightmares came he would flail away in his sleep, still fighting the enemy a half century later. For her own safety, he had had his wife start sleeping in another room.

I asked this man one day as we were visiting in my office what he was hoping for as a settlement. "Kill 'em all," he said. "That's the only settlement that will satisfy me. Line up all the sons of bitches, and kill 'em all."

Hatred ate at the man, who otherwise seemed considerate and respectful. He threw a net over anything remotely related to the war and condemned all of it. He would not ride in Japanese cars, he would not eat in "Chink" restaurants, and all Asians were still the enemy. He told me that when he had visited Hawaii, where Japanese tourists are ubiquitous, that he had refused to visit the Pearl Harbor Memorial. He said, "If I saw one of those bastards, I'd toss him in." He could not even think of forgiving the "Japs" because it would be a "betrayal" to the dead comrades he left behind.

That was the far end of the spectrum, however, and over time I came to realize what most of the men really wanted were two things: acknowledgment and consideration, even after all these years. For a good many of them, I got the distinct impression that a simple, heartfelt apology from the Japanese government and the companies that enslaved them would have ended their lawsuit then and there.

"You know, an apology would be nice," I remember Harold Poole telling me in my office. "I don't hold any animosity toward the Japanese people, none whatsoever, but I would like to see an acknowledgment that what happened, happened, and that it wasn't right. I would like to see some recognition of what went on so it doesn't ever happen again."

CHAPTER SIX

April 9, 1942
Mariveles, Bataan, Philippines

DESPITE WINNING BATAAN, the Japanese were not in an upbeat mood when they came to Mariveles to collect their surrendered prisoners. It might have been different if Corregidor Island had also been surrendered. But The Rock was still heavily fortified, defended by a garrison more than sixteen thousand strong, all of whom could fit into the Malinta Tunnel if necessary. Even though the Japanese had marched to the tip of Bataan, Corregidor—the key to the fall of the Philippines—was still beyond them, almost close enough to touch but untouchable, its gray-green hulk silently mocking their triumph.

The Japanese were impatient and angry. The Philippines had become a huge nuisance in their conquest of the Pacific, a gnat they could not quite kill. Dealing with seventy thousand prisoners of war and several thousand Filipino refugees did not help the situation.

Before they reported to Mariveles, the surrendered Allied troops had a chance to take out their frustrations—on their weapons. Along with the order to surrender, the code word "crash" was spread throughout the troops. Crash meant that anything that might be useful to the Japanese, including guns, tanks, service vehicles, fuel, runways, ammunition, airplane parts (all serviceable aircraft had been flown to Australia), maps, documents, even money, needed to be destroyed. It was the last defiant act of the defeated, and throughout the night of April 8 and morning of April 9, lower Bataan was alive with the sounds of destruction. Anything that could be rendered useless was rendered useless. Trucks were driven into the bay, ammo dumps were detonated, sand was poured into fuel tanks, buildings were set on fire. Ships in the Mariveles harbor, including the USS *Canopus*, were blown up. In disbelief that he would ever do such a thing, Harold Poole took his .45 pistol out of its case, put it on a rock, and smashed it to bits with a hammer.

"They told us to destroy everything we could," said Harold. "It was hard to cope with the reality of what was happening. What a terrible disappointment we suffered. We were American soldiers and forced to surrender. It was humiliating."

But as distasteful as surrender was, it did offer the prospect of finally getting something decent to eat. Harold told how as he and others walked through the jungle to the Mariveles seaport, they had tried to put a brave face on it.

But hope for relief disappeared quickly enough once they met the enemy. The Japanese wasted no time in demonstrating their superiority and control. "At the surrender they treated us real rough," said Harold. "They really banged us around a lot. We knew right away how it was going to be. The first thing they did was shake us down for everything we had that they wanted."

Almost before their new captives stopped marching, the Japanese soldiers began looting. They took wristwatches, rings, wallets, medals, clothing, pocketknives, books, money, cigarettes, candy, cameras, personal items, including photographs, and dental fillings. Nothing was off limits and refusal meant swift, severe consequences. Some American soldiers who resisted parting with their wedding rings wound up losing the ring *and* their ring finger. One man instinctively clutched at his eyeglasses when a Japanese soldier tried to take them off his face. In response, the Japanese soldier swung the butt of his rifle and smashed the glasses into the American's face.

Like most of the men, Harold had never seen a Japanese soldier up close, or witnessed blatant brutality and larceny on such a scale. He did not know which stunned him more, the depth of the brutality or the apparent complete lack of remorse on the part of the enemy soldiers inflicting it.

Harold had heard firsthand the stories about the Japanese soldiers' capacity for ruthlessness. When he first came to the Philippines aboard the USS *Washington*, it had been by way of Shanghai in China. The ship had made its way up the Huangpu River, escorted by a Japanese gunboat, to collect American citizens who were leaving China because of the escalating Japanese-Chinese war. Once on board the *Washington*, the expatriates told tales of Japanese torture and brutality. The so-called Rape of Nanking was the most infamous. After fierce fighting to capture the Chinese city in 1937, more than a quarter million Chinese were reportedly tortured, raped, or killed. On Bataan, soldiers fighting on the front lines told of seeing fallen bodies of American soldiers with their heads cut off by Japanese swords and tossed to the side, along with an arm or two.

It occurred to Harold and the others as they watched the Japanese soldiers file into Mariveles that undoubtedly among them were veterans who had also fought in China. These were hardened, battle-worn troops. "You could see by the way they acted that these soldiers had been through a lot," said Harold. "Some of them had probably been fighting for years."

Faced with this harsh new reality, each surrendered soldier had to come to terms with how to attempt to deal with it. As Harold watched other GIs pay the price for defiance, he made up his mind that he would not smirk or glare at a command for even a blow to the head. He would not so much as raise an eyebrow in retaliation. Whatever the order, he would obey it. No exceptions.

The day Harold met the enemy he decided that his personal mantra would be, "Take what they give and give what they take." Deep down he knew that was what he needed to do, just as he knew that his only goal was simply to survive until the ordeal was over so he could one day go back home.

"When things looked the blackest and most hopeless," he said, "that silver lining started to take shape in my mind: the only way I could fight back was to somehow see it through, whatever it was, and with the Lord's help, stay alive."

When a Japanese soldier a foot shorter than Harold walked up to him at Mariveles and without a word took his pocketknife and money—the only valuables he possessed—he stood at attention and did not move a muscle in protest.

The Japanese guards had their orders. They were to deliver the surrendered soldiers to a military camp in the province of Tarlac, some eighty-five miles to the north of Mariveles, and they were to get them there quickly. Bataan needed to be cleared. The roads needed to be open for the assault on Corregidor. The presence of tens of thousands of captured troops was a deterrent to that goal. The plan was to force-march the captives out of Bataan at a quick and steady pace, the Japanese figuring that a man—even a fat, lazy American—could easily travel eighty-five miles, part by rail, in

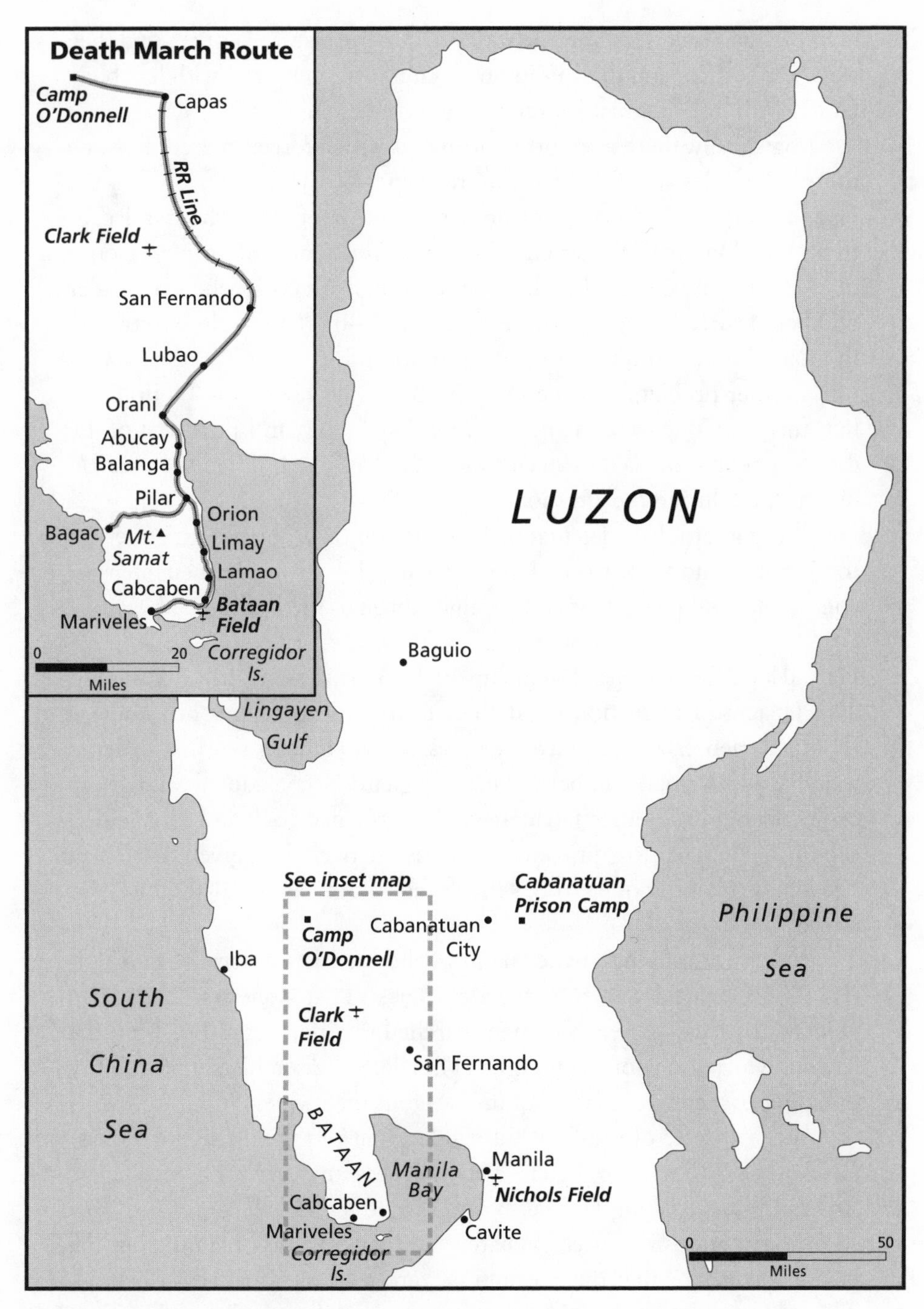

Luzon Island, P.I., circa 1942. *Christopher Robinson*

no more than four days. But the stateside Americans were not fat, and they were not healthy, and their Filipino counterparts, generally with less body fat to lose in the first place, were in even worse condition.

Logistically, there were other problems with a forced-march. For one thing, Mariveles was filled with more than twice as many people as the Japanese expected. They were prepared for about forty thousand captives. But along with the seventy thousand American and Filipino troops in Mariveles and Samac—a village on Bataan's west coast where a smaller number of surrendered troops were collected—there were close to twenty thousand Filipino refugees to maneuver around.

Another problem was the heat. It was always hot in the Philippines, but April and May were the hottest months of the year. In the heat of the day, few people worked or even moved around much. Even the carabao disappeared during the afternoon.

But to get to their destination in Tarlac on time, the new prisoners of the Japanese, no matter how large their number or feeble their physical condition, would have to march straight through the Philippine heat.

Harold left Mariveles at a decent clip on the morning of April 12, a Sunday. The Japanese had sectioned off their captives into groups of around a thousand men each and Harold's thousand was among the first ordered to move out. A small number of Japanese guards accompanied each group of prisoners, while other Japanese soldiers roamed back and forth along the road. The guard-to-prisoner ratio was relatively low, given that Japan needed the majority of its troops for the assault on Corregidor, which was already underway.

Bullets were flying at the island as the men left Mariveles and bullets from Corregidor were flying right back. That alone was enough to quicken the early pace as the men marched in a northeast direction, the bay and Corregidor on their right. They left in a semblance of military discipline, ordered to march out in lines four men wide.

At the specter of the first hill winding out of the village, some prisoners already began to falter. The Japanese may have suspected the Americans were faking fatigue, having no direct knowledge of just how short their rations had been. Whatever the case, it was obvious from the guards' demeanor that there would be zero tolerance for falling behind. The Japanese swung their swords menacingly and pushed their bayonets at anyone who slowed down. In the ranks, the prisoners prodded the slowest among them to keep up.

Harold noticed he seemed to be in better physical condition than a majority of the men. Like all of them, he had gone hungry for four months, but looking around at the others as the march began, he could see many who were tiring even more quickly than he was. His two months at Bataan Field with General George probably had not hurt. Rations there had not been anything to write home about, but rank did have its privileges and he got a little better food while he was there than when he returned to Mariveles. On top of that, he had kept himself in decent shape in the year he spent in the Philippines before the war began. He did not smoke or drink, he exercised regularly, his job kept him physically active, he had plenty of time to get acclimated to the tropical heat to the extent that it was possible, and he religiously stayed away from native women. The training films every GI had to watch when coming to the islands did not work with every soldier, but they worked with Harold. "They indoctrinated us good. They showed us what could happen if we got involved with the local women. A lot of guys did anyway, and they got venereal diseases and some other things, and it did not leave them in very good shape later on."

But sooner or later the forced-march took its toll on everyone. By the time they reached the village of Cabcaben, fourteen kilometers into the journey, the pace had slowed considerably.

National Road, the only way in or out of the peninsula, made its way along the eastern shoreline. The road's surface was hard dirt. There may once have been stones or some kind of pavement, but what the years had not destroyed the war had. The uneven surface was pockmarked with bomb craters and ruts made by tanks and other heavy machinery. Adding to the obstacle course was the occasional dead body—from both armies—a residue of the fighting that had ended just days before.

As the men in Harold's group marched through the long first day they were given no rest and no food. In the villages the natives who ventured out to the edge of the road to see the spectacle would sometimes slip a piece of bread or fruit or a handful of rice to the men passing by in the pathetic, ragged parade. But such an act of kindness was not without peril for the giver as well as the receiver. If caught, both would be beaten at best, or killed. "The guards didn't show any emotion. They'd pull their bayonet out, use it, and then just wipe it on the guy's clothes. They didn't even flinch," said Harold.

It soon became obvious that the Japanese had no qualms about killing. All the guards needed was an excuse; the slightest irritant was good enough. Harold's introduction to cold-blooded murder came early in the march when an exhausted GI stumbled and fell in front of him.

"Some of the guys would just faint, they were that weak. This guy was no more than five feet away. He was lying facedown. The guard poked him and he didn't move fast enough, so he got the bayonet right through his back."

The murder stunned Harold. "I could hardly believe what I saw," he said. "I wanted to jump that guard and grab his rifle and wrap it around his neck, and I could have in those days. I was still in pretty good shape and those guys were a lot smaller than us. I could have jumped up and wrapped that gun around his neck and he'd never have known what hit him. But you know, there was another guard behind him and he would have shot me and that would have been the end of me, see."

More death followed, and it surprised Harold how fast he became numbed to the killing. It was either that or fall apart and die yourself. There was no stopping for mourning or burying the dead. The longer the march wore on, the more bodies accumulated, and a man still on his feet had no choice but to just walk past them.

The one part of it Harold never got used to was the smell.

"You know how a dead animal smells after it's been lying out in the sun a few days?" Harold asked. "Well, the human body is four or five times worse than that, and once you've smelled it, you never forget it. But the Japanese just left them there, to rot."

Anyone attempting to move the bodies risked joining them, unless a Japanese guard on a whim decided that a body should be buried and ordered the prisoners to stop and dig a grave. Among the cruelest abuses recorded along the march was when guards ordered prisoners to bury sick, wounded men who had not yet died. Harold was never ordered to do such a thing, and he thanked God for that.

As the temperature rose, the guards seemed to increase their capacity for killing. They would sometimes ride by on horseback and take a swing at an unsuspecting prisoner's neck with their swords, trying for a complete decapitation. Other times trucks would barrel down the road aiming at the prisoners. While their captives marched, the Japanese played many killing games.

Going without food was bad enough, but in some ways the men, with their shrunken stomachs, were used to it. Much worse was going without water. Even when rations fell to starvation level during their stand on Bataan, the troops always had plenty of water to drink. There was no shortage of water in the Philippines, a tropical place with an annual four-month rainy season.

As the men walked past, they saw open wells flooding rice fields and abundant rivers flowing with fresh, clear water. But along the march no water breaks were allowed, and if a man was caught leaving National Road for a drink at a nearby stream or spigot, it could be his last. Aching for a drink, the men broke rank anyway, checking to see if the guards were out of sight before making a mad dash for a tap or a stream. Sometimes the guards stopped in the shade for a rest or talked among themselves, ignoring the prisoners. It could work if a man was quick enough.

An additional problem was that most of the water pipes in the fields were small, only about a half inch in diameter. When a pipe was spotted near the road and the guards were out of sight, several men at a time would typically rush to the water, all trying to place the mouths of their canteens underneath the half-inch spigot. For those who did not arrive first, it could take a long time and a lot of risk to get a little water.

Harold's salvation was in the form of a widemouthed bucket he shared with Nelson Quast, a friend from the 20th Pursuit Squadron. They would take turns sprinting to water pipes, and while the men with canteens fought for an opening above them, they would place the bucket below to collect the overflow. Usually, they would be the first ones back to the road. The guards never caught them.

Why they took the bucket when they left Mariveles, neither man could say. They did not carry much with them. The Japanese had confiscated most of their belongings before the march began, and they had no notice that they would be denied drinking water. "But it was a good thing we had it," said Harold. "Sometimes six or seven guys would get out there, fighting over that spigot with their canteens, and we'd get down underneath and get back quick before the bullets started to fly. Some of the men got killed going out to get water. That bucket saved our lives."

Some prisoners elected to make a run for it. The jungle could swallow a man in a second, and the guards had neither the numbers, the time, nor the inclination to chase down a runaway. For the Filipinos, especially, it was a temptation to escape. Thousands had drifted into the countryside as soon as the surrender was announced; hundreds more did likewise during the Death March. They spoke the language, they could strip off their uniforms and easily blend in with the locals, and they could find their way back to their homes with a reasonable chance of not getting caught. But for soldiers from the States it was different. Although a handful did choose to escape into the jungle, it was a much bigger gamble. A Caucasian soldier could not blend in with the native population, could not speak the language, and given the general physical condition of the men, might not even make his way through the thick overgrowth to the other side of the jungle.

So on they marched, the smart ones moving to the middle of the road, on the inside of the column, away from the random beatings of the guards.

After the first day, Harold's group was ushered into a small fenced-in enclosure on the outskirts of a village near the coast. It was after dark when they arrived. There was no evening meal, no water, and not enough room to spread out. The guards padlocked the gate and left the men to choose how they would spend the night, sitting or standing—more like cattle than human beings. Exhausted as they were, sleep, of sorts, came anyway.

No one told them where they were going. The hope among the marchers was a place where they could rest, recover, and start eating and drinking again. A high percentage of the prisoners, maybe as high as half, had malaria, a disease that even in its mildest stages required bed rest and plenty of liquids. The next most prevalent ailment was intestinal dysentery, brought on by the unsanitary living conditions and attended by stomach cramping and diarrhea. Other men suffered from diseases of malnutrition, such as beriberi, scurvy, and pellagra. Many had a variety of diseases, a kind of Philippine cocktail, and still more were carrying wounds from the war, physical as well as psychological.

From a disease standpoint, Harold was one of the lucky ones. Four months of sleeping without a mosquito net (at Clark Field, nets had been mandatory) and he still had not contracted malaria, nor had he caught dysentery or tropical cholera or any of the other diseases running through the troops. Plus he and Quast had their bucket.

They were back walking the next day at first light, around 6 AM. The sun rises and sets with monotonous regularity in a place as close to the equator as the Philippines. Days have twelve hours of daylight and nights have twelve hours of darkness, no matter what the month. The men were herded north and slightly east, as if they were walking directly into the sun. By day two any semblance of marching order was gone, replaced by a weary, shuffling gait. The men's mouths were dry, their heads down, their stomachs empty, and their skin broiled red by the searing tropical sun. They walked out of habit and duty and a survival instinct that came from somewhere deep inside; there was little else to carry them forward.

A routine emerged. The men would walk all morning, take a break when the sun was directly overhead, "for the guards' benefit, so they could rest," said Harold. Then, after finding shade and water for themselves while leaving the prisoners waterless in the sun, the guards would move everyone out until dark. The men received no food beyond what was slipped to them by the natives until the town of Balanga, twenty-five miles into the march. For most groups that was the second day. There was a second food station in Lubao, another twenty-five miles beyond Balanga. At these stops, the Japanese gave the prisoners a palm-sized ball of boiled rice and sometimes some thin soup and sent them on their way.

At an agonizing pace, the march continued through the villages of eastern Bataan, with curious but frightened villagers, hiding from the heat and the Japanese, peeking at the scene from their shacks at the edge of the road.

All along, marchers continued to die. Young men, few past the age of twenty-four, dropped like flies, their corpses scattered along and around National Road as if the devil himself was in charge of landscaping. If there was little dignity for the living, there was even less for the dead. When a body fell in the middle of the road, Japanese trucks would drive right over it.

For the men marching, every hour carried with it a maddening sameness. The Bataan Death March typified what war can do to otherwise civilized peoples. No one was there to demand decency or enforce the rules. There was no International Red Cross on the scene. There were no war crime monitors, no journalists, no judges, no juries, and certainly no PI attorneys. The only eyewitnesses were a few rural Filipino villagers, who were now effectively prisoners of the Japanese as well.

Battles were raging throughout Europe and Asia. The world did not know, could not know—had no way to know—just how far the standards of human decency had slipped in a forgotten corner of the Philippines.

Beyond Bataan, the world was very much alive. In Salt Lake City, seven thousand miles away, Harold's father still went to his accountant's job, right on schedule; his mother still dusted his room; on Sundays, his parents still sang songs of hope, peace, and forgiveness with the Mormon Tabernacle Choir; and Harold's five sisters were busy going to school, buying war bonds, and praying that their brother was alive and well in the Philippines.

When the march finally cleared Bataan Province and arrived at the city of San Fernando, capital of the neighboring Pampanga Province, Harold and the men brightened as the guards prodded them toward the railroad station in the middle of town. They had marched sixty miles on foot by this point. Now they were getting a train ride. The thought of getting off their feet and out of the searing sun was cause for celebration.

But as with everything else in their bizarre new world, looks were deceiving and hope premature. The men were made to stand on the hot railway station platform for hours as the train made runs back and forth between San Fernando and the village of Capas, twenty miles to the north. It was here that Harold received his first serious beating. While the captives waited on the platform, the Japanese brought small rations of rice that they scooped into the men's mess kits. Near where he was standing, Harold saw a bowl filled with coarse salt. Instinctively, he reached to sprinkle some on the rice. A guard hit him hard across the shoulders. "Boy, he took a club and whacked me like nothin'. That was my first personal encounter. I had it in my mind to try to not displease them, but I got whacked hard anyway."

At the station, dozens of narrow-gauge boxcars, designed to carry cattle and other animals, were strung behind ancient steam engines. Capacity for the livestock cars that measured seven feet in height, eight feet in width, and thirty-three feet in length was twenty cows or carabao. Maybe thirty human beings could fit into them with any degree of movement. The Japanese filled them with eighty to a hundred prisoners each.

"We were packed like sardines, and then they shut the doors tight," Harold remembered. Within moments, the men were thinking the unthinkable—that they would rather be back on the road, marching. For four hours, with almost no ventilation, standing so close to each other that they could not lift their arms, the prisoners sweated out the twenty miles to Capas. Those with malarial fevers coughed and wheezed and shivered, while those with dysentery-induced diarrhea defecated where they stood, the smell mixing with a hundred bodies that had not bathed in more than a week. Temperatures soared well past a hundred degrees. For some men it was too much; they either passed out or they suffocated to death. But even the dead did not stop standing until the train reached Capas and the doors were finally opened.

From Capas, the march on foot resumed for those who survived, and this time conditions mercifully improved. This was different land, friendlier than Bataan, with a relatively smooth road unlittered by bomb craters. The war had not touched here, and along the sides of the road, sugar cane grew in abundance. The men had gotten quite adept at acting when the guards were not looking, and every chance they got they grabbed for the cane. For the first time, the route turned west, away from the rising sun. Although they did not know it, the prisoners of the Japanese were nearing their destination: Camp O'Donnell.

Named for a long-since-departed landowner, the onetime farm had been turned into a military camp before the war by MacArthur to train native Filipino troops from the island of Negros. A collection of thatched-roof barracks and officers' buildings lay scattered over a large parcel of flat land. Capacity was ten thousand troops. O'Donnell exceeded that number within two days of receiving marchers from Bataan.

Harold's group staggered in at various intervals on April 18, seven days since their march began and three days longer than the Japanese had planned. They were among the first to arrive. By comparison, their journey was relatively short in duration; others would take anywhere from ten days to as long as two weeks to cover the same distance. With little food and less water, they had averaged just over twelve miles a day. Approximately sixty-five miles had been on foot and twenty miles aboard the suffocating railroad. Many who started did not finish.

Defeated, deflated, and exhausted to the point of collapse, Harold, along with the rest of the men, fell on the ground after leaving the main road and walking about a hundred yards south through the gates of O'Donnell, where the guards ordered everyone to halt. A Japanese flag, with a red dot in the center of a white background, flew over the entrance.

It was the only signal that the Bataan Death March was over.

CHAPTER SEVEN

June 28, 2000
Washington, D.C.

FIFTY-EIGHT YEARS, TWO MONTHS, and ten days after collapsing into Camp O'Donnell, Harold Poole walked of his own volition into room 226 of the Dirksen Senate Office Building in Washington, DC.

The government wanted to hear his story.

Almost seven months had passed since I recruited United States Senator Orrin Hatch to stand with Harold and Johnny Johnson on the courthouse steps in Los Angeles, pressing for justice for the veterans. In the months since, all had not gone smoothly. Hatch's presidential campaign stalled, and then died outright in the Iowa caucuses, while our quest for justice for the veterans ran into its own troubles. The case that had looked so promising had found a formidable foe: the executive branch of the United States government.

As articulated by the U.S. Department of State, it was the executive branch's position that the post–World War II peace treaty entered into in 1951 by the United States and Japan prohibited the kind of slave-labor lawsuits authorized by the Hayden Bill and now being filed by the former JPOWs in California courts. Senator Hatch learned this after writing a letter to Secretary of State Madeleine Albright, asking her to overturn "fifty-five years of injustice imposed on our military forces held as prisoners of war in Japan."

"We strongly believe that the United States must honor its international agreements, including the treaty," Hatch was told in a return letter from Albright's office. "There is, in our view, no justification for the United States to attempt to reopen the question of international commitments and obligations under the 1951 treaty in order now to seek a more favorable settlement of the issue of Japanese compensation."

To demonstrate how seriously the State Department considered its position, government lawyers from the Department of Justice, acting for the State Department, filed a legal document known as a Statement of Interest that succeeded in halting the California lawsuits pending judicial review.

Senator Hatch saw the views and actions of the executive branch not only as a slap in the face of thousands of patriotic Pacific Theater veterans, but also as an affront to the Constitution of the United States of America. Which is why the senator used his position as chairman of the Judiciary Committee—among the most powerful committees in the U.S. Senate, with jurisdiction over the Department of Justice—to convene a hearing on the matter.

Invited to participate were representatives from State, Justice, and as special guests, four former Pacific prisoners of war: Harold Poole, Lester Tenney, Maurice "Mo" Mazer, and Frank "Biggy" Bigelow. All four were in the Philippines when it fell in 1941. Lester, Mo, and Harold walked the Death March after the surrender of Bataan, and Frank was captured when Corregidor Island fell almost a month later. All four were later slaves in Japanese companies.

Harold arrived early for the hearing, stepping out of a muggy June D.C. morning into the cool Dirksen Building air-conditioning. I was already in the hearing room, along with several other mega-firm lawyers anticipating the arrival of our clients.

I pulled Harold off to a side of the room and asked, "Did you bring the Silver Star?"

"Yes, it's right here," he said, patting his suit-coat pocket.

"Could you put it on?" I asked.

I watched as Harold hesitated. He had been told to bring the medal, not wear it.

"Do you think that would be all right?" he asked.

Like a lot of things with Harold, the comment took me by surprise. In my mind, the only thing *not* all right would be not to wear it. The medal was precisely the kind of accessory you showed off because of its potential to help your case. The Silver Star was no trifle. It is the third-highest award a soldier in the United States Army can receive—only the Medal of Honor and Distinguished Service Cross rank higher. Just seeing it on a silver-haired veteran's lapel would speak volumes without saying a word. Little touches like Silver Stars win lawsuits.

The concept was obviously lost on Harold.

I put my arm around his shoulder. "Yes, Harold. I think it would be all right."

"Well, would you help me then?" Harold asked, holding out the worn cardboard box the medal originally came in a half century ago. "I've never actually worn it."

Delayed a half hour by a vote on the Senate floor, Senator Hatch began the hearing titled "Former U.S. World War II POWs: A Struggle for Justice" at 10:33 AM.

"I'm pleased today to welcome a distinguished group of witnesses to enlighten the committee on a very important issue," the judiciary committee chairman began. "Namely, the struggle for compensation of American POWs once held and forced into labor by private Japanese companies. On April 9, 1942, Allied forces in the Philippines surrendered Bataan to the Japanese. Ten to twelve thousand American soldiers were forced to march some sixty miles in broiling heat in a deadly trek known as the Bataan Death March. Following a lengthy internment under horrific conditions, thousands of POWs were shipped to Japan in the hulls of freighters known as 'hell ships.' Once in Japan, many of these POWs were forced into slave labor for private Japanese steel mills and other private companies until the end of the war. During the war, over 27,465 Americans were captured and interned by the Japanese. Only 16,000 of them made it home.

"Let me say at the outset that this is not a dispute with the Japanese people and these are not claims against the Japanese government. Rather, this is a hearing, the purpose of which is to determine whether those who profited from the slave labor of American POWs have an obligation to remedy their wrongs and whether the United States can help them facilitate a resolution."

I was seated in the back of the room with the rest of the plaintiffs' attorneys, listening as a United States senator delivered, in essence, the opening statement of our case—with the added bonus of it being carried live on C-SPAN.

The senator shifted his gaze to Harold, Lester, Mo, and Frank, who were seated directly across from him.

"Unfortunately, global, political, and security needs of the time often overshadowed your legitimate claims for justice and you were once again asked to sacrifice for your country," he said. "Following the end of the war, our government allegedly instructed many of the POWs held by Japan not to discuss their experiences and treatment. Some were even asked to sign nondisclosure agreements. Consequently, many Americans remain unaware of the atrocities that took place and the suffering our POWs endured.

"Through the years, various efforts have been made to offer some compensation to POWs held in Japan. Under the War Claims Act, our government has made meager payments of $1 a day for missed meals and $1.50 per day for lost wages and clearly, in the eyes of most, this is inadequate."

The senator paused.

"Following the passage of a California statute extending the statute of limitations for World War II claims until 2010, and the recent litigation involving victims of the Holocaust, a new effort is underway by the former POWs in Japan to seek compensation from the private companies that profited from their slave labor. One issue for the committee to examine is whether the POWs held in Japan are receiving an appropriate level of advocacy from the U.S. government. In the Holocaust litigation, the United States played a facilitating role in the discussions between German companies and their victims. The Justice Department also declined to file a Statement of Interest in the litigation even when requested by the court. The efforts of the administration were entirely appropriate and the settlement was an invaluable step towards movement forward from the past.

"In contrast, there has been no effort by our government, through the State Department or otherwise, to open a dialogue between the Japanese and the former POWs. Moreover, in response to a request from the court, the Justice Department did in fact file a Statement of Interest, which was very damaging to the claims of the POWs, stating in essence that their claims were barred by the 1951 peace preaty with Japan and the War Claims Act. This contrasting treatment raises the legitimate question of whether this administration has a consistent policy governing whether and how to weigh in during these World War II–era cases."

The senator closed his remarks with a question and an answer.

"What can the United States of America, the country these men sacrificed for, do to resolve these matters in a fair and appropriate manner? Here in the Senate, we are doing what we can. With the help of Senator Feinstein, we have moved through the Judiciary Committee Senate Bill 1902, the Japanese Records Disclosure Act, which would set up a commission to declassify thousands of Japanese Imperial Army records. And the Senate is also doing what it can to fulfill our government's responsibility to these men by including a provision in the Department of Defense Authorization Bill, which would pay a $20,000 gratuity to POWs from Bataan and Corregidor who were forced into labor. Such payment would be in addition to any other payments these veterans may receive under law, and thus would not compromise any of the claims asserted in the litigation against the Japanese companies."

Not only had the senator from Utah just spelled out our JPOW legal case, he had also thrown in the possibility of a government payment.

Hatch concluded with an almost palpable righteous indignation. Before he became a senator, he had been a trial lawyer, and it showed. In my view, he "opened" very well. His arguments made sense. Who could possibly deny these aging patriots their justice?

Without preamble, David Ogden, acting head of the Civil Division of the United States Department of Justice, moved to the microphone and cut to the heart of the debate: the peace treaty of 1951. The treaty was negotiated between Japan and the United States as well as forty-seven other Allied nations and was signed by all parties in San Francisco on September 8, 1951, six years after the end of the war. The treaty ended America's postwar occupation of Japan. It was signed by the president of the United States and approved by the United States Senate in the spring of 1952.

The treaty called for reparations and payments from Japan in a number of areas. This included the repair, where possible, of damages resulting from war aggression, as well as Japan's renouncing claims to various lands and territories, including Formosa Island (now Taiwan) and Korea. Additionally, Allied powers were given the right "to seize, retain, liquidate, or otherwise dispose of all property, rights, and interest of Japan and Japanese nationals," and it affirmed Japan's liability for any prewar debts or obligations. The treaty gave Japan back to the Japanese, ending six years of foreign occupation, but it was a costly exchange. The Japanese economy, for the most part, was drained dry. The United States alone would receive some $90 million in reparation payments from Japan, in 1950's currency.

But there was a caveat that the demands on Japan's resources would not go on interminably. As of its signing, the treaty appeared to waive all future war-related claims. The treaty was intended to be the do-all, end-all.

"It is clear from the language of the 1951 treaty . . . that the United States intended to waive its claims and those of its nationals against Japan and its nationals," said Ogden. As Senator Hatch had done earlier, he looked directly at Harold and the other World War II vets. "We admire and sympathize with these valiant men who were prisoners of war. We condemn the wartime policies of Japan and its industries that forced them into servitude. But in 1951, President Truman and the United States Senate made a carefully considered national decision that our interests would be served by a peace settlement that resolved all potential claims."

David Ogden then yielded the floor to Ronald Bettauer, a deputy legal advisor at the United States Department of State, who opened by telling the committee that he had been directly involved in both the recent German slave-and-forced-labor settlement negotiations and the development of the government's position regarding the forced-labor lawsuits against Japanese companies recently filed in California.

Bettauer told the committee that the 1951 United States–Japan treaty is what made the German reparations and Japanese reparations different.

"The fact that the treaty waived all claims is unambiguously supported by the negotiating history of the treaty, by the broad security objectives of the United States, the government at the time, and by the extensive, often excruciatingly painful deliberations that preceded the treaty's advice and consent by the Senate," said Bettauer.

The U.S. Senate approved the treaty "by a strong two-thirds majority" on March 20, 1952, explained Bettauer, and it was thereafter signed by President Harry S. Truman.

"The overarching intent of those who negotiated, signed, and ultimately ratified the treaty," said the State Department lawyer, "was to bring about a complete global settlement of all war-related claims in order both to provide compensation to the victims of the war and to rebuild Japan's economy and convert Japan into a strong U.S. ally. It was recognized at the time that those goals could not have been served had the treaty left open the possibility of continued, open-ended legal liability of Japanese industry for its wartime actions."

Bettauer testified that it was the State Department's legal opinion that language in Article 14(b) of the 1951 treaty was meant to close the door to future national versus national lawsuits, not open them.

He read the full text of Article 14(b): "Except as otherwise provided in the present treaty, the allied powers waive all reparations claims of the allied powers, other claims of the allied powers, and their nationals, arising out of any action taken by Japan and its nationals in the course of the prosecution of the war."

Hatch, who agreed with the mega-firm position that "in the course of the prosecution of war" did not cover steel mills, coal mines, shipyards, and other private companies that used JPOWs to keep their businesses running during the war years, began verbally sparring with Bettauer.

"Is that the language you're relying on then?" he asked.

"That's the basic language, yes," said Bettauer.

"How can the government waive the rights of individuals?"

"Well, I will talk a little bit about how this occurred—"

"I can see how the government can waive its rights. I can see how it can enter into a treaty. I can see how it can do all of that. But what bothers me is how can [the government] without the consent of the individual citizens waive the rights of individual citizens who have been mistreated?"

"The government has had the power to address the claims and settle these claims against foreign nations of citizens for some two hundred years under our system going all the way back I believe to the Jay Treaties," Bettauer answered. "There are many cases, including Belmont, Paine, Dames, and Moore, that have upheld the espousal power of the United States to take up the claims of the citizens and to settle them against—"

"That's right," the senator said, "If they actually take up the claims from the citizens and actually settled them, for the benefit of the citizens, then, yeah, I can see where that would apply. But here, it seems to me they just ignored the claims of the citizens other than the dollar-and-a-half a day."

"Well, I think you have to look at what the treaty intended to accomplish as a whole."

"But I've looked at the treaty and I don't see the language in there that forecloses individual suits for reparations."

"This treaty by its terms settles all war-related claims of the United States—"

"So what?"

"And its nationals and precludes the possibility of taking—"

"You mean the federal government, you mean our federal government, can just say to hell with you Bataan Death Marchers and you people who were mistreated? We're just going to waive all your rights because we have the almighty power to do so?"

"It was the decision made in 1950 in the—"

"I don't care about the decision. I'm saying can the federal government do that?"

"Yes. I think the federal government can do that."

"And actually take away their rights without giving them a chance to be heard?"

"That is, I think, an established authority of the federal government. And I think my—"

"I don't believe that. I mean, I know that you're sincere in expressing that. But I can't believe under our constitution that that is going to be upheld."

"I would suggest that it has been upheld many times."

"Upheld by whom?"

"The U.S. courts."

Hatch and the ranking Democrat on the committee, Senator Dianne Feinstein of California, shifted their attention to Article 26 of the treaty, which states, "Should Japan make a peace settlement or war claims settlement with any state granting that state greater advantage than those provided by the present treaty, those same advantages shall be extended to the parties of the present treaty."

It was the senators' contention (and the mega-firm's) that since Japan had gone beyond the treaty's provisions to help recompense forced laborers in Burma, the Soviet Union, the Netherlands, and other countries, then the United States could, and should, ask for similar treatment.

Bettauer refuted that interpretation: "The purpose of the provision was, and I'm quoting one of the documents, 'for the protection of Japan so that if other countries should make demands upon Japan, Japan would have a basis of resisting by pointing to that provision.' That was a key goal because the idea was to pull Japan away from the communist bloc. [John Foster] Dulles designed the provision to deter the Japanese from dealing on favorable terms with the Soviet Union, specifically with regard to its territorial demands.

"So, the only time that Dulles raised Article 26 was in 1956 when Japan and the Soviet Union were negotiating a peace settlement. Dulles made a public statement to the effect that if Japan recognized the Soviet territorial claims of sovereignty, Article 26 might open the way for the United States to claim comparable benefits. He explained publicly that he had inserted Article 26 'for the very purpose of trying to prevent the Soviet Union from getting more favorable treatment than the United States got.'"

"Well," Hatch said, "it seems to me that we can go back to one of my original questions, and that is how can our government take away the rights of individual citizens to sue individual companies, not the government of Japan but individual companies in Japan, for reparations for having been mistreated and forced into slave labor? Where's the justification? Where's the legal justification? Show me a case that says that these veterans have no right to go against the Japanese companies that exploited them, and abused them, and made them slave laborers?"

"Well, I have mentioned some cases and I think we're at a point where we differ on this," said Bettauer, delivering the understatement of the hearing.

"I don't know of a case in point that says that they have no right to sue those companies," said Hatch.

"The case in point for this actual treaty is currently being litigated," said Bettauer. "But the precedent is out there saying that the United States has the ability to espouse and settle claims, and we have done so multiple times over the last two hundred years . . . in the postwar period, there are probably fifteen or twenty times that we have done agreements with foreign countries and settled claims of U.S. nationals whether they have liked it or not."

It was Hatch's hearing, and he had the final word.

"We're not asking the government to pay," he said. "We're asking the companies that did the acts to pay, and some of these companies, they're multibillion-dollar companies today, which might not be multibillion-dollar companies today had it not been for forced labor during that period of time. That's the difference."

The chairman of the Judiciary Committee cleared his throat.

"I would like the State Department to go back and reassess this because I think your arguments are ridiculous."

Then he looked at Ogden from Justice.

"And Mr. Ogden, I think you ought to reassess this because your opinion is very broad, way too broad, and frankly, it's just not right. Look, I'm just a poor little country lawyer here. But I want you both to go back to reassess this. I mean, this is ridiculous. This is absolutely ridiculous."

Now Senator Hatch steered the hearing to the specially invited guests, the reason they were all here, the onetime POWs themselves—men who had been in the slave camps, who had slept on the ground, and worked for nothing but a handful of rice.

From their ringside seats, Harold, Les, Frank, and Mo had watched stoically as the senators sparred with the government experts. In a figurative sense, they were still in the Philippines, waiting on the brass to see what was going to happen. But in reality they were far from the Philippines.

They had each come home from the war, found jobs and wives, made homes, raised kids, and settled down. Harold became a mailman, Lester a college professor, Mo a food broker, Frank a cab and truck driver. Now even those careers were behind them, their children were grown, and they were not living on rumors and rice anymore, but on savings and pensions.

And finally, after all these decades, they were in Washington, D.C., to tell their story to the government.

Harold spoke first. Wearing his best suit with the Silver Star on his lapel, he looked straight at the committee members.

"Good morning, Mr. Chairman and members of the committee," Harold began. "As previously indicated, my name is Harold Wood Poole. I'm an eighty-one-year-old widower living in Salt Lake City, Utah. I have a son and a daughter and nine grandchildren. In 1940, I volunteered in the United States Army Air Corps."

He spoke plainly and sincerely, a solid, reasonable gentleman who looked the panel of senators in the eye.

Harold gave a brief history of his relationship with the Japanese, beginning with the outbreak of war, moving through the siege of Bataan, the Death March, prison camp, his hell ship crossing to Japan, and twenty months of forced slave labor for the Nippon Steel Corporation. He recounted the life-and-death statistics of the 20th Pursuit Squadron—some two hundred were alive on the day the war began, about fifty made it home three and a half years later.

"I have often wondered why I survived and why so many of my buddies did not," he said. "Obviously, these are questions whose answers are ultimately known only to God. But I attribute my survival to Him. I'm a religious man, and I believe my Heavenly Father heard and answered my prayers when I was a prisoner of war . . . and now, over fifty years later, I think I know why my life was preserved. I am here today to speak not only for myself, but also for all those young men who never came home. I'm here to ask for your help, as I seek justice not only for me, but for all of us who served and suffered, both living and dead."

Harold turned the microphone over to Frank, who introduced himself as "Frank Bigelow, former Seaman, Second Class. I am now seventy-eight years old and residing in Brooksville, Florida. I am here to speak for the POWs from World War II.

"Bullets, exotic diseases, and starvation couldn't kill us," Frank continued. "Neither could two years of slave labor, being beaten, nearly beheaded by the masters we were forced to serve. It is that strength that brings me here today. Justice is long overdue for the thousands of World War II veterans."

Frank told the senators of the fall of Corregidor, where he was stationed: "We were defending a beach when thousands of American and Filipino troops were taken prisoner by the Japanese. I knew right then that I was going to make it. When they hauled down the American flag, ground it into the earth, and urinated on it, it made me sick. I love my flag, and I love my country. I was twenty years old and half a world away from my home in North Dakota, and I contracted malaria, jaundice, and dysentery, all at the same time, and I forced myself to eat charcoal to save my life."

Frank Bigelow's slave labor had been in Omuta Camp 17, perhaps the most notorious of all the Japanese slave labor camps. Daily for almost two years he worked in a coal mine for Mitsui Mining, escorted there each morning along with hundreds of other POWs by the Japanese Army. They ate seaweed soup and tiny portions of rice and were beaten regularly and forced to work in dangerous mine shafts the Japanese would not go near. A rock in one of the shafts crushed Frank's leg, he told the senators, and his lower leg had to be amputated by the camp doctor, without anesthetic. To save what remained of the leg from infection, maggots were stuffed inside the bandage to eat the bacteria.

With that memory in the air, Mo Mazer took the microphone. He spoke of "unspeakable torture" in a Japanese copper mine owned by Mitsubishi, where his back was broken and he nearly starved to death.

"Today, I suffer numerous health problems directly attributed to the time I spent as a slave laborer," he said. "It is absolutely unconscionable that our government has awarded reparations to Japanese-American citizens who were in the United States relocation camps during World War II, many of whom were proven to be spies and Japanese sympathizers, and has ignored the plight of its military men and women who were enslaved by the Japanese.

"Those of us interned by Mitsubishi, Mitsui, Nippon Steel, Ishihara Sangyo, and many other Japanese companies suffered our own holocaust and this has never been recognized. This terrible injustice needs to be rectified as soon as possible. We who are the victims are old and dying off. We have waited too long for our private hell to end."

Lester Tenney, the "prison lawyer" of the group, spoke last.

It was Lester's grievances, as detailed in his book *My Hitch in Hell*, that got the JPOW case going in the first place. He had gone to the office of a PI lawyer named Michael Goldstein near his home in the San Diego area and asked Goldstein if he thought he had a case. Goldstein contacted his friend David Casey, who took the case to the mega-firm and the seeds of the lawsuit took root.

My Hitch in Hell was published in 1995 and told the story of a proud man embittered by continual abuse at the hands of the Japanese. Not only was Lester beaten continually by his "employers" at a Mitsui-owned coal mine, not only was he nearly starved to death, not only was he forced to shovel coal twelve hours a day, twenty-eight days a month, for nearly three years, but when he returned home at the end of the war, his wife had remarried. She thought he was dead.

"Mr. Chairman, members of the committee," he began, "in early 1942, along with twelve thousand other Americans who were fighting and defending our country on the Bataan Peninsula, I was promised supplies, food, and reinforcements by our government. As history shows, that promise was never fulfilled."

Lester was just warming up.

"During one of President Roosevelt's fireside chats made in February of 1942, we sat in our tanks and listened to him say that in every war there are those who must be sacrificed for the benefit of the whole war effort. We suddenly realized he was talking about us. We were being sacrificed and abandoned for the benefit of the overall war effort. Well, senators, we were well able to do that. After all, we were proud young men and women, serving our country, and we took an oath to protect our country at all costs.

"Well, here we are fifty-eight years later and we are, once again, informed that we are being sacrificed and abandoned by our own government. But this time, not for the war efforts but, instead, for the benefit of those large Japanese industrial giants who profited from our slave labor. I, once again, feel that I've been taken prisoner, but this time by my own country. I've been able to take the beatings, but now I have to take the beatings with words from our own country. How has this come to be? Well, the California legislature unanimously passed a statute that was enacted into law allowing claims for compensation for those veterans who were used as slave laborers to go forward in the courts irrespective of the running of the statute of limitations.

"Pursuant to this law, I, along with many of my other former POW friends, have since filed lawsuits seeking reparation, equality, and justice. Shockingly, the U.S. Department of Justice has recently filed a court submission, the effects of which would nullify the actions of the California legislature.

"The Justice Department erroneously or negligently issued a formal submission to the courts of our nation omitting the most crucial issue of the San Francisco peace treaty, and in effect, took away our rights for recovery: Section 26, known as the Most-Favored-Nation clause, which states 'should Japan make a peace settlement or a war claim settlement with any state granting that state greater advantages than those provided by the present treaty, those same advantages shall be extended to the parties to the present treaty.'

"Records of our State Department show that at least six other nations have been granted more favorable treaty terms than those given to the United States. Article 26 when properly interpreted allows victims of forced or slave labor to seek recovery for the wrong perpetrated against former prisoners of war during World War II, yet the Justice Department studiously ignores it in its statement of interest."

Lester was pleading the same case senators Hatch and Feinstein had earlier argued with Ogden and Bettauer.

"I urge you, senators, use your position within our government to correct this wrong and have our Justice Department turn away from this misguided action. Thank you for listening to my story about honor and justice and responsibility. We served our country with honor. We've had our share of injustice and now we seek responsibility from our government in allowing us to be heard in a court of justice. I have heard the statement of Mr. Ron Bettauer. The debt he's talking about can be paid by helping us or getting out of our way."

The committee had one more question for each of the former POWs: all these years later, what compelled them to pursue these lawsuits? What were they looking for from the companies that enslaved them? What exactly did they want?

"Justice is at the top of the list," said Harold, "and also I would like the information and the account of this to be incorporated in our history books. It might be a deterrent for any of this happening again."

Mo Mazer seconded Harold's words, and Frank Bigelow got more personally specific.

"What do I think the company owes us?" the big man thundered. "My leg, a couple of years of our lives, and at least miner's wages for what we did. And most of all, they owe us an apology."

Lester Tenney, the color still in his face from his recent remarks, said, "What I would like is not only the justice that we're talking about, but by getting this justice, I think we will also have an opportunity to let the citizens of Japan know, once and for all, what really happened. They are ignorant of what's happened because the Japanese government refuses to tell them. The Japanese government refuses to put it in their textbooks. Remember that in fifty-five years they've done nothing, no apology, and the Japanese companies have done absolutely nothing."

The testimony concluded with a sympathetic written comment for the former POWs from Edward Jackfert, the head of the American Defenders of Bataan and Corregidor, and a legal opinion from Harold Maier, a professor at the Vanderbilt University School of Law, who supported the senators' contention that Justice and State had misinterpreted the treaty. Each former POW was given an American flag that had flown atop the U.S. Capitol.

The next morning, headlines from coast to coast shouted the news: "WWII Slave Laborer Asks Senate Panel Why He Can't Sue" blared the *Chicago Tribune*. "POWs of WWII request lawsuits: But U.S. Lawyer Cites 1951 Treaty" said the *Washington Times*. "Former POWs Want to Sue Japanese," trumpeted *USA Today*, which ran a photo of a stern-looking Lester Tenney, and out of the 18,257 words officially recorded at the hearing, chose to use one quote from Orrin Hatch: "I think your arguments are ridiculous."

Following the hearing, the veterans were invited to a reception at the nearby House Armed Services Committee hearing room. I arranged to meet Harold there for the short walk back to our hotel. A light summer rain was falling as we left the Rayburn House Office Building. As we were about to cross the street, a policeman asked if we would stop for a moment because the presidential motorcade was about to pass and the Secret Service wanted to keep everyone back.

Soon, a caravan of cars came into view and slowly drove past. In the center of the procession was a black limousine with American flags waving from the front. Inside was William Jefferson Clinton, president of the United States.

With my mind still back in the hearing room, as I watched the president pass I thought about how he, as head of the executive branch of government, was both our problem and our solution. Every presidential administration since President Harry Truman signed off on the treaty in 1952 had stayed the party line. But that did not mean this administration could not take a serious look at the wording and interpret it in a way that would be favorable to these veterans. President Clinton could do that. Affairs of state were ultimately decided by the man riding in the limousine. Somehow, we had to get him on our side.

I was about to relay all my thoughts about the case to Harold, ready to launch into a diatribe on how we were going to convince the administration and win this case. But as I turned to face him, I saw Harold stand at attention for the president.

They don't make them like him anymore, I thought.

CHAPTER EIGHT

April 24, 1942
Camp O'Donnell, Tarlac, Philippines

AS HAROLD AND THOUSANDS MORE dragged themselves into Camp O'Donnell, their sheer numbers belied just how many bodies of their lifeless comrades were left on the eighty-five-mile trail behind them.

Ten thousand Americans and sixty thousand Filipinos started the Death March. Those are round numbers. Precise figures are impossible to calculate, due to the wide range of ways a man could die in the spring of 1942 in Bataan and the imprecise ways of keeping track. Some died in the four months of fighting, some died from fatigue and disease, some died trying to swim the two miles to Corregidor in an attempt to avoid surrender, while still others either died or disappeared into the jungle. One particularly resourceful U.S. Army private, it would be discovered months later, made his way through the Bataan jungles, across Manila Bay, and into a motorboat, which he skippered through enemy waters all the way to Australia. A few other American soldiers would be found after the war, hiding out here and there in the Philippines after helping native guerilla rebels resist and fight the Japanese.

But most marched to O'Donnell, or tried to.

Of the estimated seventy thousand who started the march, an estimated fifteen thousand died—more than seven hundred Americans and over fourteen thousand Filipinos. By the time the ordeal was over, a dead body lay an average of every thirty feet along the entire eighty-five-mile route from Mariveles to O'Donnell.

But the Death March was just the start. At O'Donnell, the dying escalated. In the absence of even a semblance of medical attention, adequate food, suitable places to rest, and sanitary conditions, attrition from the exhausting march was quick and merciless. Hour after hour, day after day, bodies piled up in the burial ravine below the camp. The corpses were all that remained of men who were either too sick or too tired to continue living.

Twenty-five thousand men, almost twice the number who died on the Death March, died at Camp O'Donnell in April and May of 1942. This included 1,645 Americans, whose numbers had dwindled sufficiently that the officers could keep precise track of the carnage, and over 23,000 Filipinos, whose numbers had not. The natives died at such an alarming rate that the Japanese finally opened the gates on the Filipino side of camp and told the ones still alive to go on home.

"They would take out the dead in a long procession every day starting about two in the afternoon and continue until after sunset," Harold said. "Eventually, the Japs could see that the Filipinos would all soon die, and this would give them a black record for treatment of prisoners of war, so they turned the remaining Filipinos free and made a big to-do of how they were the only nation ever to free prisoners of war while the war was still in progress."

But for the remaining Americans, who were *only* dying off at the rate of one per hour, there would be no clemency, or much of anything else.

The Americans' status as persona non grata had been clearly spelled out upon their arrival at O'Donnell, when the Japanese commander climbed onto an elevated platform, "so he could look down on us," said Harold, and "welcomed" the men to their new home.

Harold remembered being made to wait, bone-tired from the Death March, for hours in the sun for the speech. While they waited, the guards searched them. Anyone found carrying any Japanese items—money, clothing, jewelry, papers, perhaps a part of a Japanese flag picked up along the trail—was executed on the spot. The assumption was that the only way an enemy soldier could be in possession of such souvenirs was by killing a Japanese soldier. It was a cruel irony to endure the starvation and dehydration of the march only to be cut down when it was over because of some item that could have been ditched in a thousand places along the way.

Harold had no Japanese mementos, and he watched as others frantically stuffed paper Japanese money into their dry mouths and swallowed hard, or dug a hole in the dirt to bury other contraband. All Harold had left was the water bucket he shared with Nelson Quast. He had nothing the Japanese could hold against him, other than the fact he had personally shot down two of their planes—information he did not volunteer.

When the O'Donnell commander—a short man who wore a Hitler-style mustache—finally stepped up onto the platform, he began by informing the prisoners, with the help of an English interpreter, that they were cowards for surrendering and they had no rights.

"He said we had disgraced ourselves and didn't deserve to be alive," Harold said. "We were often reminded of this throughout our prisoner experience. They always called us cowards. Sometimes it would get to you. You'd think, 'Well, maybe I'd be better off if I'd fought to the death and got it over with.' We weren't prisoners of war at all to the Japanese. They told us because we surrendered we didn't qualify as prisoners, but only as captives. We were cowards and we were captives. It was shameful, having people call us that and not being able to say anything back."

The camp commander had given the men a crash course in the difference between Japanese and Western thinking and why their captivity was, and would continue to be, so harsh and belittling.

The World War II Japanese military adhered to an age-old Samurai warrior culture called *bushido*, which could be summed up, at its most basic wartime application, as "death before dishonor." According to the warrior code, surrender was dishonor. A Japanese soldier would rather die first.

Based on this mind-set, the Japanese simply could not relate to the wholesale surrender of the U.S.-Filipino troops. It was unthinkable. If a Japanese soldier surrendered, life afterward would be only shame and disgrace. His name would be removed from the records of his village in Japan, and his family would be ostracized. Officially, he would be nothing, a zero. His life would become a living hell. Surrender wasn't a feasible alternative to death because it was worse than death; it was much better to die in a banzai charge or aboard a suicide kamikaze plane than to be taken alive by the enemy. Throughout the course of the long war, the Allies would capture but a handful of Japanese soldiers, and almost all were either half-conscious or unconscious and unable to think straight. Bushido was why.

To the Japanese, the seventy thousand men who lined up at Mariveles were beneath contempt. Caring for them was a thankless chore, not much different than caring for barnyard animals. If anyone got out of line, they could be beaten or killed with impunity. But as with barnyard animals, there were limits to how you could vent your contempt. Mass genocide was out of the question because bushido would never allow wholesale slaughter. For the most part, those captives who did not offer a reason to be killed received disdain followed by indifference, but not death.

The relentless pace of the Bataan Death March, the almost complete lack of care at Camp O'Donnell, the arrogance and apathy of the camp commander and the Japanese guards—it was all more a case of benign neglect than contrived brutality. In their eyes, you were alive by the grace of the Emperor, but you did not deserve to be.

Bushido also explained why the Japanese did not abide by the same prisoner-of-war rules as the rest of the world. Lawmakers in most countries involved in World War II passed legislation binding their militaries to the POW rules of the Geneva Convention of 1929 that called for such basic treatment standards as adequate food and rest, adequate medical attention, correspondence with loved ones, and no forced labor. But the Japanese Diet did not pass the legislation, leaving the Japanese military to set its own standards. Those standards meant defining bushido in its most unforgiving, militaristic sense and displaying no sympathy and little mercy to what were seen as complete cowards.

At O'Donnell the half cup of watery soup at dinnertime qualified, in the Japanese view, as benevolence.

O'Donnell was a camp only by the barest definition of the word. Forty men were squeezed into each of the grass huts, which were originally built by peacetime order of MacArthur to handle sixteen Filipino trainees. Another dozen POWs would be shoved on the ground in the crawl space below the raised floor. Rifle-toting soldiers positioned in guard towers far above the ground kept watch, but in the heat, grime, and sickness, there was little to police.

There was no electricity and no plumbing. The camp latrines were long, shallow pits—"straddle trenches," the men called them—about a foot wide and two feet deep, dug in the dirt in the middle of the compound. When one trench became filled, another was dug next to it, and the old one was covered up by the new dirt. "You'd straddle the trench to do your business," said Harold. "The trenches also served as a breeding place for flies, for which we had a never-ending supply."

The camp pastime was standing in line for water. There were just three taps on the American side (O'Donnell was divided into Filipino and American areas) and nine thousand men, desperately attempting to quench their thirst after the dry horror of Bataan, waited their turn at the spigots night and day. Unlike during the Death March, water in the camp was not off limits, but there was hardly enough to go around. The water pipes were only a half inch in diameter, connected to a water tower at the edge of the compound, and they delivered water only at a trickle, in starts and gurgles. A two-hour wait for water was routine. A four-hour wait was not out of the question. Men fell asleep in line. Some never woke up.

"You'd stand in line for hours just to get a canteen full of water to drink," Harold said. "Then you'd go back and give half of it to some of your buddies not well enough to stand in line. Water was so valuable that we didn't bathe, and we hardly even cleaned our mess kits. And if we did, then we'd drink that water too."

Water for the camp tank came from a stream located about a mile from the barracks. Daily water details staffed by prisoners would go to the stream and collect the water, each man carrying a pair of five-gallon buckets hung at opposite ends of a long bamboo pole stretched across his back. Men too weak or too sick to carry the pole and buckets would volunteer for water detail anyway, in the hopes of sneaking an extra drink or two at the stream.

But at least water *was* available, if in limited supply. Other coveted items such as medicine and soap simply did not exist in any capacity whatsoever. The sick just kept getting sicker, eventually being carted off to a section of the camp that housed the hospital, which the men named "zero ward," because the chances of coming back were zero.

"There was one incident that has stayed with me continuously," Harold wrote in his memoirs. "I was on a cleanup detail in the so-called hospital area, which was more filthy than the so-called well area. The hospital barracks, as all the structures we lived in, were built up three or four feet off the ground, and due to the crowded conditions, men were placed on the ground under them as well as inside. Sick men unable to walk to the latrine were lying on board floors in their own excretion, having discarded all clothing because of its soiled condition, with big blowflies everywhere, even crawling in and out of their mouths. This is the condition I found a youth in, laying under the barracks. He was yellow with jaundice and in a coma. I knew he would not last another day, and it struck me forcibly how young he looked. He had probably lied about his age to enlist. I wondered about his mother, what she would think if she could know the sad circumstances of his passing."

Beyond burial, water, and cleanup details, there was no work for the men. Those who stayed alive suffered through the hottest heat of the hot Philippine year through long idle day after long idle day, their bodies steadily disintegrating. Daily rations consisted of a small bowl of a watery rice gruel called *lugao*, an occasional sweet potato or squash, and a quarter of a carabao—divided among the entire camp. Soldiers who two weeks before were grumbling about living on quarter-rations were now looking at those as the good old days. They had made a bad bargain, and now all they could do was stare at the baking Philippine sun and wonder if help would ever arrive. They were dazed, confused, and didn't know what to believe. Back on Bataan, their superior officers had told them help would soon arrive, even as those officers fled for Australia. And the Japanese had been even more duplicitous. For weeks while the battle of Bataan was raging, they filled the skies with flyers showing pictures of glorious food. Surrender, the leaflets promised, and this will be yours. Well, they had surrendered, and all it had gotten them was a teacup of gruel and Japanese guards calling them cowards for doing exactly what those flyers urged them to do.

As Harold awoke each day to the filth and stench of O'Donnell, he sensed through the fog of his fatigue that he needed to get away from the place. It seemed that his weight and health were deteriorating by the minute. When he lay down on the hard boards at night he could feel every rib. He had not bathed in a month. And yet, relative to so many of his comrades, he knew he had been lucky. He was still one of the men who got water for others who could not, he still had not caught malaria or dysentery, miraculously enough, and he still had the energy to swat flies off his food. Corporal Poole, United States Army Air Corps, was able to function fairly normally, all things considered. But there was death in the place, too much death. He was surrounded by it, he was a spectator to it, and daily he watched it add to its total.

Work details were being formed for labor outside the camp. The Japanese were anxious to rebuild roads and bridges blown up during the past four months of fighting, and to salvage weapons, scrap iron, steel, and other war materials scattered across Luzon. Word was disseminated throughout Camp O'Donnell: those captives desiring to join one of these details would be assigned to a group and sent on their way. They only needed to be strong enough to hold a pencil and sign up.

Harold found a volunteer list and scrawled his name. His reasoning for leaving was simple: "I thought that they could not possibly send me to a place that was worse."

CHAPTER NINE

July 1, 2000
San Diego, California

BONNIE KANE TILTED BACK IN HER CHAIR and summed up the JPOW lawsuit for me in exactly fifteen words: "If this isn't the definition of a tort case, then I don't know what is."

Ms. Kane was behind her desk at the law offices of Casey, Gerry, Reed & Schenk, a San Diego firm devoted to the practice of PI litigation—my brothers and sisters in the law. The walls of the two-story building were lined with framed newspaper articles attesting to the firm's success: "Mall Awarded $14 Million in Asbestos Case"; "Brain-Damaged Boy Awarded $6.8 Million"; "Hit Jogger Awarded $3 Million."

But in Bonnie's office, the walls were lined with book after book about World War II in the Pacific. For more than a year now, she had immersed herself in research about what the prisoners of the Japanese had endured, where they were forced to live, and whom they were forced to work for. In the process she had not only become intimately familiar with the pain and suffering incident to the Japanese captivity, she had also gotten to know some of the men who survived it. To Bonnie, the veterans of the Pacific were heroes as well as clients—she called every one of them "Mister"—and no matter what the executive branch of the United States government thought, she was convinced they were due justice. As tort law put it, these men had been wronged by not receiving their just wages, and that wrong could be righted by the Japanese companies being ordered by a court of justice to pay them the wages. It was as simple as that.

Bonnie Kane typified the reservoir of lawyers and legal resources working the JPOW case. Another half-dozen attorneys and paralegals in the

Casey firm alone were actively involved in research and strategy, and that was just the start of a network stretching from the West Coast to the East Coast.

In their wildest expectations, the former JPOWs could not have imagined legal representation on such a scale.

The official name of the mega-firm was Herman, Mathis, Casey, Kitchen & Gerel, LLP, HermanMathis for short. The firm's roots could be traced back to the tobacco company cases in the 1990s when two prominent Big Tobacco lawyers—David Casey Jr. of Casey, Gerry, Reed & Schenk in San Diego and Russ Herman of Herman, Herman, Katz & Cotlar in New Orleans—co-opted their firm's resources, along with the resources of dozens of other firms around the country, to help realize the $200 billion tobacco settlement.

Envisioning the same kind of collaboration in other cases with a national scope, Dave Casey and Russ Herman broached their idea with associates Charles Mathis of the Law Offices of Charles Mathis in Atlanta; Jim Kitchen of Kitchen & Ellis in Jackson, Mississippi; and Martin Gerel of Ashcraft & Gerel in Rockville, Maryland. Herman, Mathis, Casey, Kitchen & Gerel was born.

In early 1999, HermanMathis set up its national headquarters office in Atlanta and hired Harvard Law graduate Ed Konieczny to administer a staff of paralegals and secretaries.

All that remained was an inaugural case to get things started—which is when Lester Tenney's fifty-five-year-old World War II grievance walked through the door.

Lester was hardly the first survivor of Japan's wartime slave labor to enter an attorney's office. Over the decades, many veterans had tried to find a legal remedy for their indentured servitude. But no matter how hopeful or inventive, the cases filed inevitably collided with either statutes of limitations or the 1951 peace treaty, or both, and were dismissed.

Two things made Lester Tenney's case different. The first was Senator Tom Hayden's legislation in the California legislature that provided entrée into the California court system, giving Lester a place to sue Mitsui Mining, the company that used him as a slave.

The second was HermanMathis.

Attorney Mike Goldstein brought the case to the firm's attention after Lester had visited Goldstein's office in Cardiff-by-the-Sea, a beachside community twenty miles north of San Diego and just up the road from

Tenney's home in La Jolla. Goldstein ran a one-man PI shop not unlike mine in Palm Desert. His specialty was tire-defect cases, not World War II slave-labor grievances, which was why he turned to our mutual friend and colleague, David Casey Jr. in San Diego. Goldstein knew there were many other Lester Tenneys out there—the firm later estimated that nearly six thousand American Pacific slave laborers were still alive, along with twenty thousand–plus heirs of those not alive. The case clearly had major national ramifications.

Casey arranged a meeting with his new HermanMathis partners to discuss whether the JPOW case might qualify as the firm's flagship cause.

At first the reception was lukewarm, given the history of such lawsuits. But then the case got what all cases need: a strong advocate. Jim Kitchen developed a soft spot for the decades-old grievance, and the more the Mississippi lawyer learned about the injustices, the harder he lobbied. The case was national in scope, and with the changing legislative climate, it looked winnable. HermanMathis decided to take it on.

With the filing of *Tenney v. Mitsui & Co., Ltd., et al* by HermanMathis in August of 1999, and the hundreds of class-action plaintiffs and single-case actions that followed, the former JPOWs suddenly—and for the first time—had a formidable force behind them. For almost sixty years they had been nearly invisible. While the war in Europe was receiving the bulk of attention, they had been sent to the Philippines on the other side of the world. They had been seriously outmanned and outgunned when the war in the Pacific began in 1941. They received no additional help when they defended—and eventually surrendered—the Philippines. As captives, they were out of reach and largely forgotten. And when they came home after the war, the government asked them not to talk about their mistreatment.

The mega-firm had the assets the men needed most: resources to keep going, legal expertise, and perhaps of most significance, the hallmark of all trial lawyers, an almost pathological inability to surrender.

These were not safe, conservative, take-your-paycheck-and-go-home attorneys. These were attorneys who would take on the tobacco companies of America when everyone thought they were nuts. These were attorneys who every day of their professional lives fought national and international insurance companies, automobile manufacturers, pharmaceutical giants, governments of all sizes and levels, multinational corporations—all of them with legal departments a hundred times their size. And they only got paid if they won.

Between them, the founding attorneys of the mega-firm had tried thousands of cases and settled fifty times that many. Dave Casey held the distinction of obtaining the largest personal injury settlement in San Diego. Russ Herman and his brother Maury were among the instigators of the Castano Group that helped pioneer the Big Tobacco litigation and its historic subsequent settlements. Russ Herman was the author of *The Art of Persuasion*, a cult classic among PI lawyers. Jim Kitchen had secured one of the largest copyright-abuse verdicts in U.S. legal history, and Charles Mathis was one of the preeminent African American civil rights lawyers in the South.

But as much as they had accomplished, the PI lawyers knew that on the JPOW case, they needed reinforcements.

The international nature of the case, the war treaty, and the close interest of the federal government took the JPOW case well beyond a straightforward liability dispute. The simple tort case was really not that simple. Besides trial lawyers, it needed lawyers who knew government.

Services were secured from two of the best law firms with government lobbying experience in the country, Greenberg Traurig and Patton Boggs.

These firms were at the opposite end of the spectrum from contingency-fee practitioners: their buildings were filled with traditional corporate-attorney trappings, such as brass fixtures and crystal chandeliers and staffs that numbered in the hundreds, almost all of them paid by the hour.

Greenberg Traurig and Patton Boggs were well known to Washington insiders, with contacts throughout all three branches of government. Each firm counted among its clients presidential nominee George W. Bush—and would soon successfully defend the future president in the Florida 2000 presidential election dispute. Members of the Greenberg Traurig firm who would help with the JPOW case included Ron Kleinman, a former State Department attorney who would become the mega-firm's treaty expert and twice was awarded the Secretary of State's Superior Honor Award and Medal during his tenure there; Alan Foster, a magna cum laude graduate of Harvard Law School and, among other national appointments, the U.S. government's representative to the International Agency Dispute Resolution Centre in Paris; and Joe Reeder, a former Under Secretary of the United States Army.

At Patton Boggs, the lineup included Steven Schneebaum, a multilingual international law expert; Jonathan Yarowsky, former House Judiciary Committee general counsel and special counsel to President Bill Clinton before reentering private practice; Karen Marangi, a Stanford Law School graduate who previously worked as counsel to the Senator Patrick Leahy on the Senate Judiciary Committee; and Thomas Hale "Tom" Boggs Jr., son of two former members of the United States Congress, brother of ABC-TV newscaster Cokie Roberts, a perennial member of the *National Law Journal*'s "Top 100 Lawyers in America," and arguably the most influential Democratic lobbyist in the country.

To ensure that nothing about the JPOW case would go unnoticed, the mega-firm hired the D.C.-based public relations firm Policy Impact.

For the one-man "storefront" firm of James W. Parkinson esq. to join such a team was as unexpected as it was intimidating. I remember the first strategy meeting I attended, not long after the case was filed. We were in the Patton Boggs conference room in Washington, D.C., and I looked around the conference table at an all-star legal lineup of Dave Casey, Maury Herman, Jonathan Yarowsky, Joe Reeder, Alan Foster, and Tom Boggs. I turned to Casey, the man in the room I knew best, and whispered, "I hope they don't grade this thing on a curve."

But for all the individual assets, the real strength of the team was the sum of all our parts. We had researchers, treaty experts, litigators, strategists, and people who knew people. Everyone had a specialty. Mike Goldstein and I took the lead in securing depositions from our clients and briefing them on strategy and how the case was going. It was what we did and what we were good at.

In addition to the case's revolutionary crusade for justice, the profit potential, to be honest, was equally compelling. If Bonnie Kane's "simple tort cases" were allowed to run the course of a simple tort case, and prevail, neither the plaintiffs nor their counsel would be worrying about money anytime soon.

In a normal loss-of-wages action, damages are typically awarded by calculating the amount of the lost wages, plus interest. In Lester Tenney's case, for example, that meant calculating the number of hours he worked at the Mitsui coal mine at Fukuoka, Japan, multiplying those hours by a reasonable hourly rate, and then factoring in fifty-plus years of interest.

Lester's records showed that he was "employed" at the coal mine for nearly twenty-five months—from August 8, 1943 through September 2, 1945—with rarely a day off. He worked twelve-hour shifts. In checking comparative Japanese pay scales for coal mine laborers during that period, it was determined that Lester should have been paid an average of $1.15 per hour for each of the nearly eight thousand hours he worked. Using that arithmetic, Mitsui owed him a little over $9,000 for his services at the end of the war.

But Mitsui had not paid him at the end of the war, and after calculating a 7 percent compounding interest rate over fifty-five years (authorized under the California statute enacted as a result of Tom Hayden's senate bill), Lester's back-pay total, as of the summer of 2000, came to slightly more than $550,000.

Some POWs worked fewer hours and fewer days than Lester and some worked more. Using his case as an average and multiplying it by the 5,695 slave laborers still alive at the time the suit was filed resulted in a total of about $3 billion in wages owed by more than forty Japanese companies identified as JPOW employers.

Add in another fifteen to twenty thousand heirs of deceased slave laborers who could legally lay claim to lost wages of their loved ones, and the number climbed into the $15 billion range.

That was not all. Once in court, the men could also bring testimony about broken backs or arms or crushed ribs or any other physical, mental, or emotional distress brought about as a direct result of their employment, and use that as a basis to seek additional recompense for pain and suffering, which the California statute also allowed.

As astronomical as the numbers were, they were not unrealistic for the simple reason that many, if not most, of the companies being sued had astronomical numbers of their own. Mitsubishi and Mitsui, the largest of the JPOW employers, had emerged from Japan's postwar ruins to become, respectively, the third and fourth wealthiest companies in the world. Nippon Steel, the company that employed Harold Poole, was also enormously wealthy. And the list went on.

According to the firm's research, all of the companies the mega-firm hoped to sue were in a position to be able to pay their back wages, or at the very least sit down with their former employees and work out an out-of-court settlement both sides could live with.

But if the money and the tort laws were in place to make either a settlement or an outright victory feasible, there were also plenty of sufficiently strong problems to give pause to even the hardiest of the riverboat gambler-type lawyers taking it on. The 1951 peace treaty was just part of it. There was also a half century of friendly U.S.–Japanese business and political relations to consider, in addition to the enormous lobbying and legal power of the Japanese corporations. Not only did these companies retain some of the best public relations strategists in the United States, but as the mega-firm lawyers had already discovered, Mitsui, Mitsubishi, Nippon Steel, and the others were also represented by highly competent American lawyers of their own, and they could afford to pay them handsomely for their services.

There was not an attorney working the case who was not aware there was a distinct possibility that we might wind up with nothing.

That did not, however, slow down the effort. The mega-firm invested well over a million dollars in the first year alone, and I was personally already in for at least twenty-five thousand dollars in expenses, plus another five thousand miles on my car and hundreds of hours talking on the phone and traveling to meet clients.

A good PI lawyer knows to hedge his bets, but I was not hedging this bet, and I knew there were others working the case who felt the same way. There was an intangible to the case that would not let us turn away from the cause, or the men at its heart.

The pull of the case reminded me of something I once read in *To Kill A Mockingbird*, Harper Lee's classic 1960 novel about Atticus Finch, a southern lawyer who, against considerable odds, defends a black man falsely accused of raping a white woman. One early morning when I could not sleep any longer I pulled the book from a shelf in my library and turned to page eighty-six. Atticus explains to his young daughter, Scout, why he took the case: "Scout, simply by the nature of the work, every lawyer gets at least one case in his lifetime that affects him personally. This one's mine, I guess."

CHAPTER TEN

May 15, 1942
Cabcaben, Bataan, Philippines

HE FOUND THE BIBLE on the jungle floor, partially obscured in the dirt. It had probably been dropped by a GI who, like himself, had rushed to surrender.

Glancing from side to side to make sure he was out of sight of the guard, Harold stooped down and picked up the book. He brushed off the dust and the words *Holy Bible* appeared. The book was in excellent condition, all things considered. The pages were worn and there were several handwritten notations in the margins, but it was intact. It was a two-inch-by-three-inch GI edition of the King James Version. Harold slipped it into his pocket.

He was just outside the village of Cabcaben near the southeastern tip of the Bataan Peninsula, about five miles up the road from Mariveles. After marching eighty-five miles to Camp O'Donnell, Harold was right back where he had started.

They had hauled him out of O'Donnell in the back of a truck with dozens of other prisoners who volunteered for work detail. Leaving thousands of dying and near-dying soldiers, the truck drove south again on National Road, retracing the Death March route and passing bodies still rotting where they had fallen more than a month earlier. The Japanese were not interested in picking up the dead; they were interested in picking up scrap left behind from the fighting. All across Bataan were wrecked trucks, tanks, planes, rifles, helmets, bullet casings, and other war junk that could be salvaged and sent to Japan to be melted down and turned into new steel and bullets.

Harold's platoon, a collection of calculating Yankee opportunists like himself who seized the chance to flee O'Donnell, was billeted at an elevated schoolhouse in Cabcaben. The Japanese guards took up residence in the building above whereas the prisoners stayed outside in the shaded area below. Every day, the prisoners, eight to a guard, would scour fields, jungles, and the shoreline of Manila Bay, picking up the mangled mess created by the U.S.-Filipino troops when they destroyed their equipment upon surrender.

It was dusty, dirty, backbreaking work, performed in debilitating heat and humidity, but life away from O'Donnell was better than life at O'Donnell. There was more water here and something to do other than watch men die. But there was still too little food, almost zero sanitation, and malaria-carrying mosquitoes were thicker in the jungle.

No one was getting healthier. Every week, a truck would arrive with new volunteers and leave with men too sick or too weak to salvage scrap anymore.

As bad as the physical conditions were, the psychological conditions were in many ways worse. Defeat was everywhere. Every time a man hauled a burned-out truck chassis out of the jungle or a stripped-down M40 rifle, it was a reminder not just of U.S. defeat and Japanese victory but also of the lack of reinforcements that MacArthur had promised. The GIs had felt stranded and alone when Bataan was still theirs. Now that it belonged to the Japanese they could not help but feel complete and total isolation. They could not write home nor receive letters from home. There was no way to know what was going on beyond their small, miserable, forgotten, hot-as-hell world.

Underscoring the gloom was the silence from Corregidor. On May 6, only days before Harold's work detail arrived back in Bataan, Corregidor had fallen. The Rock had managed to hold out twenty-seven days beyond the surrender of Bataan, but then it too, facing wholesale slaughter, gave up, effectively delivering the whole of the Philippines to the enemy. Corregidor gave the Japanese another twelve thousand military prisoners, eight thousand of them Americans that they did not want, and marked yet another triumph for the Japanese assault. With the war not yet six months old, Japan had conquered or was in effective control of much of Asia and virtually all of the various territories of the west Pacific.

Harold had lost track of his pal Nelson Quast in the confusion of O'Donnell. But fortune smiled on him again at Cabcaben when he was able to hook up with another pal from the 20th Pursuit Squadron, a soldier with the same last name: E.T. Poole. Harold, E.T., and another squad mate named Jack Pool had struck up an instant friendship at Hamilton Field in California at their first squadron roll call when the commanding officer called out "Pool" and three voices answered in unison. After that, the men in the outfit gave the three Pools nicknames. E.T. was "Cess," Jack was "Whirl," and Harold was "Pocket."

That had been in October of 1940, only a year and a half ago. Now it seemed part of another lifetime.

At night, after the sun went down and they stretched out on the hard ground below the schoolhouse, Harold and the men could look across the bay at the lights of Manila only thirty miles away. It was difficult to comprehend that the city was going about its business with even a modicum of regularity. Harder yet to comprehend was that just six months ago they had been a part of that regularity, free to move about as they pleased: to hail a cab; to get measured for a suit; to walk into a restaurant and order a thick steak, cooked as they liked it, with a baked potato on the side and a slice of apple pie a la mode for dessert. And maybe have a smoke after that.

Harold remembered the day he arrived. It was November 23, 1940, Thanksgiving Day. The USS *Washington* docked at Manila Bay after a voyage that began in California on Halloween and included stops in Honolulu and Shanghai before stopping in Manila to let off the stateside troops. Two thousand soldiers stepped into a place most of them barely knew existed. Harold soon forgot the seasickness that plagued him during his first trip on the ocean. "I was instantly impressed by Manila's beauty," he said. "Dewey Boulevard was magnificent." Named for the American commander who subdued the Spanish, palm tree–lined Dewey Boulevard paralleled the bay and was an inviting corridor fronting a city filled with exotic Spanish architecture, tropical foliage, and cabs driven by carametto ponies.

Some stateside units were already in the islands, but not so many that it wasn't an event when new ones arrived. The Philippine Army Band and a sizeable crowd of natives waited at the dock to greet the troops as they walked down the gangplank.

There were fifteen million Filipinos then living in the islands and fifteen thousand Americans, the majority of them military men. The 20th Pursuit Squadron joined several other Army Air Corps units stationed near downtown Manila at Nichols Field, where the amenities included a golf course and a swimming pool.

After the regimentation at basic training in California, Harold and his mates found it easy to adapt to the laid-back ways of the Filipinos. They discovered Manila to be a warm and friendly city, particularly welcoming to GIs with dollars in their pockets. The favorable dollars-to-pesos exchange rate allowed American soldiers to live like royalty. A haircut, shave, and shampoo cost less than a dollar. A five-course meal, the best that money could buy, was two dollars. A cab and driver for a day ran two dollars plus tip. Bar drinks were as cheap as a nickel. Virtually every soldier and sailor hired Filipino servants or houseboys to shine their shoes, make their beds, clean their barracks, and run their errands. For almost the entire first year he was in the islands, Harold did not shine his own shoes or make his bed.

Other services were available, if you wanted them. Certain Filipino women practically threw themselves in front of American GIs, for a price, and all the other traditional vices—liquor, drugs, gambling—were in similarly abundant supply, along with the usual consequences—hangovers, gonorrhea, and syphilis the most common and irritating.

In the letters he dutifully wrote home every week, Harold extolled the virtues, and the occasional vices, of a place he more than once called "paradise," where he was "living on top of the world." He had plenty of "pals" and "buddies," plenty to see, and plenty to do. He liked his armament job and excelled at it, passing the air mechanics rating test on his first try, despite no formal schooling. That more than doubled his pay to eighty-two dollars a month, an amount that could get a soldier in a lot of trouble in Manila, if the soldier were so inclined. Harold was not. He was not much for clubs and nightlife, and regularly sent half or more of his draw home to his accountant father for safekeeping. He was saving for a new car for when he bid the Army adieu.

In the hot season, which seemed to be most of the year, the heat was too oppressive to work during the afternoon, so work shifts tended to start early in the morning and end by noon. Harold used his free time to get to know Manila, and after the 20th Pursuit Squadron was transferred to Clark Field, the surrounding countryside in southern Luzon. An avid picture-taker (he was the assistant squadron photographer), he packed his camera while he explored the woods and jungles, hunted in the hills, fished in the streams, went skin diving in the clear waters of Manila Bay, and ventured by car or on horseback into the interior of the island. There he discovered waterfalls; strange Christian rituals; ancient villages inhabited by *balugas* (indigenous tribes); the ubiquitous carabao, which was also known as "water buffalo" and "Filipino cow"; and the occasional python. He sent hundreds of photographs home (including a snapshot of the python for his sisters) and many souvenirs. His mother's storage room filled up with exotic knives, belt buckles, ivory carvings, and Chinese kimonos, all documentation that Nina Poole's son was having an adventure halfway around the world.

But the adventure had little to do with the threat of war, the perception of which was minimal at best. America was America, was the prevailing attitude among both the imported military and the native populace in the Philippines at the beginning of the 1940s. And the Philippines were part of America. Who in their right mind would attack the strongest nation on Earth, even though it was here, in these islands far from the country's continental borders? The men stationed in and around Manila mostly saw themselves as a deterrent to war. They were peacekeepers more than fighters, friends more than foes.

In his letters, Harold reflected that prevailing attitude. On August 31, 1941, after nine months in the Philippines and on the one-year anniversary of his joining the Army, he wrote:

> Dear Mother:
>
> I have one year up and in. Summing it all up, it didn't go so bad. I am in excellent condition. I am pretty sure that two more years will see me home, and with a little luck maybe before that . . . I read in the paper that twelve thousand men are on the way over here, and the same amount will leave here when they arrive. This all points to the fact that the United States is not very much afraid for the Philippines' safety . . . I am afraid now that we won't have any war with the Japs, and even if we did, it would be just my luck to not even see or hear any action.

In a letter two months later, dated October 29, 1941, he expanded on his skepticism of a Japanese attack:

> I don't think the Japs are foolhardy enough to start anything themselves. God help them if they do, they won't last six months against the United States.

On November 18, 1941, Harold wrote of the laid-back, almost sleepy life of a soldier in the Philippines, and of his expectations to soon leave it all behind:

> Last Sunday, I took a long hike up into the mountainous jungles, farther than I have ever been, and had a pretty good time of it. I got a notion to take a hike alone again just to remind me of the times I used to do it in the States, and slipped away by myself. You can always get plenty of guys to go with you all the time, but I wanted to go alone this once at least. You can always see and hear lots of things which you can never see when a lot of fellows are along trying to out-talk each other. I killed a snake which was around four feet long. I don't know what kind it was, but I wasn't going to take any chances with it. I found another Baluga village, and I let some of the men shoot my air-pistol, and they acted happy as a kid with a new toy. They are simple-minded people, and yet I have to admire the little fellows and the way they live off the jungles. They seem to live the same almost as they did when God put them on earth. The jungles are beautiful but deceptive, and it is very easy to get lost in all that thick foliage if you leave the beaten trails. You know that story about Tarzan? Well, I have found out that it could be true. The trees in some places are hundreds of feet high with large vines hanging down from them. These vines can be cut at the roots, and you can swing on them for all you are worth and they won't come loose. We used one of these vines about an inch and a half thick and about 150 feet long to climb up on the steep bank and dive off into the deep river. It was still there, and in good shape when I went up there this last time. I stopped off and had a nice cool swim all alone there. It was sure refreshing.
>
> Yes, the jungles are interesting and different, but I wouldn't trade them all for the hills and lakes back home. The best thing around here are thoughts of getting home and being with all the loved ones there. That is the big goal I am working for all the time. I always try to do my best, with that thought in view, and not

to do anything that would be a barrier or throwback to my getting home safely and soon.

Love, Harold

Twenty days later the Japanese attacked and war began. Less than six months after that, the foolhardy Japanese were in complete command of the Philippines.

Without a decent meal in nearly five months and hardly any food in the past month, with sleep proving more and more difficult on hip bones with no padding, Harold turned hard to the only comfort left: God.

"I knew I needed help," he said. "We all did. And we couldn't lean on each other; everyone else was as bad off as you were. So we prayed. I say 'we' because we all did I'm sure. I did real sincerely because I needed help. And I thought it would be wonderful if I could get some scriptures, not knowing where or how or anything."

He was on a routine search detail when he found the Bible. His group was scavenging an area about three-quarters of a mile off the highway where a U.S. Army field hospital once stood. It was obvious that the medics had left in a hurry, leaving debris everywhere, and there was plenty of scrap to be picked up. For several days, Harold's detail returned for more searching. Each time, coming and going, they had to step over the body of a dead Filipino soldier sprawled across the trail. The body had no head. "We tried to get the Jap guards to let us bury it, but they wanted us to work. They just left it there."

"We were coming down from the hospital, just kind of going through the jungle area, not on a trail or anything, and that's where the little Bible was lying on the ground," Harold said. "Nothing else was around, just the Bible."

"I felt bad for the soldier who lost it, if he was still alive," said Harold. "But it saved my life. A lot of guys were asking why would the Lord let all this happen, and that was bothering me too, and I found that the Bible was full of answers and comfort. The Bible tells us it might be to let us be chastised so we'll be a better person, and we'll live a better life."

The Bible was not the only lifesaver Harold found.

In their haste to vacate, the hospital staff had also left behind scattered quantities of medicines. Included were some quinine pills, the antidote for malaria that had dwindled to nonexistent status. As the incidence of malaria continued to climb, quinine pills sold for hundreds of dollars apiece on the black market—if you were lucky enough to have that kind of money and knew where to get them.

A few days after finding his Bible, Harold happened upon the quinine pills. It was not a large supply, just a handful. He quickly hid them in his pants pocket.

Somehow, Harold had lived in the jungle for six months with millions of mosquitoes and no protection and had not contracted malaria. But he had seen firsthand what the disease could do to a man. He would not sell these pills; he would keep them close in case he ever needed them.

Within days, he needed them.

Harold woke up one morning with a fever, followed by violent chills. The alternating hot-and-cold spasms—malaria's signature—continued throughout the day. The guards tried to prod him to get up and go to work, but he could barely get off the ground.

When the replacement truck arrived the next day, Harold was thrown in the back. So was E.T. Poole. "Cess" and "Pocket" were both sick with malaria and leaving Cabcaben like the scrap they had been hauling.

The truck wound its way back up the peninsula, heading north along Death March road. But Harold was not walking this time. He lay in a fetal position in a GI truck driven by a Japanese soldier.

When the truck reached the railhead at San Fernando, instead of continuing north toward Capas, and then Camp O'Donnell, it turned right, or east. It continued another thirty miles through Pampanga Province and then into Nueva Ecija Province, finally pulling to a stop in front of a large Japanese flag atop a flagpole. The guards ordered the men out of the truck. Those who were able staggered to their feet. Harold was revived enough to step out shakily under his own power. He watched as two guards grabbed E.T. and dumped him at the base of the flagpole. Harold rubbed his red eyes and looked through a blur at the enemy flag and the guard towers and grass huts beyond.

He had arrived at the entrance to the largest prisoner-of-war camp in the Pacific, a place that in time would take a position in infamy among the most deadly and notoriously inhumane camps of the Second World War.

Harold had arrived at Cabanatuan.

CHAPTER ELEVEN

August 17, 2000
San Francisco, California

FINALLY, after considerable time and effort, we got to court.

The date was August 17, 2000, and the place was a federal courthouse in San Francisco, the city where in 1951 forty-nine countries, including Japan and the United States, signed the peace treaty that was at the core of our dispute.

By this point, two of the three branches of American government had taken opposite positions on the JPOW case. The legislative branch, with Senator Hatch offering strong support in Washington, was largely on the side of the veterans, while the executive branch, with the State Department acting as spokesperson, was firm in its opinion that the 1951 treaty disallowed any such lawsuits.

A hearing to debate the issue, while entertaining a motion filed by the threatened Japanese companies asking the federal judiciary to dismiss all World War II actions against them, was scheduled by Federal District Judge Vaughn R. Walker.

It was time for the third branch of American government, the judiciary, to determine where it stood.

Since the United States Constitution clearly states that binding treaties are on equal standing with the Constitution in establishing the supreme law of the land, the debate was over the wording of the 1951 treaty. Did the treaty allow U.S. nationals to sue Japanese nationals in U.S. courts?

Everyone with a stake in the fight was represented. There were attorneys for the aging American veterans, attorneys for the Japanese companies, and attorneys from the United States Department of Justice, Civil

Division, to argue for the State Department. More than two dozen attorneys were present, along with assorted paralegals and aides.

There was only one person present, ironically enough, who was an actual principal in the fight. That was Lester Tenney, who came at the mega-firm's invitation. We sat Lester in a prominent position in the courtroom so the judge could get a good look at the face of the case.

The defendants argued first. Margaret Pfeiffer of the Washington, D.C., law firm Sullivan & Cromwell, which was representing Nippon Steel, got straight to the point.

"Your honor," she began, "Forty-nine years ago this month in this city the claims that are being brought by the plaintiffs were completely and finally resolved. They weren't resolved in a federal courtroom or in any other courtroom, and indeed, they can't be resolved in any other courtroom, because they were resolved by the negotiation that was assembled here to negotiate, draft, and sign a treaty ending the war with Japan. As part of that treaty, one of the most important features was the settlement of claims issue . . . and what was effected was a settlement and a release of claims. The allies received all of the property belonging to Japanese nationals that was located anywhere in an allied country. All of the Japanese nationals' property that was located in any neutral country went into a fund that was administered by the International Red Cross, to be given to prisoners of war who had been mistreated during the time that they were imprisoned in Japan."

Ms. Pfeiffer gave the judge a short history lesson about what the defense felt was the treaty's intended postwar purpose—an interpretation that her firm felt well equipped to explain, since John Foster Dulles, the chief architect of the 1951 treaty, was a member of Sullivan & Cromwell before he became secretary of state to President Dwight D. Eisenhower.

"The point that was very clear," Pfeiffer said, "is that it was to make certain that Japan had settled everything and could move forward to strengthen its economy. The goal of the United States for Japan was that Japanese companies would become strong, and Japan's economy would become strong, and they would be prosperous in the future, so that Japan could continue to contribute as a strong member of the free world.

"And I think, your honor, looking back forty-nine years, that it would be hard to find a better bargain struck or one that has more faithfully and fully realized the hopes of the people who did it. And they did it at the end of a very bitter war, recognizing great pain, anger, and everything else. That was the view that these people took, and it has paid off in a very strong, productive relationship between the United States and Japan."

Ms. Pfeiffer yielded the floor to Justice Department attorney David Anderson, who began with a disclaimer. "I want to stress that it is only the interests of the United States that I represent here," he said. "I do not represent the government of Japan, and I do not represent the Japanese companies."

From the bench, Judge Walker said, "I don't think there's any question about that, is there?"

"There shouldn't be," said Anderson, trying his best to sound a sympathetic note for the plaintiffs whose case he was about to discredit. "But it goes without saying that the United States deplores the kind of conduct that is alleged in the complaints here and we are here not to injure men who sacrificed for their country, but instead to vindicate the interests of the United States in carrying out an international obligation that this country made in the peace treaty of 1951."

With those pleasantries out of the way, the government attorney opened fire.

"There can't be any doubt that the power of the national government is at its zenith when you're talking about the declaration, conduct, and termination of a war," he said. "That's about the most expansive power there is in the constitution. And pursuant to those war powers, a national decision was made by the political branches in 1951 to limit claims by the United States and its nationals against Japan and its nationals. This peace treaty was of course, as every treaty is, negotiated by the executive branch. It was approved by the Senate, after extensive debate, which focused largely on this waiver of claims provision, and then the entire congress came along and enacted amendments to the War Claims Act, which provided for the disbursement of those seized Japanese assets to former prisoners of war and other victims.

"So this truly was a national decision made with the concurrence of the political branches. It's easy to sit here in the year 2000 and say that these Japanese companies are wealthy and profitable, and they should now have to account for what they did during the war. But you have to look at this peace treaty in the context of its time. In 1951, the Cold War was in full flower. You had the Korean War right on the doorstep of Japan. You had a communist regime that had just taken power in China, you had the worldwide threat of Soviet expansionism, and Japan was at the fulcrum of these geopolitical forces. The United States viewed an economically stable, anticommunist Japan as an essential ingredient of its interests in the Pacific region. Japan couldn't play that role if it were subject to continuing war claims that might stifle its economy.

"That's the only way that you could have avoided what the Allies intended not to repeat, and that was the experience of the Versailles Treaty after World War I, when Germany was brought to its knees. It's one of the causes of World War II. The Allies did not want to repeat that."

Anderson sat down. It was the plaintiffs' turn.

Our treaty expert, Ron Kleinman from Greenberg Traurig, began with a reminder that the executive branch of the government was not all-powerful and could be disagreed with.

"Let me say something about the executive branch views and the weight that this court should give them," said Kleinman. "Where a view of the executive branch is one taken between governments in diplomatic notes, is historical, and supported by consistent practice, courts give substantial deference. Where the case is presented on an amicus basis, courts commonly reject the position of the executive branch, not always, not even disproportionately, but it is not uncommon for courts to reject the views of the executive branch."

The lawyer looked at the judge. "All parties agree that you are the final decision maker," he said.

"All right, well, that's reassuring," said Judge Walker, drawing scattered laughter around the courtroom.

"Ultimately," Kleinman went on, "the court must be guided by the intent of the negotiators, forty-eight countries, not John Foster Dulles, forty-eight countries, all of whom made substantial compromises, including compromises by the United States, and you are to start by reading the clear language of the treaty."

Kleinman moved to the familiar debatable semantic ground of Article 14(b) and Article 26 in the treaty, contending, as Senator Hatch had earlier in the summer, that the phrase "in the prosecution of the war" in 14(b) did not apply to private companies using forced laborers, and that Article 26's "Most Favored Nation" clause allowed U.S. prisoners of war the right to seek a level of compensation commensurate with POWs and forced laborers from other nations who had subsequently received better treatment.

"No one tried to write Article 26 out of the treaty," said Kleinman. "Nobody authorized the United States in the year 2000 or the year 1951 or 1955 or 1957 to waive that right. The president does not have the authority to waive a right that the United States has under a treaty. It's not a political question, it is automatic."

Further, Kleinman petitioned the court that peace treaties did not, as a matter of law, supercede basic tort law.

"It has been described to me as the difference between criminal law and tort law in the United States," he said. "They operate on different planes, but the same act can be both a tort and a crime; a battery (for instance), and a wrongful death. The United States government controls the criminal law claim, and nothing that the private victim does can waive that criminal claim. The private party controls the tort law claim. Nothing that the United States does can waive the right to pursue that tort. They operate on the same facts, at two different levels, with two different rights of waiver, and in a treaty, under international law, the United States would not be expected to waive both the criminal level rights and the tort level rights. They are two very distinct matters."

With that, Judge Walker thanked the participants and without a nod to the left or the right, banged his gavel, bringing the hearing to a close. From start to finish, it lasted one hour and fifty-five minutes.

After the hearing, I joined Kleinman, David Casey, Joe Reeder, Bonnie Kane, Mike Goldstein, Maury Herman, and Lester Tenney in the federal building cafeteria to compare notes. We agreed that it was hard to read the judge, who indicated he would rule on the issue shortly, probably within a month. No one was turning cartwheels, but no one was throwing in the towel either. We also all agreed on another thing: this was definitely new legal ground we were plowing.

We commiserated with one another on the difficulty of facing a lineup of not just some of America's top corporate attorneys, but also one that had the U.S. government batting cleanup. By our count, seventeen private attorneys had been in the courtroom, all working for various Japanese corporations and not one of them, we were sure, making less than $300 an hour. And yet, with the exception of Margaret Pfeiffer and one or two others who made short clarifications, they all sat in the seats and made their hourly wages while Anderson from Justice made their case for them.

I considered the incongruity of a legal battle pitting the United States government against the very men who helped preserve that government. More loyal, patriotic, law-abiding Americans would be hard to find. I felt comfortable in saying that. I knew these men. I had signed them onto the case by the dozens. I had been to their houses. They had been to my office. They had remarkable stories to tell. Manny Eneriz, a devout Catholic, had me mesmerized when he told me about standing on a ladder in the hold of a crowded hell ship where starving, suffocating men were on the verge of a riot until Manny led them in the rosary. Such tales were legion with the men.

They were not ashamed of who they were or what they had done. Nor had they turned their backs on their country. They wore their patriotism on their sleeve. When I was having trouble finding Tom Nixon's home in Ramona, California, I called him on my cell phone for directions. "Turn at the gas station, come up the hill and when you see two flags, that's my house," he said. I turned at the gas station, came up the hill and there were two huge flags, one the Stars and Stripes and one the United States Marine Corps flag, waving in the breeze.

I started taking my father along on recruiting trips so he could meet some of his fellow World War II vets. When I took him to meet Homer Boren in Scottsdale, Arizona, we visited about the case and then said our goodbyes at the door. On my way to the car, I realized my father was not with me. I looked back at the front porch and saw Homer and my father saluting each other in farewell.

That's the caliber of men we were representing against their own government.

Judge Walker's verdict came by fax.

It was early September and Lupe walked in my office with the disappointing, but not entirely unexpected, news.

The executive branch prevailed—on all counts.

In dismissing all World War II–era forced-labor lawsuits, the judge established that, first, the federal judiciary had jurisdiction over state courts in the matter, "because these actions raise substantial questions of federal law by implicating the federal common law of foreign relations."

And second, that, "the court concludes that plaintiffs' claims are barred by the Treaty of Peace with Japan."

The judge was not persuaded that either Article 14(b) or Article 26 allowed the POWs their day in court.

Of Article 14(b) he stated: "To avoid the preclusive effect of the treaty, plaintiffs advance an interpretation of Article 14(b) that is strained and, ultimately, unconvincing. Although the argument has several shades, it comes down to this: the signatories of the treaty did not understand the Allied waiver to apply to prisoner-of-war claims because the provision did not expressly identify such claims, in contrast to the corresponding Japanese waiver provision of Article 19. Article 19(b) states that the Japanese waiver includes 'any claims and debts arising in respect to Japanese prisoner-of-war and civilian internees in the hands of the Allied Powers'. That the treaty is more specific in Article 19 does not change the plain meaning of the language of Article 14. If the language of Article 14 were ambiguous, plaintiffs' *expressio unius* argument would have more force. But plaintiffs cannot identify any ambiguity in the language of Article 14. To do so would be to inject hidden meaning into straightforward text."

As for the argument that Article 26 allowed American prisoners of war to petition for a better settlement, the judge wrote in his opinion that "without deciding whether the evidence plaintiff cites of other agreements implicates Article 26, the court finds that that provision confers rights *only* upon the parties to the present treaty, i.e., the government signatories. The question of enforcing Article 26 is thus for the United States, not the plaintiffs, to decide."

In a general summation, the judge wrote that the court was satisfied that the 1951 treaty settled the matter of claims against the Japanese.

"The court does not find the treaty language ambiguous, and therefore its analysis need go no further," he wrote. "Counsel for both sides have proved themselves skilled in scouring these documents for support of their positions, and that both sides have succeeded to a certain degree underscores the questionable value of such resort to drafting history. Nevertheless, the court has conducted its own review of the historical materials, and concludes that they reinforce the conclusion that the Treaty of Peace with Japan was intended to bar claims such as those advanced by plaintiffs in this litigation.

"The official record of treaty negotiations established that a fundamental goal of the agreement was to settle the reparations issue once and for all. As the statement of the chief United States negotiator, John Foster Dulles, makes clear, it was well understood that leaving open the possibility of future claims would be an unacceptable impediment to a lasting peace:

> Reparation is usually the most controversial aspect of peacemaking. The present peace is no exception. On the one hand, there are claims both vast and just. Japan's aggression caused tremendous cost, losses, and suffering . . . On the other hand, to meet these claims, there stands a Japan presently reduced to four home islands which are unable to produce the food its people need to live, or the raw materials they need to work. Under these circumstances, if the treaty validated, or kept contingently alive, monetary reparations claims against Japan, her ordinary commercial credit would vanish, the incentive of her people would be destroyed and they would sink into a misery of body and spirit that would make them easy prey to exploitation. There would be bitter competition (among the Allies) for the largest possible percentage of an illusory pot of gold."

The judge closed his order with a reminder of who won the war and what that meant for the world in general, and for the plaintiffs, specifically.

"The Treaty of Peace with Japan, insofar as it barred future claims such as those asserted by plaintiffs in these actions, exchanged full compensation of plaintiffs for a future peace," he wrote. "History has vindicated the wisdom of that bargain. And while full compensation for plaintiffs," hardships, in the purely economic sense, has been denied these former prisoners and countless other survivors of the war, the immeasurable bounty of life for themselves and their posterity in a free society and in a more peaceful world services the debt."

It was not easy calling Harold, Homer, Tom, Manny, and the rest of the men. I did not want to have to be the one to inform them of another setback. But I did not want them to hear it on TV or read it in the newspaper, so I went straight to the phone.

Do not lose hope, I told the vets. We were already in the process of filing an appeal. The loss at the district court level was not unexpected.

We were prepared to take the case all the way to the United States Supreme Court.

I was pleased, but not surprised, that to a man the clients took the news in stride. Not a single former JPOW quit the case—or fired his lawyer.

CHAPTER TWELVE

June 2, 1942
Cabanatuan Prison Camp, Philippines

LEFT ON DEATH'S DOOR at Cabanatuan, Harold Poole caught a break when he was *not* put in the prison camp hospital.

He was sicker than anytime in his life, his body racked continuously by alternating spasms from fever and chills. But he could at least walk, and that spared him the fate of his buddy, E.T. Poole, who was sent to Cabanatuan's so-called hospital. St. Peter's Ward, the prisoners sardonically called it, a place where the sick mingled with the sick, got sicker, and died. The few inmate doctors there could usually identify what a man had but without medical supplies could do little for him.

Harold was sent to the central barracks, where he collapsed on a thin straw mat atop a board bunk and managed to swallow more of his quinine pills. He was fortunate that he had contracted the noncerebral form of malaria. Cerebral malaria attacks the brain and almost always results in a coma followed by death within two or three days. Noncerebral malaria attacks the body and, especially with the help of quinine, is survivable.

For centuries, malaria had plagued the tropics. It was known to wipe out entire villages before science identified the cause of the disease, a microscopic parasite carried by mosquitoes. In time, it was discovered that a natural alkaloid drug found in the bark of the cinchona tree could kill the parasite. That drug was called quinine. In the 1940s, the largest supply of quinine in the world was in Java, where large cinchona plantations produced 95 percent of the world's needs. But even though Java neighbored the Philippines, the war cut off the supply of quinine. At Cabanatuan the only quinine was on the Japanese side of the compound. On the prisoners' side, it had to be smuggled in.

Within a week, Harold's quinine began to work. Within two weeks, most of his malarial symptoms were gone. Only when he came out of his stupor did Harold learn that E.T. had died not long after he entered St. Peter's Ward. Harold had to absorb the loss of yet another friend and member of his outfit. The sting was soothed a bit a few days later when he looked up to see his old friend Nelson Quast walking into the compound. He had not seen Quast since they shared the water bucket during the Death March. "Boy, it was good to see him," said Harold. They moved their straw mats side by side in the prison barracks. The 20th Pursuit Squadron was not dead yet.

With the malaria gone, Harold looked at his new circumstances for the first time. For a moment, he thought they had sent him back to O'Donnell. He recognized the disease, the smell of death, the ever-present flies, and the cruelty. But from the other prisoners he learned that O'Donnell was in the process of being abandoned and this was its replacement. All O'Donnell prisoners—the ones still alive—were being transferred to Cabanatuan.

Like Camp O'Donnell, Cabanatuan was originally built as a training camp for the Philippine Army. The first prisoners sent to Cabanatuan were the eight thousand U.S. troops who surrendered at Corregidor. Those men had been paraded through the streets of Manila as a demonstration to the populace of Japanese military might before being sent fifty miles north to the new prison camp outside Cabanatuan City.

The men from Corregidor thought they were in pretty sorry shape until they watched the sick, emaciated prisoners from O'Donnell stumble in. Many of the walking skeletons from O'Donnell were unrecognizable to fellow soldiers who had known them well just months before.

Harold and the others were a graphic representation of what happens when the most basic standards of nutrition and hygiene are ignored. The battling bastards of Bataan had diseases caused by malnutrition and dehydration: wet and dry beriberi, cystitis, pellagra, hypoproteinemia, and scurvy. They had rampant dysentery, the result of two months of completely unsanitary living conditions. They had the tropical parasitical diseases dengue fever and malaria. And as a kind of final insult in a place where no one could escape each other's presence, they had the communicable diseases of diphtheria, jaundice, and hepatitis.

Young American men, some not yet twenty years old, were being rendered lame, crippled, blind, and insane by diseases medical science had long since whipped into submission. The problems plaguing the men were easily preventable: the vitamin B in a ripe apple would clear up the beri-beri, vitamin B12 would take care of the pellagra, vitamin C would cure the scurvy, and eating off a clean plate with clean hands would fix the dysentery. These soldiers did not need doctors; they needed their mothers.

By the summer of 1942, the military captives held in the Philippines were mostly Americans, with a small percentage of British and Dutch POWs, and almost no Filipinos. Thousands of native soldiers who had fought the Japanese were back in their villages. They were captives of the Japanese in the sense that everyone in the Philippines was captive, but otherwise free. Only those who had come to the Philippines from other lands, for the express purpose of defending it, were confined.

At Cabanatuan, the death toll continued. In June, 740 prisoners died, followed by another 786 men in July. The high was 60 men in one day—more than one dead soldier every half hour. By the end of August, more than 2,000 Americans were dead, bringing the number of U.S. deaths since the surrender of Bataan less than five months earlier to over 4,500. Of the 10,000 who started the Death March, nearly one in every two was already dead.

Most died from wounds or disease, or a combination of both. But some simply lost hope. An image from Cabanatuan that would stay with Harold all his life was of a fellow prisoner crossing the compound with a glazed-over look in his eyes. The men in camp called it "the stare." The man sat on a bench opposite Harold, seemingly physically healthy by the way he walked, and then, seconds later, he keeled over, dead. "He'd given up," remembered Harold. "His hope was gone. It was more than he could take. That's how much the mind can control the body."

The malaria reduced Harold to barely more than a walking cadaver. When the Japanese weighed him shortly after recovering he sneaked a look at the scale and noticed that he weighed 97 pounds—almost half his normal 180. Thoughts of death haunted him continually. "In the back of your mind you'd always think, 'well, I'm next,'" he remembered. "But I wanted to lick this thing and I wanted to lick these people. To do that, you had to stay alive."

The ninety-seven-pound weakling was assigned to burial detail. Every afternoon, Harold and three other prisoners would load a few bodies at a time on top of an old wooden door. Each would take a corner of the door and carry the bodies to the burial pit about a quarter mile away on the far end of the prison compound. It was heavy, sweaty—and in the mid-summer rainy season—slippery work.

There was no ceremony to it. At the edge of the pit, the men would set down the door, pick up a man by the arms and legs, and toss it onto the pile. Then they would shovel loose dirt on top. In the rainy season, the rain would turn the dirt to mud and the next day there would be arms and legs sticking out, as well as bodies scattered here and there after wild dogs had sorted through the skeletons.

"At first, we laid the bodies out all nice and even. But after a while they got so deep we just threw them in any old way to get them in there."

They buried the bodies naked, salvaging all clothing by boiling it in a fifty-five-gallon barrel. "Some of the bodies weren't in very good shape. A lot of these guys had diseases. One day we carried out a guy and I had a hold of his wrists and another fella had his ankles and when we went to throw him in the hole, the skin of his wrists came off in my hands. That's how bad some of those bodies were."

Slowly but surely, however, the living started to catch up with the dying. The men were not marching every day from sunup to sundown anymore, and there was water to drink, and regular if meager rations. Prisoners continued to die from fatigue, hunger, disease and depression every day. It would not be until December, seven months after Cabanatuan opened, that a twenty-four-hour period would pass without a single death. But the pace had slowed and a kind of bare-bones routine began to surface in the camp.

In the shadow of death, signs of life emerged. A society of sorts formed amid the mud and the heat and the flies. Personalities revealed themselves. Social cliques developed. The barracks took on a kind of unorderly order, the pathways between them were named: Main Street, Broadway, Fifth Avenue. Showing the resilience of a Philippine weed, a black market emerged. Quinine pills and chocolate bars could be had, for steep prices few could afford. So could tobacco. As meager as the men's possessions were, stealing became a problem. Some men would take anything and do anything in an attempt to remain healthy and alive. "Treat a man like a dog, he'll respond like a dog," said Harold.

But the humanity of the men also shined through. They were beaten down but not beaten. Groups were organized to produce plays, vaudeville and otherwise, for the camp's entertainment. Books magically appeared, in English, including some of the classics, and a camp library was established. Church services were held. The Navy steadfastly kept track of the time, clanging an iron at the top of every hour without fail. And always, day in and day out, rumors of the war slipped through the barbed wire, keeping the door open to gossip and, with it, hope. The captives of Cabanatuan heard about Allied battleships bearing on the Philippines across the Pacific and bombers on the way from Australia. The reports came on good authority from someone who knew someone who knew a man who worked on the docks in Manila. As the prisoners idled away their days, they clung to such optimistic reports as if they were gold.

That a place like Cabanatuan even existed was evidence that the Japanese were resigned to containing, as opposed to exterminating, the enemy troops they captured. If a man could survive on rations of a couple of handfuls of rice and an occasional cup of watery gruel every day, he could live. The camp rules were simple: stay inside the barbed wire and do not cause problems. The penalty for breaking the rules was death.

The prisoners were divided into groups of ten and told that if any of the ten escaped, those left behind would be executed. No exceptions. Harold was put in charge of one of these groups of ten. It was his responsibility to report "all present" to the guards each night. The moment his group was formed, he gathered the other nine men around him. "If anybody plans to leave, tell us all about it," he said. "Then we'll make a group decision. Either we all go or none of us go."

As far as Harold knew, no one in his group even thought about escape. There really wasn't anywhere to go in a country isolated in the Pacific Ocean that was already completely occupied by the Japanese. Harold shared the nervous confidence of many of the men: that America would one day rescue them. Despite everything that had happened, he continued to believe America's might would eventually prevail. "The Yanks would have to take care of Hitler and Mussolini in Europe first, but eventually they would avenge the defeat in the Philippines. I just knew they wouldn't leave us sitting there," he said.

There were those who could not resist the urge to leave, however, even if the intent wasn't to escape outright. Shortly after Cabanatuan opened, five American prisoners bribed two Japanese guards into letting them crawl under the fence at night to get food from the Filipino natives. The guards would get a portion of the food, and other valuables, in exchange for looking the other way as the prisoners left and returned. The plan worked well for a time, but one night a guard not in on the ruse uncovered the plot. The next day as the camp population was lined up to watch, the five Americans were shot—along with the two Japanese guards. As a reminder of the consequences of not obeying the rules, the decapitated head of a Filipino native involved in the deal was displayed on a tall post beyond the camp's north fence line, where all the prisoners could see it.

Beyond the camp's gates, Philippine life continued much as it had for centuries. In the distance were rice fields and farms, and on the road that passed out front, Filipinos traveled to and from Cabanatuan City, the provincial capital of fifty thousand people, paying scant attention to the prison camp in the distance.

Life on the outside was far from stress free. The Japanese imposed martial law throughout the Philippines and kept a military presence in the barrios. But it was only the men inside the gates of Cabanatuan—where they slept on boards in almost suffocating heat and humidity, and knew no privacy and little nourishment, and where staying alive was the only real pastime—whose lives had been turned completely upside down.

They spent their days with one goal: to make it to another. They walked in slow, deliberate steps to conserve their energy. They ate their rice one grain at a time. Their conservation was everything, but even it was economical.

In the fall of 1942 the months of the rainy season dragged on with maddening monotony. The men inside Cabanatuan had little to do. Harold went on burial details and read his Bible. To protect the book, he took a small piece of tent canvas, and with a makeshift needle he made out of a key to a corned beef can, he stitched a cover. Life was as slow as it was hungry.

At the start of December, a year since the war began, the Japanese decided to put the prisoners to work clearing an overgrown field of about three hundred acres adjacent to the camp. Once the clearing was finished, crops were planted, and Cabanatuan had a farm.

The farm work was all manual labor. But with more than 2,000 prisoners, there was plenty of manpower. All prisoners able to stand under their own power became farmhands. The days were divided into two shifts, the first from sunrise to midmorning and the second from midafternoon to sundown. In between, the prisoners returned to camp for a midday ration and rest.

One day the men would chop down cogan grass as tall as they were. The next day they would gather the grass into piles and burn it. Then, by hand, they would plow, plant, and weed all over again, with a guard always nearby ready to deliver a beating to anyone caught slacking.

Harold, like all the men, despised the farmwork. Weak from malnutrition and squalid living conditions, they were in no shape for physical labor.

But it was not long before he saw that there was a redeeming side to planting rice, eggplant, okra, corn, carrots, and other crops, even if he had had no choice in the matter.

"That farm work was a blessing in disguise," Harold said. "The sun is really kind of an antiseptic. There we were, out in the fresh open air and sunlight, using our muscles. In the compound we were subjected to all kinds of vermin: body lice, fleas, bedbugs, mosquitoes, and always the big old blue flies around the straddle trench. In the fields, we were away from all that. I'm sure working at that farm helped save our lives."

Harold Poole models his work uniform at Clark Field, Philippine Islands, in 1941.
Courtesy of Harold Poole

The men of the 20th Pursuit Squadron pose in front of their barracks at Nichols Field in the Philippines in 1941. By war's end, barely one-fourth were still alive.
Courtesy of Harold Poole

Harold Poole inspects a Lewis .30-caliber, air-cooled machine gun similar to the one he used to shoot down a Japanese dive bomber from Clark Field on December 8, 1941.
Courtesy of Harold Poole

Technical Sergeant Poole in 1946.
Courtesy of Harold Poole

Congressman Mike Honda (D-California) and Harold Poole (shown at his home in Salt Lake City) found a connection through their World War II experiences. As a child, Honda lived in a U.S. internment camp for Japanese-Americans. *Courtesy of Lee Benson*

Harold Poole talks with Senator Orrin Hatch (R-Utah) before Poole testified at Hatch's June 2000 Judiciary Committee hearing on the Bataan veterans' issues. *Courtesy of James Parkinson*

Senator Joe Biden (D-Delaware) poses with attorney Maury A. Herman. Together with Senator Orrin Hatch, Biden coauthored legislation designed to compensate Bataan survivors for their slave labor and to elicit Congressional recognition of their sacrifice. Herman and his Louisiana firm, Herman, Herman, Katz, and Cotlar, LLP, served as key members of the mega firm that represented the men. *Courtesy of James Kegley*

Preparing to testify at the committee hearing in June 2000 are (front row, left to right) veterans Ed Jackfert, Les Tenney, Frank Bigelow, Mo Mazer, and (second row, far right) Harold Poole.
Courtesy of James Parkinson

Attorney Bonnie Kane, whose legal and historical research and analysis were the basis of the JPOW case, poses with Harold Poole at the hearing. *Courtesy of James Parkinson*

Author and attorney Jim Parkinson (back row) stands with members of the 20th Pursuit Squadron in front of the Mormon Tabernacle Choir prior to a September 2002 broadcast honoring the veterans. Clockwise from Parkinson: George Idlett, John Bristow, Gene Jacobsen, Joe Moore, Harold Poole, and Jim Huff. *Courtesy of Tom Smart*

During a December 2002 visit to the Philippines with Poole's son-in-law, Paul Warner, Harold Poole and Jim Parkinson pose before a sign in Mariveles that marks the beginning of the Bataan Death March route. *Courtesy of James Parkinson*

Harold Poole leans on the 69-kilometer marker along the Death March route, one of many placed by the Filipino-American Memorial Enterprise. *Courtesy of James Parkinson*

In the distance atop Mount Samat, a memorial cross commemorates sacrifices made on Bataan.
Courtesy of James Parkinson

This memorial on the National Road in Bataan depicts the brutality on the Death March.
Courtesy of James Parkinson

At the Capas National Shrine a towering obelisk commemorates the site of the notorious Camp O'Donnell, where 54,000 POWs were incarcerated and 25,000 Filipinos and 6,000 American servicemen died. *Courtesy of James Parkinson*

Paul Warner and Harold Poole view replicas of Camp O'Donnell guard towers and POW quarters at the Capas Shrine. *Courtesy of James Parkinson*

Harold Poole gazes out of a barracks replica very much like the one in which he was held captive in the spring of 1942. Through the window some of the 31,000 trees that have been planted at Capas can be seen, one for every man who died there. *Courtesy of James Parkinson*

Harold Poole and Paul Warner stand next to the memorial at Capas erected by the Battling Bastards of Bataan. *Courtesy of James Parkinson*

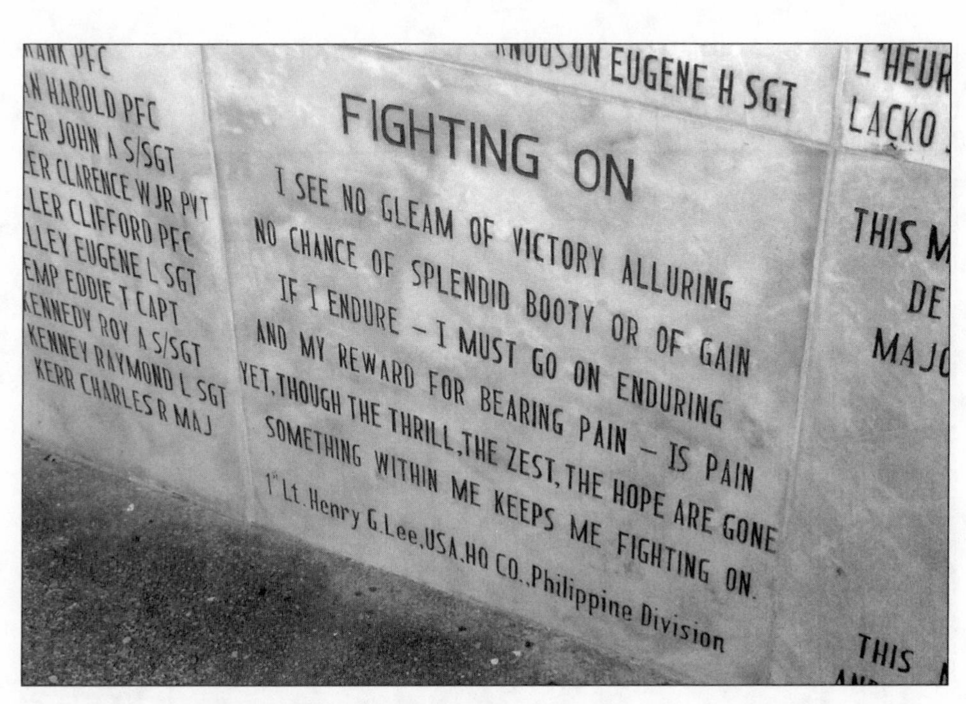

A soldier's poem etched into the Capas memorial reflects the sentiment of the men who fought and survived on Bataan. *Courtesy of James Parkinson*

Cement bags litter the front of the then-partly-finished Cabanatuan War Memorial at the entrance to what was once the Pacific Theater's largest and most notorious POW camp. Cabanatuan Prison Camp was also the site of the biggest POW rescue in U.S. history, dramatized in the 2005 film *The Great Raid. Courtesy of James Parkinson*

At the American Cemetery in Manila, 17,206 crosses and Stars of David mark the final resting place of soldiers who never made it home. *Courtesy of James Parkinson*

Key legal team members David Casey Jr. and Bonnie Kane, among the first to represent the JPOWs and lead the formation of the mega firm, are pictured here with Lester Tenney in San Diego, California. *Courtesy of Dennis Mock*

Tom Boggs, Jonathan Yarowsky, and Karen Marangi (members of the Patton Boggs legal team) were part of the mega firm that represented Harold Poole and thousands of Bataan Death March survivors.
Courtesy of James Kegley

Members of the legal team—(left to right) Jim Parkinson, Maury Herman, Joe Reeder, Allen Foster, Steve Schneebaum, and Ron Kleinmann—pose in the offices of Greenberg Traurig in Washington, D.C. *Courtesy of James Kegley*

Michael Goldstein, an attorney who practices in Cardiff-by-the-Sea, California, launched the project, introducing former POW and slave laborer Lester Tenney to David Casey. *Courtesy of Michael Goldstein*

CHAPTER THIRTEEN

March 22, 2001
Washington, D.C.

IN THE SAME SUMMER that Harold Poole was settling in behind the barbed wire of Cabanatuan, an infant named Mike was settling into his own form of confinement—in Colorado.

Mike Honda was born in Stockton, California, on June 27, 1941, less than six months prior to the bombing of Pearl Harbor. Before his first birthday, he and his three brothers and sisters and his parents, Byron and Fusako Honda, were ordered by the U.S. government to leave their California home for the Amache Relocation Camp in southeast Colorado. There, in a remote dustbowl twenty miles west of the Kansas border, the family was housed in a guarded compound and forbidden to leave.

The lone indictment on the Hondas was that they were of Japanese descent.

Across the country, and especially on the West Coast, there was a fear of Japanese spies and saboteurs. Within hours of the attack on Pearl Harbor, President Roosevelt issued Presidential Proclamation 2525, the Alien Enemies Act, granting the government emergency authority to round up any and all "alien" suspects—U.S. citizenship notwithstanding—and restrict their movements. Two months later, in February of 1942, Roosevelt issued the even broader-based Executive Order 9066, effectively paving the way to confine all of the country's more than one hundred and twenty thousand Japanese American citizens, among them the Hondas.

Mike was too young to carry any cognitive memory of the long, dusty train ride he and his family took under military guard from California to Colorado. He would only hear about his father's leveling the ground and building the barracks they would live in, and pounding in the fence posts and stringing the barbed wire around the camp's boundaries. Byron Honda was an American-born, college-bound man forced to build his family's own prison.

The Hondas were interned for slightly more than two years until Byron volunteered as a language specialist in the Naval Military Intelligence Service, a move that got the family out of prison. The Hondas first moved to Boulder, Colorado, and then Chicago, where Mike's father taught Japanese to Naval Intelligence officers. Byron Honda was a spy all right, a U.S. spy.

As fate would have it, Byron's son Mike would grow up to become a United States congressman. In the fall of 2000, at the age of fifty-nine, he was elected by the constituents of California's Fifteenth District in the San Jose area to his first term in Washington, D.C. This was just weeks after Judge Vaughn Walker had ordered the JPOW cases dismissed from federal court. Outwardly, there was no correlation between the JPOW court decision and the election of the Japanese American politician to the U.S. House of Representatives. But as anyone involved in the case would soon realize, the JPOW cause had an unexpected and invaluable ally in Congressman Honda—a man who understood what it meant to be a pawn in the machinery of government and war, and the importance of righting wrongs, no matter how dormant.

Almost before he had finished unpacking, the freshman legislator let the JPOW lawyers know that he considered Judge Walker's ruling erroneous, and he was prepared to use his new position to help any way he could.

Mike Honda's knowledge of and sympathy for the former JPOWs preceded his arrival in Washington. As a California state assemblyman he had dispatched his chief of staff, Keith Honda, to a 1999 symposium at Stanford University dealing with Japanese atrocities during Japan's conflict with China in the 1930s. Not only did the staffer return with information about such horrors as the "Rape of Nanking" and the importing of Chinese "comfort women" who were forced to service Japanese soldiers, but with details about thousands of U.S. servicemen who were imprisoned and used as slave laborers by the Japanese during World War II.

Honda's research into Japan's wartime behavior resulted in his sponsoring a California State Assembly Resolution, AJR-27, that called for an official apology from Japan for its inhumane wartime acts. The non-binding state resolution dovetailed nicely, as it turned out, with Tom Hayden's effort on the senate side of the California legislature. Although Nazi war crimes were Hayden's specific target, Honda and Hayden collaborated to make the language of Hayden's Senate Bill 1245 broad enough to cover war crimes committed by "Nazi Germany and her allies," thus opening the door for legal remedies against the Japanese as well the Nazis.

All his life Mike Honda had been a patron of seemingly lost causes and a crusader for the little guy. After the war his family had returned, penniless and without possessions, to Santa Clara County as sharecroppers, growing strawberries. Refusing to let an unjust past cloud his future, Mike graduated from high school and college, and then, inspired by JFK, volunteered for a Peace Corps assignment in El Salvador. Later, he became a teacher, and by 1975, the vice principal of a middle school in Sunnyvale, California.

Even as his personal and professional life prospered, the injustice at the internment camps he and his family had once been part of nagged at him, and in the mid-1970s he was among the earliest pioneers in a crusade known as the Japanese Redress Movement. The objective was to secure a measure of justice for the more than one hundred thousand people who had been stripped of their belongings and dignity, uprooted from their homes, and placed behind bars without due process. After more than a decade of hard, often acrimonious negotiations, in 1988 the United States Congress passed the $1.25 billion U.S. Civil Liberties Act.

The Act awarded every World War II internee $20,000 from the United States people and its government and, of greater importance, an apology delivered by President Ronald Reagan on behalf of the American people.

Twenty thousand dollars could not make up for fifty years of lost economic opportunity or pay for enduring humiliation caused by the internment. But it did put sincerity behind the official apology. "It let people know they mattered," the congressman said. "Almost immediately, I saw it make a huge difference in how people who had carried the wounds of abuse the majority of their lives looked at themselves."

The Civil Liberties Act also brought out into the open details of internment-camp history, information that for decades had been pushed aside and not mentioned either in textbooks or polite society.

Honda felt strongly that the former JPOWs had suffered a similar injustice and deserved their own apology and acknowledgment. The best vehicle for them, he believed, was the United States system of justice, where they could meet the companies that once enslaved them in a court of law.

To combat Judge Walker's ruling that, pending appeal, canceled such opportunities, once he got to Washington the congressman got to work on a House of Representatives resolution. He found an ally in veteran California Congressman Dana Rohrabacher, who not only had seniority and influence in the House, but also had a relative who had once served in the Philippines. The California legislators made quite a team: the ultraliberal Honda from Silicon Valley in his first term in Washington, and the ultraconservative Rohrabacher from Huntington Beach in his seventh term.

In March of 2001, only two months into the congressional term, Honda and Rohrabacher jointly introduced House Resolution 1198, the "Justice for United States Prisoners of War Act of 2001."

HR 1198 was more forceful than Senate Concurrent Resolution 158 that had been introduced by Senators Orrin Hatch and Dianne Feinstein in the United States Senate the previous December. Hatch and Feinstein's SR 158 called on the executive branch "through the Secretary of State or other appropriate officials to facilitate justice and fairness on behalf of the prisoners of war of the Japanese and the companies that used them as slave labor." The resolution passed the House and the Senate by unanimous consent in late 2000.

The Honda-Rohrabacher resolution bypassed the executive branch entirely, taking aim at the judicial branch by spelling out why U.S. courts should not only hear the lawsuits being brought by the former JPOWS, but why the courts should specifically interpret Articles 14(b) and 26 of the 1951 peace treaty in the JPOWs' favor.

"The people of the United States owe a deep and eternal debt to members of the United States Armed Forces held as prisoners of war by Japan during World War II for their heroism and sacrifice on the nation's behalf," HR 1198 stated. "The pursuit of justice by members of the United States Armed Forces held as prisoners of war by Japan during World War II who were forced to provide labor without compensation and under inhumane conditions through lawsuits filed in the courts of the United States, whether otherwise supported by applicable standards established by Federal, State, or international law, is consistent with the interest of the

United States and should not be deemed preempted by any other provision or law or the Treaty."

On March 22, 2001, the bill was presented on the floor of the House with signed support from twenty-nine representatives. Within a week, one hundred and thirty-seven representatives, nearly a third of the House, had signed on from both sides of the aisle and both sides of the cultural divide. (Sheila Jackson Lee, an African American Democratic congresswoman from Texas, told Dana Rohrabacher, a white Republican congressman from California, "I don't agree with you on anything, but I agree with you on this.")

As the bill's visibility increased, Mike Honda was repeatedly asked why a Japanese American would fight so hard for men imprisoned during the war by his own race.

"This isn't about race and it isn't about Japan bashing," the onetime resident of the Amache Relocation Camp answered. "It's about reconciliation and what's right."

CHAPTER FOURTEEN

January 1943
Cabanatuan Prison Camp, Philippines

HE DREAMED of rotting fruit.

When sleep finally came at Cabanatuan—usually induced by exhaustion more than anything—Harold went back home to Utah: to his grandfather's orchard at harvest time. The trees were full of fruit. There were apples, pears, peaches, and apricots everywhere. But Harold's focus was not on the fruit hanging on the trees' branches, but on the ground, where the overripe fruit had fallen. No one ate this fruit, not with all the good stuff still in the trees. It would either be left where it was to rot, or it would be fed as slop to the pigs. In his sleep, Harold reached for the fruit on the ground . . . and then, invariably, he would wake up.

Of all the plagues afflicting the prisoners, none was more constant, more maddening, or in the end more defeating than the lack of food. Beatings and diseases came and went. They either killed you or they did not. But hunger was always there, waiting, vulturelike. "The ultimate torture," Harold called it.

Rations at Cabanatuan consisted of twice-daily servings of a ball of steamed rice smaller than a man's fist. At the evening ration, carabao meat, vegetables, fruit, or a thin soup would sometimes be added, but only rarely and in ridiculously small amounts. The men simply never had enough to eat.

Thus, food became their obsession. It was what they dreamed about, what they fantasized about, what they discussed incessantly. "In normal times, soldiers sit around and talk about women and liquor," Harold said. "But we didn't talk about women and liquor at all. We talked about food."

Men who had never cracked an egg, let alone followed a recipe, were now avidly discussing exotic concoctions they would whip up in the kitchen once they got home. Nothing was too extreme. "A guy would be sitting there and out of the blue he'd say, 'Milky Way pie,'" remembered Harold, "and then he'd go into all the details of melting down Milky Way bars and making them into a pie. The guys would do that all the time."

They challenged each other to eating contests when they got back to the States and bragged how much they could and would eat in one sitting. No one would outeat them. No one! They talked of their favorite meals and their mothers' cooking and Sunday dinners with roast beef and enormous ice cream desserts until they nearly drove one another crazy. But they were powerless to stop.

Harold's personal waking fantasy was a smorgasbord. With every one of his ribs visible, he would mentally entertain himself by envisioning table after table piled high with every kind of food imaginable—and he free to load his plate with all of it.

Then he would expand his fantasy to include his dream family—a pretty wife and happy kids—and his dream car, which had to be an Oldsmobile. In his mind's eye he could see them all loading into the Oldsmobile at dinnertime, and driving to a smorgasbord. On a good day, he could stretch out that fantasy at least until the next meal, when it would invariably disappear into a tiny ball of rice covered with flies.

Besides dreaming about food, the men constantly searched for new places to find it. They supplemented their rations wherever with whatever they could. If they went outside the camp on a work detail—to gather wood, perhaps, or to the farm—they could sometimes get something extra to eat from a Filipino native who took pity on them. Smuggled food also occasionally found its way into the camp's black market. Nothing was sneered at. Rats became a much sought-after delicacy, known to the prisoners as "Cabanatuan beef." But after the first couple of months at camp, rats were hard to come by.

Anything that moved, with the exception of flies and mosquitoes, was fair game. One afternoon Harold and Nelson Quast managed to corner a small animal they spotted running through the camp. They quickly killed the animal, skinned it, dressed it out, cut it up in a gallon bucket, boiled it over a small fire, and ate the whole thing in one sitting. That night they boasted that they had dined on "Filipino rabbit," one whose last word was "meow."

"I found that a hungry man can eat anything he can get past his eyes," said Harold.

Over time, the starvation diet turned the men into little more than walking skeletons. No one was spared. Even the most inventive and larcenous among them became seriously undernourished. Fortunately there were no mirrors, although seeing the desperate look in a neighbor's eyes was seeing your own. "Ghost-looking faces," Harold called them. "But there were no tears. Tears wasted water that you didn't have to waste."

If you couldn't eat and you couldn't cry about it, the one thing you could do was pray. For Harold, it continued to be his only real source of sustenance.

"You could pray standing up, you could pray lying down, you could pray wherever you wanted, and they never knew you were doing it," he said. "They couldn't stop you from praying."

He prayed constantly, for anything and everything. It was his secret weapon and his only hope that he could somehow make it through. "When you see your body wasting away and you've got sores on your hips because you're sleeping on boards, and all around you is decay and dying, you can't help but wonder, 'How long is this going to last?'" Harold remembered. "I prayed that I could put up with it."

Although he was raised in an active Mormon home where prayer was part of each day's activities, Harold had never turned to God like this. When he was not praying, he read the Bible from cover to cover and then read it again. The guards were constantly taking the book from him, but they always gave it back, something Harold considered nothing short of a reoccurring miracle. Because of the numerous handwritten notations scribbled in the margins—his and the previous owner's—he was always sure that the Japanese, who were notorious for confiscating anything with English writing on it, would keep it for good. But time after time, his good book kept returning.

He also read the Book of Mormon while he was at Cabanatuan. For months, Harold had prayed that he might find a copy of the Latter-day Saint scriptures. Then one day he started talking to a prisoner from Arizona named Franklin East who was Mormon and had served a two-year proselyting mission before the war. East had managed to hang onto a copy of the Book of Mormon through the Death March and had brought it with him to prison camp. He loaned the book to Harold, who for the first time in his life read it from start to finish.

The scriptures gave him solace that he was far from the only person to ever go through hard times. Some of the men turned away from religion, wondering how God could exist and allow the kind of pain and suffering they were experiencing, but Harold's faith and dependence on a higher being only increased. Without prayer and God's words, he would be in Cabanatuan quite alone, and he was sure he could not make it alone.

If it was God's will, he would see this through, and he saw repeated indications—the scriptures, the quinine pills, the friendship and timely appearances of Nelson Quast and Everett Poole, the farmwork—that it just might be God's will. It seemed like every time he was nearing rock bottom, he got just enough good fortune to be lifted back up.

If one key to prison camp survival was trusting in God, another was never trusting in the guards. Although their contempt settled over time into a kind of scornful indifference—no more were men being run through with a bayonet for getting a drink of water—the guards still seized upon any opportunity for a beating. For Harold, it came natural to stay as far from the guards as possible, and he managed to keep his beatings to a minimum. But for others it came just as natural to test the guards. Sometimes they would get away with it—for the most part, soldiers assigned to guard duty in the Philippines were the least trained and worst disciplined in the Japanese Army—but when they did not, the results could be devastating.

Harold remembered one guard who was particularly abusive and animated. "He'd jump up and down and tell us to work hard, and we couldn't really understand what he was saying," Harold said. "He'd stomp around like Donald Duck, so that's what we called him."

Some of the men called him "Donald Duck" to his face. When the guard asked in broken English who Donald Duck was, he was told that it was a famous American movie star. The guard was as pleased at the comparison as the POWs were pleased at their joke. All went well until the day the guard discovered the truth. He remembered every prisoner who had referred to him as Donald Duck, rounded them up, and had them all beaten.

"If you did the least thing out of line, you'd get hit," said Harold. "I got hit but I never broke a bone. A lot of them did. One guy picked up a little piece of soap in the tool shed where you got your shovel or hoe. They caught him with that soap and broke his arm."

There was virtually no fraternization between guards and prisoners. East was East and West was West, and not for one minute did the Japanese let the prisoners forget it. Harold remembered one occasion when the guards rounded up all the men and showed them a film of the bombing of Pearl Harbor. For the American GIs, the setting was almost surreal—thousands of them sitting cross-legged on the dirt, surrounded by Japanese soldiers, watching footage of the U.S. battleships at Pearl Harbor being blown to bits.

After the film, the Japanese allowed the prisoners to take over the stage and present a variety show. As the guards looked on impassively, various U.S. soldiers performed skits, songs, and comedy routines. The Pearl Harbor film had served as their warm-up act. Such was life at Cabanatuan.

As the months passed, Harold and the men noticed a change in the guards' demeanor. They became edgier. They walked with less of a swagger. The reason for the change in attitude, the men came to understand, was almost always due to a downturn in Japan's war success. "They were poor losers. When something in the war wasn't going well," said Harold, "they would take it out on us."

By the summer of 1943 they were taking it out on them quite often.

Japan was not losing the war by any means, but the Allies were beginning to hold their own. Several islands taken by the Japanese had been regained, and the battle for the Pacific had become less lopsided. The prisoners at Cabanatuan usually heard this first by way of rumors filtering in from the Manila docks; verification usually came later in the form of a guard's outrage.

Harold absorbed the shifting war news with his characteristic cautiousness. If the Allies really were on their way to retake the Philippines, he reasoned that it might not go well for the Allied forces—meaning himself and his fellow inmates—who were already there.

"I figured if the Yanks started to invade this island, the Japs just might kill all of us, just for spite," he said.

But a prisoner did not necessarily have to be in the Philippines when the Yanks returned. For months work details had been leaving Cabanatuan for Japan, where manpower was needed in Japan's factories, shipyards, and mines. Any prisoner was free to volunteer for such duty, and his offer was almost never refused. After weeks of deliberation, Harold decided he would be better off leaving Cabanatuan, just as he had once decided it would be wise to leave Camp O'Donnell.

He found the work list by the commandant's office and put down his name as a volunteer to work in Japan.

On September 18, 1943, after more than seventeen months as a prisoner of the Japanese and fifteen and a half months at Cabanatuan, Harold was escorted out of the prison-camp gates. Brown from the sun and dressed in cut-off trousers and wooden sandals he had made, he walked under his own power and climbed in the back of a truck with dozens of other men. He weighed slightly more than a hundred pounds, and all he carried with him was the worn Bible in its homemade canvas case.

There was little traffic on the roads, and the truck quickly covered the fifty-mile distance to Manila. At the docks, the prisoners were escorted to the *Taga Maru*, a cargo ship that was one of dozens of commercial vessels the Japanese government used to transport prisoners of war to Japan from 1942 through 1945. After the war these ships would become known as hell ships. Harold Poole and his fellow comrades fleeing Cabanatuan were about to find out why.

CHAPTER FIFTEEN

Summer 2001
Orange County, California

BY EARLY SUMMER OF 2001, two years since the first lawsuit was filed, the JPOW case was beginning to register in the court of public opinion. And in that court, I liked to point out to the men, there was no question we were winning.

The case, and the former JPOWs, got great press. Newspapers, magazines, and television news shows lined up to interview our clients and extol their virtues. *Parade*, the nation's largest magazine with a circulation of thirty-seven million, ran a cover story in June of 2001 with the headline, "They Should Have Their Day in Court." Pictures of the JPOWs, then and now, were published—a skeletal prisoner in a coal mine alongside a photo of the same man as a white-haired grandfather—along with details of the Bataan Death March, the hell ship crossings to Japan, and the brutality, starvation, and death rates of the slave camps. In a sidebar to the lead story, information was included about Mike Honda and Dana Rohrabacher's proposed Justice for U.S. Prisoners of War Bill and a quote from Honda that the JPOWs should be allowed to "survive our judicial system."

It didn't hurt that the veterans were from "the Good War." Since the early 1990s, all things World War II had been enjoying a nostalgic revival. A number of golden anniversaries were held between 1991 and 1995, commemorating everything from Pearl Harbor Day to D-day to VE-day and VJ-day. In their wake came a flood of new media. TV news personality Tom Brokaw's book *The Greatest Generation* heaped unabashed hero status on the World War II GIs and was the best-selling book in America for eighteen straight weeks in 1999. *Flags of Our Fathers*, a book that told the tale of the famous photograph of the American flag being raised by marines on Mount Suribachi during the epic battle for the Japanese island of Iwo Jima, was another bestseller in 2000. At the front of the publishing stampede was author Stephen E. Ambrose, who from 1992 until his death in 2002 published eight books on World War II. Ambrose's *Band of Brothers* was made into an Emmy-awarded cable television miniseries by Steven Spielberg and Tom Hanks. The Hollywood icons had previously made *Saving Private Ryan*, a 1998 movie about D-day that was nominated for an Academy Award for Best Picture. Another 1998 film, *The Thin Red Line*, about the battle for Guadalcanal, was also nominated for Best Picture. *Saving Private Ryan* and *The Thin Red Line* were the first major movies made about World War II since *A Bridge Too Far* in 1977.

The movie *Pearl Harbor* followed in 2001—thirty-one years after the release of the definitive Pearl Habor epic, *Tora! Tora! Tora!*—unearthing long-dormant details of the Japanese attack and introducing Army Air Corps Lieutenant Jimmy Dolittle's sneak air raid on Tokyo in April of 1942 to a generation of Americans who never knew it happened.

In 2001, author Hampton Sides published his book *Ghost Soldiers*, a riveting account of the rescue at the end of the war of the prisoners at Cabanatuan. In *Ghost Soldiers*, millions read—many for the first time—of the horrendous treatment of American soldiers in the Philippines.

Reaching less of a mainstream audience, but more damning in its content, was a book published in 2001 by Linda Goetz Holmes, *Unjust Enrichment: How Japan's Companies Built Postwar Fortunes Using American POWs*. Holmes laid out the details of the use of prisoners of war as employees/slave laborers in Japan. She described the brutal working conditions, the profits the companies were able to realize with a nonpaid workforce, and the postwar success of Mitsubishi, Mitsui, Nippon Steel, Kawasaki, and other Japanese companies.

Equally hard-hitting were books by Gavan Daws and Van Waterford, titled, respectively, *Prisoners of the Japanese: POWs of World War II in the Pacific* and *Prisoners of the Japanese in World War II*.

This influx of information about the dark side of the war in the Pacific brought with it an outpouring of genuine sympathy for all JPOWs, living and dead. It mirrored a revival of sympathy for victims of Nazi Germany's World War II brutalities in Europe. The fall of the Berlin Wall and reunification of Germany in the early 1990s set the stage for more exposure of Nazi war atrocities than ever before. One highly publicized exposé dealt with the discovery of hundreds of millions of dollars of Jewish money that had been stolen by the Nazis and deposited in Swiss banks in the 1940s. The banks were reluctant to part with their reserves, but public and legal pressure was so intense that eventually the banks returned the money to the original Jewish owners, or their heirs, along with more than a half century of interest.

The question that naturally followed regarding prisoners of the Japanese was, if Swiss banks could hand over money unlawfully gained during the war, then why not Japanese corporations? Why should companies such as Mitsubishi and Mitsui not have to settle their war debts as well?

As the media posed its questions, virtually every veterans organization in the country lined up in support of the JPOWs, including the Veterans of Foreign Wars of the United States, the American Legion, the Disabled American Veterans, and the Jewish War Veterans of the United States of America.

"The VFW is outraged that the U.S. government has failed to support the fair and just compensation of these former POWs who were ruthlessly exploited by Japanese companies during World War II," wrote Robert E. Wallace, executive director of the VFW, in a letter sent to every member of the United States Congress. "These former World War II POWs sacrificed much for our country, and have asked for little in return. The Veterans of Foreign Wars of the United States supports fair and just compensation for injuries suffered by all American POWs at the hands of their Japanese captors, and particularly for those who were forced to perform slave labor by private Japanese companies."

The American Legion pledged full support of its 2.8 million members for HR 1198, stating, "The survivors of Bataan have been waiting more than fifty years for closure and justice. They will get neither without the support of the government that they served with indescribable fortitude... considering Germany has apologized for its wartime injustices and the U.S. government has paid reparations to Japanese-Americans who were forced into internment camps, the relief sought by Bataan survivors and their families is the very least the Japanese can do."

For bluntness, nothing topped the statement from Colonel Herb Rosenbleeth, executive director of the Jewish War Veterans, who wrote: "JWV is unique among our fellow veterans organizations because we are veterans and of the Jewish faith. We are, therefore, very painfully aware of the meaning of wartime slave labor, as millions of our coreligionists in Europe served the filthy Nazi bastards in this capacity. We also support, we demand, we expect adequate and fair compensation for the veterans in the Far East, or their survivors or descendants, who were used as slave labor during World War II."

But if the veterans, the media, growing numbers of legislators in the United States House of Representatives and the United States Senate, and the public at large were vocal in their support of the POWs, the State Department still was not. A number of heavy political hitters stepped forward to support the executive branch, including former Secretary of State George P. Shultz, who wrote to Congressman Henry Hyde, the chairman of the House Committee on International Relations, to express his concern about Honda and Rohrabacher's bill. That legislation, Shultz contended, "would fundamentally abrogate a central provision of a fifty-year-old treaty, reversing a long-standing foreign policy stance. The treaty signed in San Francisco . . . involving forty-nine nations could unravel. A dangerous legal precedent would be set."

"I express my opposition to the bill against the background of tremendous sympathy for the problems of the United States citizens who have in one way or another been harmed, many severely, in the course of war and its sometimes dehumanizing impact," Shultz wrote. "But the bill in question would have the effect of voiding the bargain made and explicitly set out in the treaty of peace between Japan, the United States, and forty-seven other countries."

Shultz defended the wisdom of those who drafted the treaty, especially "the clear-eyed and tough-minded John Foster Dulles, who later became Secretary of State for President Eisenhower . . . [and who] chose to do everything possible to cause Germany and Japan to become democratic partners, and as the Cold War with the Soviet Union emerged, allies in that struggle."

Shultz noted that he personally served in the Pacific during World War II with the Marines. "I had friends," he wrote, "friends close to me . . . killed practically beside me. I do not exaggerate at all in saying that the people who suffered the most are the ones who did not make it at all. I have always supported the best of treatment for our veterans, especially those who were involved in combat. If they are not being adequately taken care of, we should always be ready to do more. But let us not unravel confidence in the commitment of the United States to a treaty properly negotiated and solemnly ratified with the advice and consent of the U.S. Senate."

In an op-ed article in the *Washington Post*, three former ambassadors to Japan, Walter Mondale, Thomas Foley, and Michael Armacost, coauthored a guest editorial that expressed in public what Shultz privately expressed to Hyde.

"As former ambassadors to Japan," they wrote, "we are extremely concerned about a little-noticed measure that is working its way through Congress. If adopted, this amendment would undermine our relations with Japan, a key ally. It would have serious, and negative, effects on our national security.

"The provision in question certainly has an honorable purpose: to help former U.S. POWs. But in pursuing that aim, this amendment would abrogate one of America's most important treaties, the 1951 San Francisco Treaty, which ended World War II in the Pacific. That treaty is the cornerstone of U.S. security arrangements in the Pacific, for it provides the legal and political basis for related bilateral agreements that have allowed the United States to station troops in Japan for a half century. The San Francisco Treaty anchors other bilateral and multilateral security agreements on which the United States depends.

"In a well-intentioned effort to be responsive to our former POWs, Congress has considered passing legislation that would essentially require courts to entertain the POWs' lawsuits. These bills take different forms, but any measure that provides a basis for these lawsuits would certainly violate an essential provision of the San Francisco Treaty.

"Congress certainly has the authority to award further compensation to our World War II veterans. Such federally mandated payments would not be inconsistent with the San Francisco Treaty."

The editorial opinion of the former ambassadors was answered in a *Post* op-ed piece coauthored by U.S. senators—Democrat Tom Harkin of Iowa and Republican Bob Smith of New Hampshire—who argued that support for the World War II veterans "neither impinges upon our relations with Japan nor abrogates the 1951 peace treaty with Japan in any way. The American POWs are not suing Japan; they are suing private Japanese companies. Even more important, the views of Messrs. Foley, Mondale, and Armacost, and of the State Department, are not actually conducive to good, long-term relations between the United States and Japan. As has been widely commented upon by the press, Japanese–American relations would actually be best served by an immediate and forthright recognition by Japan of its wartime past and an apology and compensation by the Japanese companies to these heroic veterans for their labor and suffering."

Senators Harkin and Smith represented a prevailing sentiment of JPOW sympathy among the legislative branch that escalated by summer's end into an amendment attached to a budget bill that barred federal agencies, including lawyers from the justice department, from intervening in any civil lawsuits filed by former prisoners of the Japanese against companies that enslaved them. Backed by Harkin, Smith, Orrin Hatch, Dianne Feinstein, Dana Rohrabacher, Mike Honda, and others, the amendment provision passed overwhelmingly in first the House and then, on September 10, 2001, the Senate. All that remained was the signature of President George W. Bush to turn the action into law.

But before the budget bill made it to the White House, two things happened. First, on the day following the Senate vote, came the September 11 terrorist attacks. Next, the JPOW amendment litigation was removed from the budget bill before it ever arrived at the president's desk—an action almost without precedent in Washington congressional history. On only five previous occasions had language been stricken from a bill after it had been passed by both the House and Senate.

One critic, Iris Chang, author of "The Rape of Nanking," openly accused the executive branch of orchestrating the amendment's demise. In an op-ed piece that ran in the *New York Times*, Chang wrote, "The White House succeeded in having the provision struck in a conference committee; the Bush administration feared it might interfere with gathering international support for the war on terrorism."

Meanwhile, nothing had happened on the legal front since Judge Walker's ruling the previous fall. In late June, with our appeal to Walker's ruling pending, there was a brief ripple of enthusiasm that an out-of-court settlement might be reached when the California Superior Court helped set up an exploratory settlement meeting between the two sides. A retired federal judge in San Diego was retained to act as mediator. The possibility of a settlement brought mega-firm attorneys from around the country to San Diego armed with documents to impress the judge. But we didn't get to impress him, or even try, because lawyers representing the Japanese corporations flew to San Diego only to inform the judge that their clients did not wish to settle under any circumstances. They billed their clients for the trip to and from San Diego just so they could tell a retired federal judge no in person.

The aborted mediation meeting made it clear that any expectation we harbored that the Japanese companies would extend, at the very least, a belated apology—and a meaningful apology might have ended the case then and there—was only hopeful thinking. In a book by Thane Rosenbaum, *The Myth of Moral Justice*, I had read about the modern honor code in Japan's judicial system. In his book Rosenbaum writes that, "Japan is a nation that virtually exists in a constant state of contrition and repentance. Criminal defendants are sometimes released even if they would have otherwise been found guilty, because the prosecutor, or the court, became convinced that the accused displayed sufficient remorse, acknowledgment, and sympathy. Article 248 of the Japanese Penal Code, in fact, gives the prosecutor discretion not to institute formal criminal proceedings, or even file charges, if the accused has apologized in a way that is both meaningful and sincere."

We obviously were not dealing with the modern Japanese penal code, or, for that matter, the Japanese court system.

In an attempt to shut down the game for good, the corporate attorneys petitioned the California state courts to follow the lead of the federal courts and dismiss all JPOW cases left in the state system. They filed a plea of demurrer, a legal maneuver that asks for the outright dismissal of a lawsuit on the grounds that even if the statements in the complaint of the opposing party are true, they are legally defective.

The demurrer hearing was set for October of 2001 before Superior Court Justice William F. McDonald in the city of Santa Ana, California.

All the familiar parties reported to Justice McDonald's courtroom at the appointed time. The usual small army of corporate attorneys was there, as was a government attorney, Amy Allen from the Department of Justice, who did most of the talking. As her colleague had done in federal court, Ms. Allen opened by delivering a disclaimer: "We'd like to make it clear that the United States is in no way here attempting to represent the interest of Japan or Japanese corporations or to injure or to in any way stand in the way of individuals who sacrificed for their country." After which the DOJ attorney added, "But we do have to stand in support of our obligation under international treaties."

The mega-firm had done its homework and come up with a new wrinkle in the meaning of the much-discussed Article 14(b). Allen Foster from the Greenberg Traurig firm produced historic documentation for the court showing that a parenthetical sentence had been deleted from the text of 14(b) before the wording was approved. After the sentence, "Except as otherwise provided in the present treaty, the allied powers waive all reparations claims of the allied power, other claims of the allied powers, and their nations, arising out of any action taken by Japan and its nationals in the course of the prosecution of the war," the deleted parenthetical read: "(Including claims arising out of the treatment accorded by Japan to its prisoners of war and civilian internees)."

If that parenthetical phrase had been allowed to stay in, it would have definitively prohibited future claims by prisoners of war and civilian internees, explained Foster, who then added, "That parenthetical was taken out and the reason it was taken out, your honor, is because the Dutch wouldn't do the deal. The Dutch recognized that, regardless of how important Japan was to the postwar world, regardless how down it looked like Japan was . . . the Dutch realized it couldn't be done. Their constitution did not allow the taking of private property without compensation. And so, of course, they said to John Foster Dulles, 'We won't sign.' They were the monkey wrench and John Foster Dulles had to do something about this. The Dutch also, by the way, had a political problem as well as a legal problem. They had a hundred thousand civilian internees that had been in Dutch portions of the Far East. They had to broker both their own single legal problem and their political problem. And so John Foster Dulles brokered an exchange between the Dutch and the Japanese, in English."

That exchange, it was our contention as plaintiffs, allowed the removal of the parenthetical phrase, thereby opening the door for Dutch POWs and civilian internees to later file claims, should they choose, against Japanese nationals—a door also open to American POWs and civilian internees should they choose to do likewise.

When Alan Foster sat down, I could see from the troubled looks on the faces of the numerous defendant attorneys that he had told them something they did not know.

Among those watching in the courtroom was one of our JPOW clients, Frank Dillman. We brought Frank to the hearing for the same reason we had taken Lester Tenney to the earlier San Francisco hearing—to let the judge see exactly who this case was about.

Frank Dillman was a United States Marine who was on Corregidor the day it surrendered. Before that he was stationed in Shanghai, China, helping protect American expatriates living there. His regiment, the Fourth Marines, was transferred to Subic Bay in the Philippines just six days before the war began. After the fall of Corregidor he was first imprisoned at Cabanatuan, and then rode in a hell ship to Japan where he endured two-plus years of humiliation and abuse at a Mitsubishi-owned copper mine.

I first saw Frank when I arrived in the corridor outside the courtroom. His wife was with him, and another family member, a daughter I believe, to help both of them get around. The daughter had Frank's lunch money in an envelope so she could remind him when it was time to eat. Frank had obviously arrived at that forgetful time of life.

But he had not forgotten what happened in Japan. While Frank was sitting on a bench waiting to enter the courtroom, a reporter sat down next to him and started asking him questions. I did not hear all the interview, but I did hear Frank whisper, "Every time I see one of those Mitsubishi sons of bitches I get so goddamned mad." He then went inside the courtroom alongside a team of Mitsubishi lawyers.

During the oral arguments, the old marine sat stoically by his wife and daughter, twitching his big hands as his own government's lawyer, Amy Allen from the DOJ, who looked like she could be his granddaughter, stood up and sided with Mitsubishi.

When the hearing ended, I watched as Frank and his wife approached the big double door at the back of the courtroom. As fate would have it, the entourage of defendant lawyers was approaching at the same time from the other direction. One of the corporate attorneys opened the door so Amy Allen could exit first. Just then the government lawyer looked up and saw the Dillmans. She stopped abruptly, and without a word, stepped back in deference to the World War II hero and his wife.

CHAPTER SIXTEEN

September 18, 1943
South China Sea

HAROLD'S BRIEF RETURN to the Manila docks presented him with a far different city than the one he had left two years before. That Manila was peaceful, a blend of old Spanish architecture and new American-style buildings made of steel and glass. The Pearl of the Orient, the city was called, an emerging Asian jewel fronted by the region's finest harbor. The only reminder of conflict was an old Spanish galleon half-sunk in Manila Bay, a remnant of the Spanish-American war.

Now, signs of conflict were everywhere in a city occupied once again against its will by a foreign power. Japanese soldiers patrolled the streets. Nothing escaped their touch, including MacArthur's ornate penthouse in the Manila Hotel, once a symbol of the country's high hopes for military independence and now the residence of the Japanese commander in charge of "liberating" the Philippines. Nichols Field, Harold's first home, was now a Japanese air base, its runways smoothed and resurfaced by the very air force that had blown them up.

Not unlike Harold Poole, the Philippine Commonwealth had become a war casualty itself, an island nation caught in the crunch between two much larger and more powerful nations. It was not the first time. Not since the third century had the islands been under home rule. They had been controlled by Hindu-Malayan empires from Sumatra, Indochina, and Borneo; and then by the Chinese beginning with the early Ming dynasty; and then by Muslims from Borneo; and then by the Spanish, whose three-hundred-year term as landlord ended with the short-lived 1898 Spanish-American war that put the United States of America in charge. The American plan to bring full independence to the islands on July 4, 1946, had proceeded on pace until the outbreak of world war. Now a new ruler occupied Manila.

Despite the relatively close geographic proximity of the two countries and Japan's aggressive nature, the Japanese had little ruling history over the Philippines. For a short time in the sixteenth century Japan claimed rights to the Philippines and forced the Spanish to pay tribute to the emperor, a kind of sophisticated extortion. But Spain flexed its muscles and was soon in full control again, and demands from the Japanese palace stopped. For the most part the island nations of Japan and the Philippines had coexisted peacefully as disassociated neighbors for thousands of years. They shared neither customs nor roots: the Filipino lineage traced back to the Malay, the Japanese to Jomon and Yayoi cultures from central Asia.

All that changed, however, with Japan's militaristic ambitions that began flickering at the beginning of the twentieth century, fueled initially by a desire for more room.

With its population crowded onto a landmass of one hundred and fifty thousand square miles—a space the size of California with four times the people—Japan first expanded beyond its traditional borders at the turn of the twentieth century when it "acquired" the island of Formosa from China, annexed Korea, and added several seaports from Russia. The stakes of aggression were raised in 1931 with a westward march into Manchuria, a part of mainland China.

In their eagerness to develop an expansionist identity that could somehow fit with the new and the old, the Japanese brought to the front a brutal form of militarism based loosely, but doggedly, on their two-thousand–plus year history of dignity, honor, and fealty to an emperor who, Shinto lore had it, was a son of the gods. The new militarism held that it was by divine appointment that the Japanese were meant to command the eastern hemisphere, and every Japanese by right and duty of birth had a sacred charge to help build the empire's expanding borders. In essence, all of Japan became an army, seventy-four million strong and endowed by the almighty.

Clothed in this Asian version of manifest destiny and armed with a death-before-dishonor code of living and fighting borrowed from the ancient samurai and upgraded to suit their new designs, the Japanese sharpened their swords and manhandled the Chinese throughout the 1930s with a brutality unimaginable in centers of civilization halfway around the world. In Paris and London and Washington, D.C., in Moscow and Stockholm, indeed, even in Berlin, people gasped as they sipped their tea and coffee and read reports of the Japanese atrocities that made their way into modest newspaper headlines printed below the fold. The Chinese claimed that in Nanking alone at least two hundred and fifty thousand people perished at the hands of Japanese brutality, many of them raped and tortured, their heads hung on poles with looks of horror still in the eyes.

The East, it was becoming apparent to anyone paying attention, was no place for a Westerner, not with Japan on the rampage, carrying high its "Asia for the Asians" banner.

If the Philippine Commonwealth—and the Americans sent to protect it—should have seen its turn coming and prepared its defenses accordingly, it was not the only place slow to react. Japan's rampage through the Pacific was the equal of, if not superior to, Hitler's rampage through Europe: quick, decisive, and full of righteous indignation. Emperor Hirohito and his minister of war, Hideki Tojo, were as convinced of the superiority of their race and their right to rule their neighbors as Adolf Hitler was convinced of the superiority of the members of the Aryan race and their right to rule the world.

By surprise and stealth, and with the blessings of the emperor, the Japanese steamrolled through the Pacific. After screaming "Tora! Tora! Tora!" (Tiger! Tiger! Tiger!) at Pearl Harbor they never looked back. The Philippines and everywhere else soon discovered that it was no small challenge to subdue a foe for whom surrender was not an option; whose troops were willing to, as one historian wrote, "literally fight to the last bullet and bayonet."

The Japanese soon discovered that the people they were fighting did not have a similar do-or-die mindset. Once conquered, its enemies wanted to live. After rousting the British in Malaya and Hong Kong, the Dutch in the East Indies, the French in Indochina, and the Americans in the Philippines, they were left with prisoners of war by the hundreds of thousands—and none of them with the good bushido sense to just die.

In the first days of the war, the foreign POWs were mainly kept close to the battlefields where they were caught, used begrudgingly by the Japanese in salvage and cleanup work and road- and airstrip-building. Some were used to drive the big military supply trucks the Japanese gained as a result of their victories.

But as the war wore on and the demands on Japan's able-bodied male population increased, the leaders in Tokyo recognized a use for the POWs in the home islands, where they could alleviate the critical need for laborers in the mines, factories, and shipyards.

In the fall of 1942, Allied prisoners of war, along with captured civilian workers, began being shipped to Japan to work for Japanese industry as an ambitious POW manual-labor program took shape. Emperor Hirohito wrote a telegram that was sent on September 8, 1942, to "All Transportation and Communication Chiefs" to begin the initiative: "Due to a serious shortage of labor power in Japan, the use of white POW is earnestly desired. Therefore it is required to render considering to send some white POW to Japan by every returning ship (including both transport and munitions ships). It is also desired to send as many personnel as possible by every means such as by loading them on decks."

The POWs-as-slaves enterprise brought in workers from throughout the Pacific. Dozens of merchant ships and passenger vessels were drafted into the Emperor's service as POW transports. These vessels were never marked with POW letters or a red cross—the symbol of the International Red Cross which would have given them immunity from Allied attacks—and they continued to ply their regular trade transporting cargo, livestock, and paying passengers. Since the POWs were added cargo, more often than not, there was no place for them. They would typically be thrown into holds in the bottoms of the ships, the place no one else wanted, where air, water, food, sunlight, and toilets were in short supply. The ships quickly earned their distinction as hell ships.

Harold was one of eight hundred and fifty prisoners steered onto a rusting cargo ship with *Taga Maru* painted in black on its bow. It was a medium-size oceangoing vessel weighing 2,868 tons empty. The men were taken belowdecks for the fifteen-hundred-mile ocean crossing by way of Formosa to Honshu, Japan's principal island. Harold and about two hundred and fifty others were placed into a separate compartment, apart from other cargo holds and any other passengers, where wooden slats covered the cold steel of the boat's hull, with just enough space for each man to lie down at night but no room to spread out. There were no blankets and only a scattering of dim electric light bulbs that cast a half-dark glow on the heaving hold, effectively blending day and night into one.

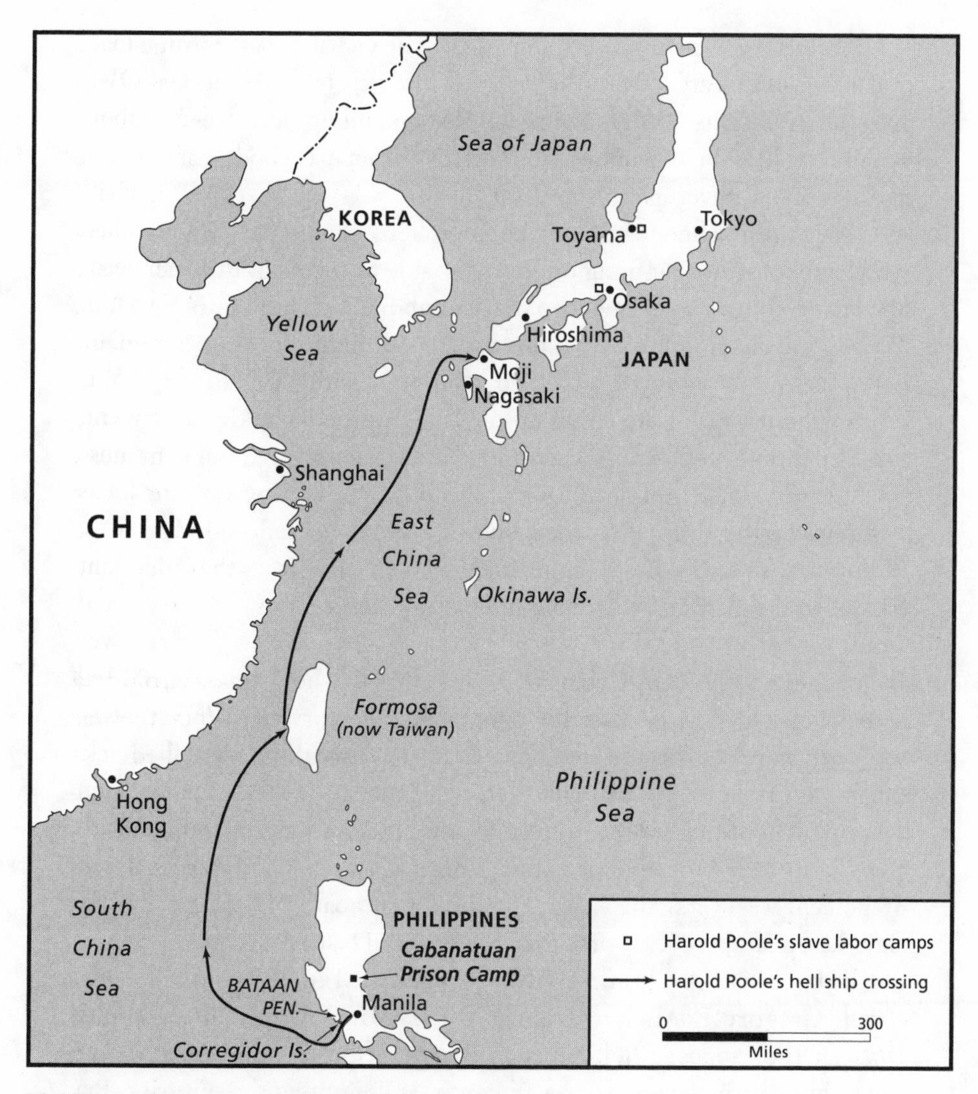

Philippines-Japan, circa 1945. *Christopher Robinson*

Rations were even more minimal than at Cabanatuan. Steamed rice and a thin soup were lowered at irregular intervals from the deck above in five-gallon buckets. "We'd divide the rice up among ourselves," remembered Harold. "We'd count out the kernels so that everybody got the same amount. They never gave us enough."

The *benjos* where the men could relieve themselves were rickety wooden platforms that hung out over the side of the ship. Prisoners were allowed to climb a steel ladder to the deck above and climb into the benjo. "When you did your business it fell straight down into the water," remembered Harold. "And if you weren't careful, so would you."

Some men made the climb up the ladder; others could not or would not. Conditions in the hold deteriorated into an unsanitary, pungent mess. The guards would not set foot in the holds, consenting only to lower and retrieve the five-gallon food buckets. When a dead body had to be removed, which was often, the prisoners would carry it up the ladder and hand it to the guards, who would pitch it into the sea.

By stepping away from Cabanatuan and aboard a hell ship, Harold had actually managed to increase the odds against his survival. When the war was over, statistics showed that of an estimated fifty thousand Allied prisoners who traveled by hell ship between January 1, 1942, and July 18, 1945, 21,039 of them died, from suffocation, starvation, sickness, exhaustion, or an Allied torpedo or bomb. The hell ship casualty rate of almost 50 percent was worse than casualty rates for combat, for prison camp, for slave labor camps, even worse than the Bataan Death March.

In his book *Death on the Hellships* published in 2001, military historian Gregory F. Michno compared the crowded, unsanitary conditions of the Japanese hell ships to the notoriously inhumane African slave ships of the sixteenth, seventeenth, and eighteenth centuries. But at that, the Japanese hell ships produced far more deaths than the slave ships, since the slave ships did not have to deal with wartime activity during their voyages.

Nearly six decades after they occurred, Michno's book detailed many hell ship disasters for the first time in print. Time after time, unmarked ships filled with thousands of Allied prisoners were torpedoed by unsuspecting Allied warplanes or bombed by Allied submarines. The most egregious voyage involved the *Arisan Maru*, a freighter that left Manila in

October of 1944 with 1,802 American POWs on board. Shortly after the voyage began the ship took three direct torpedo hits from an American submarine. The Japanese abandoned ship and clubbed the prisoners with oars to keep them from getting into their lifeboats. Just nine POWs survived, making the wreck of the *Arisan Maru* America's largest single disaster at sea during the war.

By the fall of 1943, Allied planes were hitting a Japanese ship on average every other day, and the *Taga Maru* could have met a similar fate as the *Arisan Maru* or any of scores of other hell ships that encountered torpedoes from Allied submarines or bombs from Allied aircraft. But that did not happen because of a force more dangerous than any of the Allies' weapons: a typhoon.

Not long after clearing the relative safety of Manila Bay, the *Taga Maru* ran into wind, rain, and high seas. It was typhoon season (in Asia, hurricanes are called typhoons) and this was the introduction to a big one. Soon, the ship was pitching and heaving in the waves, alternately rising and plummeting with violent shudders.

In the hold, the men grabbed onto anything they could for support, including each other. Afraid to move, afraid to even think about the few inches of steel between them and the raging seawater on the other side, they shook and shivered day and night until the worst of the storm was over.

But even when the ship stopped its violent trembling, the seas did not quiet down. Almost until the *Taga Maru* came in sight of Formosa, where the ship would stop to refuel before the final leg to Japan proper, the storm persisted.

"In the long run, I guess the storm saved us from getting hit by our own submarines," remembered Harold. "It was just so rough. The submarines could not get near the surface to fire torpedoes. The huge waves would have thrown them out of the water."

Their stomachs empty and reeling, and pale as ghosts, the American prisoners had nonetheless made it to Japanese territory and would remain in that protection as their sea journey continued northward to Honshu.

By the time the *Taga Maru* reached the seaport town of Moji on the northern coast of Honshu, Japan's principal island, fifteen days since leaving Manila, seventy POWs had died on board—from suffocation, dehydration, or disease—but that still meant more than 90 percent of the ship's prisoners were alive and able to disembark on their own accord. By hell ship standards, a healthy crossing.

As Harold placed his first footprint on Japanese soil, he knew little to nothing of the extent of the deaths on board his ship or any other hell ship for that matter, just as he had known little of the deadly statistics along the Death March or at Camp O'Donnell or Cabanatuan. He knew that dying and discomfort were all around him. He knew many other prisoners had succumbed, but he did not know the details. None of the men did. They were stuck in a war vacuum, oblivious to any bigger picture than their existence. They had just one identity. They were still survivors.

The Japanese ushered the men into a large building where they were ordered to remove their clothes and shower in disinfectant. Each prisoner was issued a new set of clothes, Japanese military issue. After that a line of doctors administered a variety of shots with no explanation as to what they were for.

After being washed, prodded, and poked as if they were livestock coming in from the Philippines, Harold and about four hundred others were boarded onto a train and sent into Japan's interior. The train's windows were painted black. No one knew where they were going; no one wanted to think about where they had been.

CHAPTER SEVENTEEN

July 10, 2002
Palm Desert, California

ABOUT THREE YEARS INTO THE CASE, we almost lost Harold. Not in a physical sense. Harold was healthier than I was. "One of the secrets to a long life," he told me, "is eating to live instead of living to eat. A lot of people live to eat, see."

At eighty-three Harold still kept his own home, drove his car, and went about his business like he always had, if a bit slower. He could even squeeze into his old army uniforms if he had to.

We almost lost him as a client.

I got a call in my office late one afternoon from my good friend and Harold's son-in-law, Warner, who as usual got right to the point.

"Harold's quitting the case," he said. "He read President Hinckley's book and he called me and told me he's quitting. Parky, you need to talk to him."

I called Harold. He had indeed just finished reading a new book written by LDS Church President Gordon B. Hinckley, *Standing for Something*. In the book, Hinckley writes about forgiveness and not attempting to right every wrong through fights and lawsuits. Salvation comes from within, not without, the church leader counsels. Jesus taught to turn the other cheek and love those who despitefully use you.

As obedient a Latter-day Saint as you will ever find, Harold took the advice to heart. He had forgiven the Japanese long ago. He decided he did not need to push the point any further by suing them.

I told Harold I agreed with President Hinckley when he talked about turning the other cheek and about not suing over every wrong. But I also contended there were some fights that needed to be fought so they would not get pushed under the rug, and they could serve notice that some things would not be tolerated. If the LDS Church did not believe in lawsuits, I asked, then why did BYU have a law school, and why did I attend it?

"This isn't about turning the other cheek," I said to Harold. "You already did that. You turned the other cheek, and you forgave. What this is about is justice. Jesus never said to do away with justice. He said justice is necessary. Without it there can be no real mercy. Mercy doesn't preclude justice; it demands it. If you don't stand up for what is right, if you don't do everything you can to make sure history doesn't repeat itself, is that fair? Is that right?"

The irony was that Harold wasn't talking about leaving because of how long it was taking or how much difficulty we were experiencing in court, the very problems that were causing me concern, and the ones I thought would cause our clients to leave.

As Harold listened, I reviewed the case. We had won exactly one legal round to date. That had come when Judge McDonald overruled the defendants' demurrer, which had been filed the previous October. Judge McDonald's ruling led to an appeal by the defense to the California Fourth District Court of Appeals in Santa Ana, where a hearing was held in early June in front of a panel of three judges. This time a sharp young Department of Justice attorney named Doug Hallward-Driemeier spoke for the government. He said the 1951 peace treaty barred our lawsuits, because the plaintiffs were officially prisoners of war when the alleged damages occurred. "Their status as prisoners of war is essential to their claim," he said. "And if they were part of the war, then how could their activities not be related to the war?" It was the catch-22 we had been bumping up against for three long years.

The hard part for our clients was having to hear over and over again the legal arguments that essentially said that what they went through did not matter. It was what they had been told at war's end when they returned home and were ordered not to talk about what happened "over there," and it was what they were being told now.

These good men wanted someone to say that what they did mattered. That is what they were fighting for. They were not opportunists looking for a quick buck. They were not suing for slipping on an imaginary banana peel. They were not abusing the system. They wanted the system of justice to care. But the court hearings went straight to the legal issues and flew right past what the old veterans were really after.

I said to Harold that I knew it had to be galling for the veterans to find themselves in courthouses in the good old USA, the land of their dreams, sitting across from representatives of the companies that once heaped scorn and abuse on them, and listen to lawyers from their own government argue against them.

What we needed was someone like Oliver Wendell Holmes or Louis Brandeis—legendary jurists I had learned about in law school—who could come up with legal wisdom that transcended the black-and-white of the law and would produce a solution compliant with morality. Forget the semantics of the treaty, the double-talk, the legal loopholes, and do the right thing.

I guess I got a little carried away with Harold, spilling out all my thoughts and frustrations. Usually, it is the client who rails against injustice and the seeming impenetrability of the law. But he patiently listened to what I had to say, and then said in a sympathetic tone that, all right, he would not quit the case after all.

But he did clarify exactly why he was staying in. "It is for the people who didn't come back," he said. "And it is so generations to come can know what happened so hopefully it will never happen again."

"It's not about the money," he added. "If there is ever any money, it would just go to the kids, and money someone hasn't worked for usually doesn't come to much good."

CHAPTER EIGHTEEN

October 5, 1943
Hirohata Steel Works, Hirohata, Japan

AS WAS THE CASE WITH industries throughout Japan, the Hirohata Steel Works was experiencing serious labor shortages as winter approached in the second year of the great world conflict. Part of the Nippon Iron & Steel Corporation, the Hirohata mill was located fifty miles west of Osaka near the shores of the Inland Sea. Two hundred and fifty miles to the east was Tokyo. Fifty miles to the west was a city called Hiroshima.

With millions of Japanese men away fighting the enemy, elderly men and women were the only sizeable segment of the population left to liberally pick from, and war sacrifices or not, there were many jobs at a steel mill elderly men and women could not do.

But the mill's manpower problems began looking up the morning of October 5 as five hundred young men, including Harold, came marching up the road to the front gate, reporting for work.

Months earlier, every one of these new "workers" had been trying to stop the Japanese from winning the war; now, they were taking over shifts at the steel mill for the very soldiers they had been fighting.

Harold was placed with a multinational group of prisoners at Hirohata. They were housed at a prison camp north of the small town of Hirohata, a half-hour walk from the steel mill. Seven days a week, Japanese Army guards would march the prisoners in formation to and from the mill. Their commute would take them along a winding rural road where Japanese farmers worked the fields.

"The land was flat, near the seacoast," remembered Harold. "Every day, we'd walk straight down the road. There were a few bicycles, but not many cars. On the shoulders of the road they raised vegetables."

Because of the low supply of workers and heavy war demands on steel production, shifts at the mill were lengthy. A short shift was ten hours. The work was hard and dangerous: loading blast furnaces, stoking fires, hauling steel beams and equipment. The kind of work you couldn't pay a man to do.

Some prisoners filled out pay sheets, and the names and service numbers of the men, along with the terms of their employment, were recorded by the mill's bookkeepers. But these were paper documents only. As Harold, for one, could personally attest after giving twenty months of his life to the production of steel at Hirohata, there were no actual paydays.

The worker's "benefits" included one day off a month, when they were marched five miles to a stream to do their laundry.

On top of the backbreaking work, the prisoners were required to perform military exercises in the morning and in the evening. "They'd have us left face–right face, forward march, all that," Harold remembered. "We'd do that after we'd worked all day. I can tell you we sure didn't need the exercise."

Each prisoner was given a number, which he would answer to at roll call. Harold's was 221, "Ny hyaku niju ichi." No soldier or mill supervisor at Hirohata would ever know him as anything else. Whenever a prisoner's number was called, the proper response was to bow and answer, "Hai." A prisoner did not have to worry about who needed to bow lowest, based on one's status in life, because there was no status lower than captive. "We had to bow, stiffly from the waist down, to anyone, civilians, executives, soldiers. If you didn't do it right you got banged by a club," said Harold.

Camp conditions were as spartan as in the Philippines, but much colder. In the winter months, temperatures regularly fell below freezing. Each prisoner was issued one thin blanket and a straw mat for a mattress. Bunks were wooden planks in unheated wooden barracks. The prisoners would periodically be herded to a large cement tub for bathing, where they would be sent in groups into the water. The water was warm to start with. The farther back your position in line, the colder and dirtier it got. There was almost never any soap.

The guards exhibited the same mixture of arrogance and indifference as in the Philippines. A smirk or a shrug merited a beating. More egregious offenses gave the guards the opportunity to inflict what Harold remembered as their special "blue" punishment. "There was no water pressure and their only means of fighting fire was to have big tubs of water around," Harold explained. "In the wintertime these tubs would get ice on top. If somebody did something the guards didn't like they'd make him strip down and put him in that tub. They'd turn blue. Sometimes they'd pass out. They had tortures that they used on us like that."

But the number one torture in Japan, as in the Philippines, was food deprivation.

Despite the need for strong workers in the mill, rations consisted of a small serving of rice and a cup of thin soup in the morning, a midday meal at the mill of more rice, and an evening ration again of rice and soup—less than eight hundred calories a day for steel mill laborers sometimes working double shifts.

Consequently, there were a lot of missed shifts. Harold guessed that, on average, at least a hundred men would miss work every day. But there was a penalty for missing a shift. "You could tell them you were sick and they'd say that's fine but they'd cut your rations in half," said Harold. "And we weren't getting half what we needed. They'd think we were goldbricking, but the guys were really sick. The way they did it, the sick only got sicker."

One disease that ran rampant through the camp was stomach worms caused by eating contaminated food. Harold described the parasites as "big white worms as thick as a night crawler."

The camp hospital had medicine to kill the worms, but in order to get the medicine, a guard had to see proof of the disease. "You had to pass one of those worms and take it in as evidence," remembered Harold from personal experience. "You'd see a lot of guys digging around in the latrines. We'd rinse them off a little so we just had the worm, but it came out of a bunch of crap, I'll tell you."

The rate of camp deaths decreased from the Philippines, but men still died, and there was still no sanctity for the dying. As in the Philippines, the prisoners themselves were charged with removing and disposing of the bodies. In a place as crowded as Japan, that meant cremation. "There was a big oven where they did it," said Harold. "Usually they'd pick two guys to take the body over, one to stoke the oven and one to throw in the body and make sure it burned. I didn't ever have to do that, fortunately, but for the ones who did, it was pretty traumatic."

At that, the number of deaths at Hirohata were minimal compared to many of the work camps in Japan. One reason might have been the worms the men ate.

These were not the big white worms that gestated in their stomachs and made them sick. These were dead silkworms that became a regular staple of the evening ration. "The Japanese would dry them and give them to us to eat," said Harold. "They still had the legs and eyes. Sometimes they'd take the bugs and dump them in with the rice and sometimes they'd grind them up and use them as gravy. We called that our bug gravy. We laughed about eating worms. But I think the protein in those silkworms was real helpful to us."

"We ate everything," said Harold. "Sometimes we'd get fish heads in our soup, with the eyes still in them. We'd eat them right down. We didn't throw away anything."

Harold never left a meal satisfied, save for one time shortly before Christmas of 1943 when the Japanese inexplicably allowed the prisoners to receive Red Cross care packages.

According to war rules drawn up at the 1929 Geneva Convention, which Japan did not ratify, prisoners of war were to be given Red Cross packages on a regular basis. Although the Red Cross distributed its packages to Japan's prison camps, Harold got just two in the entire war, one in the Philippines just before Christmas at Cabanatuan, and one a year later at Hirohata. Inside were chocolate, canned fruit, condensed milk, and cigarettes.

Harold, a nonsmoker all his life, traded his cigarettes for four full rice rations from other prisoners who wanted the smokes.

When his twenty-fifth birthday arrived on December 20, 1943, he collected all his extra rice rations, loaded his plate, and began to eat. Although the helping of rice was no more than a normal-sized portion back home, his stomach had shrunk to the point that halfway through the pile of rice he discovered there was no more room. His stomach was full to the point of bursting. He had to cover what was left and push it under his mattress, leaving it until the next day. When he pulled the plate back out, he was delighted to find that what he had not finished was still there.

The inmates at Hirohata were not the only inhabitants in Japan being worked hard, fed little, and treated harshly. At the height of the war, according to Linda Goetz Holmes in *Unjust Enrichment*, Japan had a network of 169 work camps supplied with POW labor. Tens of thousands of troops and civilians from Australia, Great Britain, the Netherlands, Canada, and the United States had become an integral, if unwilling, part of the Japanese work force. Approximately twenty thousand American prisoners labored in at least seventy-nine of the camps. The biggest of the employers were Japanese family conglomerates known as *zaibatsus*, including Mitsubishi, Mitsui, NNK (Nippon Iron & Steel, Harold's employer), and Kawasaki Heavy Industries.

The work camps were located throughout Japan's expanding empire, wherever there was coal, copper, or lead to mine, ships to unload, steel to make, textiles to weave, and factories to run. The majority of the camps were centered in Japan's four main islands—Honshu, Hokkaido, Shikoku, and Kyushu—but the network spread out to eventually include work camps in Korea, Thailand, parts of Japanese-controlled China, Java, Formosa, and as far north as Manchuria. All were directed by Japan's Prisoner of War Information Bureau in Tokyo. POWs were the property of their companies during the day and the Japanese army by night.

Brutal, dangerous working conditions were a staple of the camps. Among the most notorious was the Miike Coal Mine operated by the Mitsui zaibatsu near the central Japanese city of Omuta. Thousands of POWs were sent into mine tunnels that had been sealed off for more than twenty years, some stretching seven hundred feet underneath Omuta Bay. Cave-ins were common. Of the nearly two thousand men who worked at Omuta; one hundred twenty-six died, about one a week. Of those who survived, few left without a permanent disability.

At the Mitsubishi-run Osarizawa Copper Mine in northern Honshu, prisoners worked twelve-hour days in mine tunnels so cold icicles were permanent fixtures on the ceilings. At the POW complex in Mukden, Manchuria, where the Mitsubishi zaibatsu oversaw textile and machinery manufacturing factories, POWs made artillery pieces that would be used against the Allies. Next to the factories, in a place called Harbin, was Unit 731, where Japanese doctors used Allied prisoners for medical experiments.

King of the torture camps, in terms of sheer size and scope, was the moving chain gang that built the Burma-Siam Railway through 225 miles of dense Java jungle. Some 61,000 Allied prisoners of war were utilized, including 668 Americans, of whom 133 perished. In all, 13,708 POWs—nearly half of them British—died while working on the railroad. Many more died in the immediate aftermath from exposure and lingering injuries.

Of 133,000 Allied prisoners of war taken by the Japanese, 36,000 died in captivity, a death rate of 27 percent. American-only mortality rates were even higher. Of 29,350 American JPOWs, 10,360, or 35 percent, died. Many of the American deaths occurred before the captives even had a chance to become slave laborers. Seven hundred Americans died on the Bataan Death March, for instance, another 1,645 at Camp O'Donnell in the Philippines, another 3,000-plus at Cabanatuan and other prison camps in the Philippines, and another 3,000 or more during hell ship crossings. Only a little more than half of the American POWs—19,986 of 29,350—actually made it to Japanese slave camps. Of these, 1,375 perished and 18,611 lived to be liberated, for a slave-camp death rate of 7 percent, meaning that for those who made it all the way to slave status, the odds of staying alive actually improved.

In sharp contrast, prisoners of war fared considerably better in the European Theater, where Geneva Convention POW rules were more strictly observed. Of some 236,000 Allies taken prisoners by the Germans and Italians, about 9,000 did not return, for a death rate of less than 4 percent. In Nazi Germany's POW camps, 1,213 Americans died out of 91,376 held captive, for a death rate barely over 1 percent.

But unlike in Europe, Japan's prison camps extended the captives virtually no rights. Soldiers became slaves, powerless to do anything but obey their masters. In Europe, prisoners were allowed to organize and allowed to at least air their grievances. They were allowed to develop social networks and exert some semblance of control over their living conditions. And they were prohibited from hard labor. In Japan it was just the opposite. Laboring in the mines, mills, and factories overwhelmed all else. Even in the Philippines, there had been the occasional variety show and camp interaction. But in Japan there was little if any of that. The men were too tired to socialize. What little free time they had, they used to rest. "When you get that low on energy, you think before you move," said Harold, who spent most of his days at the steel mill loading limestone, coal, and scrap iron into a blast furnace. "If you're going to go somewhere, you plan it out. Every step matters."

The cumulative effect of continued neglect was the biggest threat to a man's health. One day at the mine could not kill a man, but a hundred in a row, with too little food and too much cold, could. The attrition almost killed Harold.

He first came down with a case of dry beriberi, causing his legs to swell and his energy to lessen. After several days pulling himself out of bed, he woke up one morning and found he was too weak to move. He was carried to the hospital, where he was diagnosed with pneumonia.

Beyond offering sympathy, the camp doctor, a fellow POW, could do little. He had no medicine. Harold was sent back to his bunk, to live or to die.

For a week, he barely moved. Several times the guards, convinced he was dead, wanted to haul him to the camp crematorium. But his buddies bent down near Harold's mouth and verified he was still breathing. After two weeks, he was back on his feet, well enough to resume his shifts at the mill.

"I was so sick I seriously wondered if I was going to make it," Harold remembered. "It was the closest I came to dying."

Other than furtive glances from passersby on their morning and evening commute, contact with the outside world was practically nonexistent for the prisoners. They received no letters from home and had no assurances that the letters they wrote would ever make it out. Some men stopped writing altogether, considering it a waste of time. Harold, however, did not. "If there was a chance, no matter how small, that my folks could know I was still alive, I was going to take it," he said. The Japanese did not permit long letters, and everything got censored, but month after month Harold resolutely wrote to his folks and handed the letters to the guards for mailing. Only one ever actually made it to its destination.

It was in October of 1944, nearly two years since his parents first received the telegram that he was alive and a Japanese prisoner, that Stanley and Nina Poole opened their mailbox and saw, to their disbelieving eyes, a postcard from Japan:

> Dear Folks:
>
> I am well, and everything's the same. Sure hope someone there can have me a nephew! Hunting season here again and getting my blood stirred up as usual! Time goes quite fast, and the longer this lasts, the more determined I become to see it through. No words could express how happy our reunion will make me.

Great consolation comes from Bible scriptures such as Hebrews 12:5–9. My faith is strong and I know God will answer all our prayers in the future. Be patient and remain faithful always.

Love, Harold

The reference to hunting season was meant as a code to his parents. "I thought by talking about hunting it would assure them I still had my wits about me," said Harold, "and that I planned on one day coming home." It was the same with the references to the Bible and prayer, signals from Harold that he had not given up.

Not all prisoners shared Harold's hope and faith, however. Captivity tended to turn a man toward God with open arms or away from God completely. Concerned when he saw some of the men floundering, Harold sat down with a sheet of Japanese writing paper and wrote an open letter to his fellow prisoners.

When he was finished he passed the letter among the men. Eventually, a prisoner working in the camp office was able to produce a typewritten transcript, in English, which was posted at the entrance to the barracks.

Trials and Tribulations
April 25, 1945
Dear Fellow Associates,

I would like to bring to you a message found in our Holy Bible. I have heard so many of the men remark about our present condition of tribulation, and why we must go through it all. What awful sins have we done that we deserve such prolonged punishment? Maybe some of us have done things in the past that would justify such treatment, but maybe we can find the true answer in our Bible. In this world we find a contrast for everything, night and day, hot and cold, sweet and sour, and so on. Also there is the contrast of good and bad that governs the happiness and success of our lives. We must have the cold in order to appreciate the warm. We must have the darkness to enjoy the sunlight. Therefore, we must have the bad to really appreciate the good.

Many of the fellows have lost faith in God, because they say, "Why would God allow such tribulation to go on all over the world, that this war condition brings?" It might shock some of us to know that Jesus Christ, the only begotten son of God, said,

"Think not that I come to send peace on earth; I come not to send peace, but a sword." (See St. Matthew 10:34 and St. Luke 12:51).

It is the case again of the good and bad. Christ came and gave us the good and true methods of living that we should follow in this life, to bring us happiness and contentment, and to prepare us for the life to come. The teachings of Christ were so true and simple that many people couldn't comprehend them, and many heated arguments began to follow. Christ brings us peace and happiness of the spiritual kind if we will accept and follow his doctrines. (See St. John 14:27 and 16:33).

Now the question arises, what must we do to live a life of righteousness? The greatest commandment is to love God with all your heart, mind, and soul, and the next is to love thy neighbor as thyself (See St. Matthew 22:36–39 and St. Mark 12:28–31). In doing this, we would accomplish all of the laws of righteousness, and there would be eternal peace and happiness the world over.

We are the children of God, and he looks after us and teaches us as we progress along in this life, much the same as a father watches over his own son. Now we find that the father who loves his son, chastises him, and spares not the rod of corrections while he is young (See Proverbs 13:24, 19:18, 22:15, and 23:13); as a matter of course, God sees fit to chastise us, both for the wrongs we have done, and to keep us from doing wrong in the future. In Revelation 3:19, he says, "As many as I love, I rebuke and chasten; be zealous therefore and repent." Hebrews 12:5 says, "My son, despise not thou the chastening of the Lord, nor faint when thou art rebuked of him, for whom the Lord loveth he chasteneth, and scourgeth every son whom he receiveth." Psalms 44:12 says, "Blessed is the man whom thou chastenest, O Lord, and teachest him out of thy love." Job 5:17 and 18 say, "Behold, happy is the man whom God correcteth; therefore despise not thou the chastening of the almighty; for he maketh sore, and bindeth up; he woundeth, and his hands make whole." And Romans 5:3–5, in the words of the apostle Paul, says, "We glory in tribulations also; knowing that tribulations worketh patience, and patience, experience, and experience, hope, and hope maketh not ashamed; because the love of God is shed abroad in our hearts by the Holy Ghost which is given unto us."

So now we find that maybe after all, we are not so bad off and our tribulations may be wonderful blessings in disguise, to prepare us for a beautiful happy future.

I pray that we may all bear these thoughts in mind constantly, and have complete faith in God for our safe and happy deliverance to the beautiful shores of our Land of Liberty.

Always remember that faith and prayer in righteousness will obtain anything (See St. Matthew 21:21 and 22). Let us all try to develop a better spirit of cooperation, and join our faith and prayers for a speedy arrival of that blessed day when we may be called "free men" and be delivered to our home and loved ones once again.

Harold W. Poole
221

Not long after Harold distributed his letter, he and about a hundred other prisoners were lined up, counted off, and loaded into a truck. They were being transferred.

No explanation was given for the abrupt move, but it did not surprise the men. For months, prisoners kept leaving the mill and they were not replaced. The guards were becoming more impatient and even more harsh in their treatment. The prisoners could only hope that it had something to do with the sounds they heard with more and more regularity at night: the unmistakable sounds of airplane engines, and of bombs hitting the ground. The Allies must be attacking Japan, they reasoned, because it made no sense for Japan to be attacking itself. And if the Allies were attacking Japan, as long as the bombs missed them, it could not be a bad thing.

Harold and the others had no idea where they were going, and as usual, the guards did not offer any information. At least they were not leaving by foot or by ship, and no one was sorry to be leaving the steel mill. Things seemed to be looking up as they left Hirohata—and the prevailing winds coming from the direction of nearby Hiroshima City—behind.

CHAPTER NINETEEN

Fall 2002
Pasadena, California

DAVE CASEY'S LONG, BLACK law-firm limousine rolled to a stop at the entrance of the Richard Chambers Federal Appeals Court in Pasadena, California. The chauffeur opened the door for the passengers inside: Lester Tenney and his wife, Betty.

If anyone deserved limo treatment it was Lester. He had been fighting the fight longer than any of us—a lot longer. He had first contacted the government about getting even with the Japanese companies for their exploitation of prisoners in 1946, shortly after his release from captivity, when his wounds were fresh, and a peace treaty with Japan was still far in the future. "I wrote the government and asked them about claims against the companies," said Lester. "They wrote back and told me not to do anything personally, that they were aware of what went on, that they were taking care of it, and they'd get back to me."

What irritated Lester, maybe more than anything, was that no one had ever gotten back to him. He sat back and watched as first the 1951 peace treaty was signed and then, slowly but surely, the Japanese companies that used prisoners as slaves became huge international successes.

He picked up the pieces of his life, got married, graduated from college, taught finance as a university professor, and raised a fine family, but the injustice of what happened in Japan, to him and to so many others, never left him.

In many ways, as both a captive and a plaintiff in the JPOW litigation, Lester Tenney was the polar opposite of Harold Poole. As a prisoner of war, Lester constantly rubbed against the grain. He gave what they took but did not always take what they gave. After surviving the Bataan Death

March, he escaped from Camp O'Donnell and joined a band of guerrilla fighters in the Philippine jungle until he was recaptured and sent to Cabanatuan. He was one of the first prisoners of war sent by hell ship to Japan, where he was put to work in a Mitsui-run coal mine that gained a reputation as one of the most inhumane slave camps of them all. Defiant and resolute by nature, Lester never did anything or went anywhere peacefully. He came home a marked man, literally.

He never really stopped fighting or protesting. He published his book *My Hitch in Hell* in 1995 hoping it would be a catharsis, but getting it all out on paper did not heal everything. After the book was published, he moved on to pursue legal action against the Japanese—the catalyst that had brought the nationwide legal cause together.

Agreeing to be the first name on the lawsuit was just the start of it for Lester. Whatever we asked as his lawyers, he would do. He made numerous appearances at courthouses and congressional hearings and he was constantly doing media interviews. Besides appearing on several network television news programs, he was featured in a four-page spread in the Christmas Eve 2001 issue of *People Magazine*: "Lester Tenney's 60-Year War." His book also got plenty of attention. At a Memorial Day 2002 ceremony on the Washington Mall, actor Charles Durning read excerpts from *My Hitch in Hell* before introducing the author to speak to the crowd of thousands.

Everywhere Lester told his story, it was sympathetically received. But after more than three years of trying, the one place he still had not been able to personally tell it was in a court of law.

Today in Pasadena would be no different. Lester was our agreeable courtroom prop, but he would not be allowed to speak. Only attorneys could talk on the record as a panel of three federal appellate court judges entertained oral arguments relating to the appeal of Judge Vaughn Walker's year-old ruling that had dismissed all JPOW cases from federal court.

The hearing quickly moved into another round of semantic squabbling over the definition of the phrase "prosecution of the war." Did the slave labor performed by the JPOWs qualify as part of the war effort—as the defense contended—or did it not, as those us on the plaintiffs' side believed?

Our designated spokesperson, Steven Schneebaum of the D.C. firm Patton Boggs, was asked directly by Judge Stephen Reinhardt, "If a company makes missiles, is it involved in prosecution of the war?"

It was a tricky question. A yes answer would leave open the question whether coal, steel, copper, and other products the POWs helped produce were not also directed toward Japan's war effort—and if they were, the treaty would successfully exempt them from further compensation. But since coal, steel, and copper, it could easily be argued, were obviously materials that could be used for implements of war, answering no would strain the point of just what could constitute involvement in prosecution of the war.

Caught between this legal rock and hard point, Schneebaum deliberated before tentatively saying, "Our answer would be no."

By now, after more than two years of uphill battling, it was a familiar feeling to sense that we were not scoring points. But just as the defense table was getting comfortable, Judge Reinhardt turned his laser stare on the defendants.

"Why do you dance around the German settlements?" asked the jurist of the Justice Department lawyers from Washington.

The question was in reference to the difference in the U.S. government's legal posturing in regard to World War II slave-labor lawsuits against Nazi Germany and against Japan.

The so-called "Holocaust cases" involved millions of private citizens, some of them Americans, who were forced into labor during World War II for companies operating as part of Adolf Hitler's Third Reich. At the height of the war, these companies stretched across Europe and supported the Nazis out of fear or fealty or both. As with the companies that used Allied POWs in Japan, the Nazi-affiliated companies stayed in business during the war years largely because of the availability of cheap or unpaid labor. Some used concentration camp labor, usually Jews, and these were declared "slave laborers," while others used private citizens who lived in their own homes, a combination of Jews and other races and nationalities, and these were declared "forced laborers." In all, more than ten million people were used as slave or forced laborers during World War II by the Nazi regime.

In the 1990s, in concert with the fall of the Iron Curtain and Berlin Wall and outright collapse of the Soviet Union, a reunified Germany began to see and feel the need to address the wrongs of its Nazi past. Throughout the decade, the German government paid a number of war debts to reconciliation foundations and other groups. Adding to the wave of righting Nazi wrongs was a huge settlement by Swiss banks to German war victims, primarily Jews, who had their fortunes seized by the Nazis during the war and deposited in Switzerland. As time wore on, PI lawyers in the United States who helped ignite and then participated in the Swiss bank affair began to see the possibilities of hauling German companies doing business in the United States into U.S. courts to face their war sins. These companies included, among many others, such giants as Ford, Chrysler-Daimler, Bayer, Volkswagen, Siemens, BASF, and Deutsche Bank. The lawyers signed clients, class actions were organized, legislation was lobbied for and passed (including Tom Hayden's bill in California), and lawsuits were filed, the first in early 1998 in New Jersey.

Before they could proceed, the courts needed to know where the United States government stood on the matter. The Department of State was asked if the suits could go forward in America's famously open centers of litigation. Or were there political resolutions from World War II that halted their progress in the American court system?

The State Department's answer was neither yes nor no.

In a 1999 letter to New Jersey federal judge John W. Bissell, Acting Assistant Attorney General David W. Ogden clarified the position, or nonposition, of the executive branch as it related to the Holocaust cases:

> Dear Judge Bissell:
>
> Thank you for your letter of November 23, 1999, inviting the participation of the United States as amicus curiae in the cases Elly Gross v. Volkswagen, A.G., et al. and Emanuel Rosenfeld v. Volkswagen, A.G., currently pending in your court.
>
> The United States has a strong interest in the correct interpretation and application of the various treaties that are implicated by the parties' pleadings in these cases. Nevertheless, for the reasons set forth below, we must respectfully decline to participate at this time.
>
> As the Court may be aware, multifaceted negotiations to resolve the claims asserted in these cases, as well as other similar claims against German industrial firms, banks, and insurance companies, have been underway for more than a year. The talks are being led by Deputy Secretary of the Treasury Stuart E. Eizenstat, on behalf of the United States, and by Count Otto Lambsdorff, Special Representative of the Chancellor, on behalf of the Federal Republic of Germany. Participants in the talks include not only

> counsel for the parties before Your Honor, but also other plaintiffs' attorneys, representatives of German industry and their counsel, victims' organizations, and the governments of Belarus, the Czech Republic, Israel, Poland, Russia, and Ukraine.
>
> These negotiations are currently at a very delicate stage. At the most recent round of talks, held in Bonn, Germany in mid-November, the various parties seemed within striking distance of a comprehensive agreement, an agreement that would, among other things, result in the consensual dismissal of the pending litigation. The United States is hopeful that these talks, given their very advanced stage, can reach fruition within the next eight weeks. As a result, we are reluctant to take action now that might interfere with achieving that objective.

The settlement talks, unencumbered as they were by U.S. government legal interference, would reach a fruition of massive and unprecedented proportions. On July 17, 2000, the Foundation for Remembrance, Responsibility and the Future was signed into being by the German Bundestag, or parliament. That foundation and others set up by assorted businesses and the governments of France and Austria—where the foundation was called "Reconciliation, Peace and Cooperation"—raised $8 billion to be paid as settlements to forced and slave laborers of the Nazis as well as other wartime victims. The money was a combination of governmental and business contributions. In Germany alone, some 6,542 companies—including many that had not even been in existence during the war—stepped up to "signal their historical and moral responsibility."

With the money in place, an organization was established to adjudicate more than 1.5 million expected claims, with bureaus in Poland, Ukraine, Russia, Belarus, and the Czech Republic as well as at the Jewish Claims Conference and the International Organization for Migration.

With such a large number of deserving recipients—only survivors, and no heirs, were included in the payoffs—the $8 billion amounted to an average payout of about $5,000 for each forced laborer and $7,500 for each slave laborer. Along with the money came another payoff in the form of apologies from German President Johannes Rau and Austrian Chancellor Wolfgang Schuessel.

"I know that for many it is not really money that matters," said President Rau on the day the German Foundation settlement was announced. "What they want is for their suffering to be recognized as suffering and for the injustice to them be named injustice. I pay tribute to all those who were subjected to slave labor under German rule, and in the name of the German people, beg forgiveness."

A key provision of the settlement was that it would halt, once and forever, any and all legal claims against companies that once associated with the Nazis. By the summer of 2001 all significant cases had been dismissed by the courts, paving the way for "prompt payment" to the 1.5 million recipients.

"From its inception, this has been at its heart a German company initiative," Stuart Eizenstat, the U.S. diplomat who brokered the deal, said in July in Berlin. "It was this generation of enlightened German industrialists and financial leaders who were willing to meet the moral responsibility for the actions of their corporate predecessors. For sure, there were practical and legal dimensions to their actions, given the pendency of class actions against them in the United States, one of their largest markets. But it would be unfair and misleading to suggest that this was their sole motivation for the actions they have taken. They have contended from the start that they bore no legal responsibility today. Indeed, there are a variety of legal hurdles to any recovery in U.S. courts. But German companies sued in U.S. courts have clearly assumed a moral responsibility, thereby setting a standard for good corporate citizenship . . . This moral dimension is further demonstrated by the contributions of literally hundreds of German companies who have absolutely no legal risk in U.S. courts or elsewhere."

After praising corporate Germany, Eizenstat, an attorney himself, turned to the role U.S. lawyers played in the settlement.

"We must be frank," he said. "It was the American lawyers, through the lawsuits they brought in U.S. courts, who placed the long-forgotten wrongs by German companies during the Nazi era on the international agenda. It was their research and their work that highlighted these old injustices and forced us to confront them. Without question, we would not be here without them . . . For this dedication and commitment to the victims, we should always be grateful to these lawyers."

Finally, Eizenstat turned to the role of the U.S. government.

"Why has the U.S. government taken such a direct role in the settlement of private lawsuits and in helping to shape the German Foundation for Remembrance, Responsibility, and the Future? It is because we were asked by the German government to work as partners with them in facilitating this historic initiative, and all parties to the litigation agreed to our participation. It is because of President Clinton's determination to expeditiously help in their lifetimes those who were victims of German companies and German government injustices, many of whom are American citizens. It is because of our national interest in addressing any tensions in our relationship with Germany, one of our most important in the world, arising out of prolonged litigation and threats of sanctions.

"The United States for fifty-five years has supported Germany's efforts to provide justice to victims of the Holocaust and Nazi era, to Jews and non-Jews alike, wherever they lived. This effort has been a continuation of these governmental efforts. U.S. occupation forces passed the first compensation and restitution law to address the wrongs done to victims of Nazi persecution in the early postwar period. This law was later largely incorporated into Germany's domestic legislation, which was encouraged by the United States, and reached millions of Nazi victims in the West. Payments from the German Foundation will add another five billion dollars to the one hundred billion (in current dollar terms) in compensation, restitution, and pensions that have been paid and will continue to be paid by Germany for acts arising out of the National Socialist period.

"Our role has been to work cooperatively with Germany as a catalyst and partner to help achieve some justice for far more people and far more rapidly than could ever be achieved in our courts, and to create a mechanism to help German enterprises achieve legal peace in the United States courts."

In his 2003 book on the subject, *Imperfect Justice*, Eizenstat called the huge multinational Holocaust settlements a "massive alternative dispute-resolution process."

"We developed novel concepts," Eizenstat wrote, "that may have applicability in future mass violations of human rights, like 'rough justice' to pay mass numbers of victims, rather than the individualized justice that courts provide."

Eizenstat noted that the German cases inspired other victims and lawyers to consider their legal possibilities. "Class-action suits by . . . American POWs against the Japanese clearly took their inspiration from the Holocaust cases," he wrote.

But the Japanese cases had not received the same treatment, from the courts or the executive branch.

It is true that the Holocaust and Japanese cases were hardly parallel. In many ways, they were apples and oranges. Significantly, all of the more than ten million people used as forced or slave laborers by Nazi Germany were civilians, while almost all of the more than twenty-five thousand Americans used as forced or slave laborers by Japan were part of the military. Just as significant was the difference in respective postwar treaties signed by America with the Nazis and the Japanese. Nothing as explicit as the 1951 San Francisco Treaty between the United States and Japan was signed between the United States and Germany, due in no small part to Germany's fragmented geography and politics in the aftermath of the war.

Also, it was Germany that asked for America's help in making amends, followed by Austria and then France. Governmental and business leaders in the onetime Nazi strongholds wanted the assistance of the United States. In Japan, neither government nor industry indicated any desire for redress, repentance, or redemption.

That this was the case was not surprising. Although they were once wartime allies, Germany and Japan were worlds apart during World War II, and six decades later they remain worlds apart. Postwar Germany has moved as far from Hitler and its Nazi past as possible, effectively reducing Hitler to a mutant despised in the very place it was spawned. Successive politicians and businesses, as well as the general German population, want nothing to do with the philosophies and the men who waged World War II on Germany's behalf. In Japan such separation from the past has not been so easily accomplished or desired. While Japanese feudalism and the militarism it produced was disarmed by the ratification of a new Japanese constitution in 1947 that reduced the emperor to largely symbolic status, there is still, in fact, an emperor on the throne who is given more than a measure of respect (when Hirohito, the war emperor, died in 1989, U.S. President George Bush attended the funeral). Japan is still Japan. Divorcing its wartime past from the present is complex, delicate, painful, and in some cases, impossible. Mostly, as the dearth of history books and discussions on the subject inside Japan attest, the subject is ignored. To disrespect the past is to disrespect the present.

But for all the differences between German Nazism and Japanese Militarism, one question emerged from both sides of World War II: did those people who were forced to labor during wartime have a right to sue for back wages from the companies that did the forcing? What the appellate court wanted to know in Pasadena was if the United States Department of Justice, as spokesperson for the Department of State, was consistent in the way it answered, or did not answer, that question.

Begging the same question were California congressmen Mike Honda and Dana Rohrabacher, cosponsors of the United States Prisoners of War Justice Act, who held a House hearing on the POW matter just days before the Pasadena court oral arguments.

"Perhaps most shocking is the fact that the U.S. State Department is opposed to the veterans' efforts, rather than helping them resolve this matter," Mike Honda said at the outset of the House Judiciary Committee hearing held on September 25, 2002. "This is especially tragic given the key leadership role the United States has played recently in resolving similar claims brought by civilian slave laborers in Germany."

From the State Department, William Howard Taft IV defended the sanctity of the 1951 treaty. Taft, whose great-grandfather William Howard Taft was the twenty-seventh president of the United States, and before that, the first civilian governor of the Philippine Islands from 1901 to 1904, explained that the treaty prevented the government from taking a nonparticipant legal position as it had in the Holocaust cases.

"In short, the [State] Department supports justice for U.S. prisoners of war," said Taft, "but it does not support H.R. 1198 and would oppose its enactment . . . The United States should assume that our POWs, together with all other veterans, should receive full and fair compensation for their service. Special hardships connected with that service, such as those suffered by POWs, should be considered in determining what compensation is proper . . . we owe it to those who serve to do our best to establish an equitable system that takes into account the many different situations they experience."

Lester Tenney testified at the hearing and reminded everyone that Pacific Theater veterans were now dying at the rate of three men per day. If justice was to be served, it should be served quickly.

"I am not looking for any sympathy," Lester said, "nor seeking any glory. All I really want is justice. We were very proud of the medals we were awarded while defending our country's freedom, but they have very little meaning if the government of today denies us the right we fought for yesterday. We were there for our country when they needed us. Now we need our country to be there for us."

At the hearing's conclusion, I sought out Congressman Honda, whom I had never met. I wanted to shake his hand and thank him for his support. Our conversation turned from case strategy to the courage and character of the former JPOWs themselves. We agreed that they are good and honest men, fighting at this late stage of their lives for justice and not much else.

"I have a client in Salt Lake whose only real concern is if I'm going to go broke on this case," I told the congressman.

He responded, "I'm going to Salt Lake this weekend. Do you think I could meet this man?"

On a Saturday morning three days later, after landing at the Salt Lake City International Airport, Mike Honda caught a ride to the downtown Sheraton Hotel, where I had arranged for him to meet Harold in the lobby.

This was no press conference for the case or publicity stunt to drum up votes for the congressman, who was running for his second term. There were no reporters or cameras or public relations people present. Honda had flown to Salt Lake to help a fellow Democrat, Utah Second District Congressman Jim Matheson, in his bid for reelection. But before he went to Matheson's luncheon rally, he took the time to meet and talk with Harold.

After the congressman and the veteran shook hands, Honda told Harold of his own wartime imprisonment. Since he was a small child when that occurred, he could not use that experience to personally relate to what the POWs of the Philippines went through, but what he could relate to was the need to make things right. That was what motivated him to fight so long and hard for the 1988 internment apology and payments from the government in the Civil Liberties Act—an experience he compared to "moving a rock up a mountain"—and it was why he was fighting so long and hard for his Justice for United States Prisoners of War Act.

"I see this century as a century of reconciliation," Honda told Harold. "The last couple of hundred years, all we've done is fight. This is not about Japan bashing; it's about reconciliation. It's about private companies enriched by slave labor paying their debts. It's really not reparations.

If you work for somebody and you're not compensated, you have the right to get paid."

Harold nodded his agreement. "We appreciate what you're doing," he said. "We want you to know that. It's wonderful to have you on our side."

"We're looking at 9/11, Iraq, a whole generation of armed people," the congressman said. "How can we do that without taking care of our veterans? You should have your day in court. You should not have to survive the very same government that you defended."

Congressman Honda clasped his two hands together and held them aloft. "When people say 'I'm sorry,' our bonds are so much stronger."

The men talked for their scheduled hour, and then beyond. Harold told the congressmen that he had worked for the post office for thirty years and the congressman told Harold his World War II veteran father had also worked for the post office after the war. Honda's aide, Isaac Yamagata, repeatedly told the congressman that he was running late for his next appointment, to no avail.

When the two men finally stood, Honda put his arm around Harold's shoulder. "It has made my day to meet you," he said.

He had one more request of Harold: "I'd like to have my picture taken with you."

The congressman was dressed in the Hawaiian shirt and shorts he had traveled in, but he would be changing into a suit. Would it be all right, he asked, if he came by Harold's house later in the day, properly attired, and they could take their photo?

Harold gave directions to his home and early that evening, as the sun was reflecting off the mountain peaks of the Wasatch Mountains, Yamagata and Honda swung into the driveway. Yamagata took photos of the two men as they posed arm-in-arm in the driveway, after which Harold loaded down his visitors with apples from a tree in the backyard, and then pulled out his box of war souvenirs and showed off his prized war mementos: the Bible he had found in Bataan and his Silver Star.

"I'm flattered that you've come," Harold said as he walked Honda and Yamagata to their rental car. "Congressmen don't come by here every day, you know."

CHAPTER TWENTY

May 28, 1945
Nagoya Sub Camp #9, Toyama, Japan

HE BECAME A SHIPYARD WORKER and unloaded freighters in the harbor town of Toyama on the Sea of Japan, about a hundred miles north from Hirohata.

"It was just a seaport, not too big a one at that," said Harold. "We mainly unloaded food. They'd get us up just after daybreak and we'd start working. There was a lot to do."

POWs from various camps had been recently recruited to Toyama, including a hundred or so British soldiers who were brought in from Singapore. Harold and the others from Hirohata brought the camp population to about 350. The new work camp where they were housed was located at the edge of town not far from the docks.

The need for workers was immediately obvious. Freight lay scattered across the docks, waiting to be organized and hauled. Cargo holds were in disarray, with sacks of food piled on top of coal, limestone, and scrap iron. It was all very un-Japanese-like and was another indication that the Japanese war effort itself was in disarray.

Almost nightly since the POWs arrived, the sound of bombs exploding could be heard in the distance.

One night, Allied planes dropped hundreds of fliers alerting the residents that the town was about to be bombed. The fliers gave the precise date and time of the approaching nighttime attack. As they worked at the docks, Harold and the other prisoners heard the townspeople discuss the details. The news both thrilled and frightened the POWs. The thought of Allied bombs on their way was all they had hoped for. But that did not change the fact that their camp was unmarked.

On the day of the bombing, Harold watched the population of Toyama evacuate. "It was pitiful to see a Jap mother with a little baby strapped on her back and one or two other little ones clinging to her skirt as she pulled a little cart with what belongings she could take," he said. "I'm sure most of them had no place to go, but just wanted to get out of town before it was burned. The civilians always suffer in any war."

In many ways, Harold observed, the Japanese people were not in much better shape than the prisoners of war. They too were on rations for food and plenty of other things, and when it came to knowing what was going on, they appeared to be kept completely in the dark. "The whole time, the Japanese people were told they were winning the war," said Harold. "That's what they kept on hearing, no matter what was happening."

The night of the attack, the men at the prison camp looked on from their barracks. "We watched the Yanks flatten out the town," said Harold. "There were no Japs around. The guards had all taken cover in air raid shelters. The American B-29s came over one at a time, fifteen minutes apart, dropped bombs, and left. Not one anti-aircraft shot was fired in opposition, nor was there any air resistance at all."

Some bombs hit near the prison camp, which was just far enough out of town to be spared. One came so close that a piece of shrapnel flew into the kitchen and lodged in the wall. But otherwise the camp was untouched. "We could have been hit. But we had no marks, nothing," said Harold. "But oh goodness, it lifted our spirits seeing those B-29s. They flew pretty high and they'd leave these wide vapor trails. They were something to see. Nobody got much sleep that night."

When morning came, the POWs kept their celebrating to themselves as the guards emerged from their shelters, rounded everyone up, and marched to what little was left of the town to begin a massive cleanup.

The work at the docks was backbreaking, especially for men with bad backs to begin with. There were no days off and the prisoners paced themselves as best they could. Through years of captivity and forced labor, they had learned the fine line between working so slow that they would rate a beating and so fast that they would collapse. A seasoned prisoner of war had a sixth sense about when the guards or company honchos were around. Survival demanded a keen awareness of when to work and when to rest. This was even more true at Toyama, where the chaos and the constant threat of enemy bombs made the guards and honchos more edgy and ornery than ever.

In other ways, conditions had improved. There were no more mandatory military exercises morning and night as there had been at Hirohata; it was summertime now, meaning more comfortable weather; and while rations remained woefully inadequate, heaven smiled on the prison shipyard workers by providing soybeans to supplement their diets.

The soybeans arrived one day on a big freighter. Many of the sacks of soybeans lay on top of scrap iron and ore in the bottom of the hold, where they had broken open, scattering soybeans everywhere. The Japanese offered a sack of soybeans to the men if they finished the job by the end of the day. The prisoners took the bargain, made the deadline, and hauled the beans back to camp, where someone with a smuggler's heart got a brainstorm. With all the loose soybeans down at the docks, why not devise a way to scoop them up and sneak them into camp? The men tied strings to the bottom of their underwear and the next day at the docks, when no one was looking, they stuffed loose soybeans down their pants and cinched the strings. When their shift was over, they walked to camp in underwear full of soybeans.

"Everything worked fine until one day one of the men had a string break on him, and beans were scattered all over the road, ending our little scheme," said Harold.

But the men had already enjoyed several days of extra nourishment, and the punishment that followed was barely noticeable. After a cursory effort to find the instigators of the crime, the Japanese just let it go. There were times when smuggling soybeans would have been a capital offense. Now, the attention of the guards was diverted elsewhere. "They were too anxious for us to stay in shape and get those ships unloaded," said Harold. "They weren't thinking about too much else."

Rumors that the war was ending flowed constantly through the camp. The biggest rumor was that Germany had already surrendered. The men did not know whether to believe it (it was in fact true; the Germans had surrendered on May 8, 1945, three weeks before Harold arrived at Toyama), and even if they did dare to believe such a thing, they were not sure if that made Japan more dangerous, or less.

For Harold, World War II ended in quiet.

He was in his bunk the morning of August 15, 1945, feeling the familiar numbness in his hips and legs after another hard night's sleep, when the preternatural quietness of the morning came over him. No one had awakened him. There had been no stick in his side, no guard demanding that he get to his feet.

Instinctively, he knew the war was over.

And he knew Japan had not won.

The guards said nothing. The shipyard honchos came by to announce there would be no work that day, and the prisoners were left in their barracks. The next day, there was also no work, and the guards served the men all the rice they wanted to eat. It was as close to a formal surrender declaration as they would get. But the signs were all there, even if no one on the Japanese side was saying it out loud.

"Among the men it just came down the line, 'The war is over! The war is over!'" said Harold. "We were slapping our backs and carrying on. We were so happy. We didn't know what to do. It was just unbelievable."

Harold remembered one of the guards handing the prisoners a can of paint so *PW* could be painted on the barracks roof, designating prisoner-of-war camp. "They said there were reconnaissance planes looking for us," he recalled. "So a couple of the guys ran up on the roof with the paint."

After that, the guards laid down their guns and fled.

"They just dropped down like a wet rag," said Harold. "We told them to run and they ran."

Watching the Japanese soldiers turn and flee was a final lesson for the POWs about the vast gulf between East and West. When the Japanese fought, they fought as one; and when they gave up, they gave up as one. They had been playing by rules of war all along, but they were *their* rules of war. They had battled the world on Japanese terms, not America's terms or England's terms or even Germany's terms. As soon as the emperor sent out word that the war was over, it was over. No one kept fighting. No one. In the snap of a finger, guards who had been dominating, belligerent, intolerant, and cruel became docile, humble, and self-effacing. These guards were still soldiers, they were still armed, they were still on their homeland, and they were in considerably better physical condition than the emaciated men they had been guarding. But they laid down their weapons without delivering any final blows, warnings, or insults. They simply bowed, turned around, and scrambled off.

During the war, the Japanese had avoided surrender at all costs. At the battle of Okinawa, in one of the more graphic examples, over one hundred thousand Japanese troops chose to die in the face of an overwhelming Allied offensive rather than surrender. In the island's underground caves, another twenty-seven thousand chose to suffocate rather than surface and surrender. It had been that way for nearly four long years, at every battle, on every front. But when the emperor surrendered, all the Japanese surrendered. It was allowed. It was the way of bushido.

Even when provoked, the Japanese declined to fight. Shortly after the guards abandoned the Toyama prison camp, Harold was with several GIs when they passed one of their former guards on the roadside. One of the American soldiers attacked the guard viciously, taking out years of pent-up frustration. The Japanese soldier responded by covering his head and making no attempt to fight back. The former POW might have killed him, if only he had had the strength.

No sooner had the *PW* dried than the B-29s came into view again. The new Superfortresses—an upgrade from the B-17 Flying Fortresses the men had admired in the Philippines and thought could not possibly be improved—parked above the prison compound and opened their bomb bays. The men below, out of instinct, flinched before realizing the "bombs" were 55-gallon drums filled with supplies and attached to parachutes.

As soon as the drums landed on the ground, the men opened them. The contents were not to be believed: canned milk, corned beef, tins of peaches packed in thick syrup, Hershey chocolate bars, whole cartons of Camel cigarettes, plus personal hygiene items including shoe laces, sewing kits, soap, razors and razor blades, combs, shaving cream, toothpaste, soap, and toilet paper, all compliments of Uncle Sam.

"We had American food again," said Harold, "and all we could eat! It was like heaven."

Instructions attached to the shipments designated how much food and clothing should be distributed per man, but the men found the orders unnecessary. There was more than plenty to go around. They took everything back to the mess for general consumption. They had lived so long sharing practically nothing that they would have no trouble sharing more than they thought possible.

Several men took pieces of the parachutes that dropped the supplies, dyed them red, white, and blue and stitched the pieces together to make an American flag. When it was finished, they ran the Stars and Stripes up the flagpole where only days before the Flag of the Rising Sun had flown. With time on their hands while awaiting their evacuation orders, they explored Toyama. The only military activity in the area was conducted by the Allies. Things could still go wrong, however, such as the U.S. fighter plane on reconnaissance from a nearby aircraft carrier that flew too low to the ground and hit a wire. The plane crashed, killing the pilot and breaking both legs of the gunner.

The air force flew in a transport plane to a landing strip a mile or so from the prison camp to take out the dead pilot and assist the injured gunner. Seeing all this activity from camp, Harold and another soldier, an old friend from Bataan named Zimmerman, set out on foot to investigate.

As they were walking, a truck full of Japanese passed them. Harold and Zimmerman waved their arms for the truck to stop.

"We climbed in and told them to take us to the airstrip, and, by George, they did!" said Harold. At the airstrip, they met nonprisoner American soldiers for the first time in more than three and a half years.

"What a sight it was for us to see those stateside Yanks," remembered Harold. "They looked so big and strong to us who were skin and bones. They gave us chocolate bars, which we ate with relish. The sergeant asked us if we could tell the Japs there to move a lot of stuff out of the hangar. 'Boy, can we ever!' we told him, and did we enjoy bossing those Japs around some more."

As the cleanup operation was mopping up, the pilot pointed to the transport plane.

"Come on, climb aboard," he said, his eyes absorbing the pitiful sight of two fellow soldiers who were nothing but skin and bone. "We'll fly you out of here. There's plenty of room. You've been here long enough."

It was a tempting offer, a chance to leave a place where the wrung-out prisoners had known nothing but misery and go to a place where, the pilot promised, they would very soon have a hot meal, an even hotter bath, and a bunk with a mattress, things they had been dreaming of for what seemed like forever. They could do it. They were free. No one would stop them. The Yanks won. They could begin their journey home.

But their friends were still back at camp, friends they had suffered with and survived with, friends they had encouraged to stay alive and nursed back to health when they were beaten or sick and who had done the same for them, friends they had gone through the brutal war of imprisonment with.

"We told him thanks," said Harold, "but that we'd go back to camp and go out with our buddies."

CHAPTER TWENTY-ONE

September 6, 2002
Salt Lake City, Utah

THE FIRST 20TH PURSUIT SQUADRON reunion I attended was to find clients; the second, to reunite with friends.

After three years working "the case," I felt like one of them: James Parkinson, 20th Pursuit Squadron, legal counsel.

The reunions were of recent vintage. Like most World War II outfits, the men of the 20th who had made it home had gone their separate ways when the war ended. Of the 225 men in the unit when the war started, just 67 survived the war, a casualty rate of slightly more than 70 percent.

Coming home in 1945 was great, but it was not easy. Returning POWs filled an uncertain niche, not quite conquering heroes and not quite dead. They had spent the war as imprisoned, surrendered soldiers, loading ships and shoveling coal. They were wounded, but not in the conventional way. They came home limping, with bad backs, shattered ear drums, broken bones that had not been set properly, if at all, and brought along a dizzying array of unseen parasites. They flinched every time they heard a raised voice. In postwar America, no one held tickertape parades or made movies about that.

The siege of Bataan, as the details became widely known and documented, was given its due as an example of profound sacrifice and courage. War historians labeled it a significant factor in slowing Japan's momentum during an otherwise mostly unbridled rampage through the Pacific to start the war.

But medals for heroism did not go to the men who fought it. A total of three Congressional Medals of Honor were awarded for the battle in the Philippines: one to General Douglas MacArthur, whose myopic leadership left the Army underequipped in the first place; one to General Jonathan Wainwright, who from Corregidor ordered the men on Bataan not to surrender when they were out of food and bullets; and one to Lieutenant Commander John Bulkeley, the pilot of the PT boat that delivered MacArthur and other officers from the Philippines to Australia.

No one who had been in a prison camp got a medal for valor. No purple hearts were awarded for beatings sustained behind barbed wire.

The United States military contributed to the returning JPOW's identity crisis when many were greeted upon arrival on the West Coast with orders not to talk about the details of their incarceration. Peace negotiations were underway with Japan, and in light of the atomic bombs America dropped on Hiroshima and Nagasaki, the less talking about the past, the better. MacArthur, the men were informed, was heading the negotiations in occupied Japan. Dugout Doug himself. The man whose actions had helped produce the JPOWs' nightmares was now in charge of a production that would ensure their story would not be told.

It was not until 1991, twenty-seven years after MacArthur died and fifty years after the start of the war, that the first 20th Pursuit Squadron reunion was held. So many other World War II groups were holding golden anniversary get-togethers that the 20th followed suit.

The men told me they were surprised at how good it made them feel to see each other again. Even though they had spent little time together, relatively speaking, during the war, and a lifetime had passed since the war ended, they discovered in one another a connection that would not fade and one that they had been unable to find with anyone else—wives and children included.

So they continued holding the reunions, which became annual affairs, held in one or another squadron member's hometown.

For 2002, they chose Harold's.

Of twenty-two squadron members still alive (there were thirty-two for the 1991 reunion), eleven were healthy enough to make the trip to Salt Lake. Harold was there, of course, escorted by his daughter, Linda. The others included Fran Agnes and his wife Marlene from Everett, Washington; John Bristow and his wife Betty from Sacramento, California; Jim Huff and his wife Anella from Napoleon, Ohio; George Idlett from Herndon, Virginia; Bill Mitchell from Rockport, Texas; Don Newbold from Preston, Idaho; Gene Jacobsen and his wife Barbara from St. George, Utah; Johnny Johnson and his wife Evelyn from Sandy, Utah; Grant McDonald and his wife Evelyn from Bountiful, Utah; and Joe Moore from San Antonio, Texas. A fighter pilot, Moore had been the outfit's commander and was not taken as a prisoner of war. He got out of the Philippines before surrender when he was ordered to fly a P-40 to Australia.

I had requested a luncheon spot on the men's schedule so I could give a group presentation of how the case was going. That was my official motive. My ulterior motive was I just wanted to see the men again, and I was willing to spring for lunch to do it. At that, I almost did not make the cut. The men were in high demand. Among those who lobbied for a place on the itinerary were Mayor Rocky Anderson of Salt Lake City, who hosted a dinner; the Air Force commanders at nearby Hill Air Force Base, who hosted a tour of the base and the post museum; the local Olympic organizers, who arranged for a ski jumping show at the Utah Olympic Park where the Winter Olympics had recently been held; and as a final coup de grace, the Mormon Tabernacle Choir, which reserved seats of honor for the men at the choir's weekly Sunday morning radio and television broadcast.

Everywhere they went, the men were toasted. The air force brass saluted them, and the crowd at the Olympic Park gave them a standing ovation. But it was at the Tabernacle Choir broadcast that the old soldiers were given a hero's salute that transcended time.

Sunday morning before the performance, the men were ushered through a side door of the 135-year-old Mormon Tabernacle on Temple Square and escorted to their seats. The choir's weekly live television and radio performances began in 1929, when Harold Poole's parents were members of the choir, and nothing, including two world wars, has stopped them.

Just before going on the air, Craig Jessup, the choir conductor, introduced the veterans, explained who they were, and asked them to stand, prompting a warm reception from the capacity audience of six thousand people. Then at the end of the half-hour broadcast, Jessup asked the audience to please remain in their seats. "We don't usually do this," he said, "but we'd like to perform a song for our special guests." He turned to the men and asked if they would please stand again. "We'd like to sing for you 'The Battle Hymn of the Republic,'" he said.

The 325 members of the choir proceeded to sing a rousing rendition of the song that once won the Tabernacle Choir a Grammy. At the finish, as echoes of "*His peace is marching on*" lingered in the hall, a hush settled over the crowd and the choir members, still standing and unprompted, looked directly at the row of veterans and began to applaud. The conductor turned and smartly saluted as the audience rose to its feet to join the ovation. The men of the 20th Pursuit Squadron, who spent the war behind enemy lines, brushed aside tears as they soaked in a thank-you sixty years in the making.

My luncheon followed the choir concert. I waited as the men settled into their seats, then tapped a water glass to get their attention. "Sue and I would like to welcome you all here," I said, gesturing toward my wife who stood beside a computer and video screen set up in the corner. "I have a presentation that will give you an update on the case, and I'd like to answer any questions you might have." I paused for effect, and then said, "But if I know anything, I know not to get between you men and food. So let's eat first!"

The men retreated to the buffet lines, where everything from fresh shrimp and prime rib to waffles and custom-made omelettes were piled high.

I watched these gallant gentlemen as they held their wives' hands and walked economically toward the door. I looked at the filled water glasses in front of each of their plates. Just that much water on the Death March, and who could say how many more men might be with us?

After lunch, I booted up my PowerPoint presentation and explained to the men the different strategies the mega-firm was mounting on their behalf. I explained the lobbying on the congressional front, and the work the public relations firm was doing with the media. I told them our attorneys were still optimistic the 1951 peace treaty would ultimately not be a problem. I cited for them the details of a recent court ruling in Japan that had gone in favor of several Chinese civilians who had sued the Japanese companies that used them as slave laborers during World War II.

I desperately wanted to keep their spirits up, but even as I put the best face of the case forward, I knew these men, after all they had seen and been through, were not fools. We had been at it for over three years now. No one was going to persuade them that they were not still fighting an uphill battle against their own government. In my mind I could see the same faces, much younger and much leaner, listening to General Douglas MacArthur explaining to them in Bataan that reinforcements and supplies were on the way. Just hang on.

But if some things had not changed, plenty had. No one was confusing 1942 with 2002. Least of all Harold Poole, a man sitting comfortably and at peace in his hometown, surrounded by his old army buddies.

There had been long days, months, and years, all of them knew, when thoughts of such a reunion were almost too cruel for a man to entertain: freedom, food, friends, family. They were all just so many impossible dreams that would sometimes invade your thoughts when you were lying on a hard mat in the hot Philippines—and would imagine dining at an all-you-can-eat smorgasbord with your family and driving home in your very own Oldsmobile.

Sixty years beyond those fantasies, as he bid farewell for another year to his lifelong friends, kissed his daughter, and thanked Sue and me for the fabulous smorgasbord he had just eaten, eighty-three-year-old Harold Poole walked to the hotel parking garage, slid behind the wheel of his blue 1998 Oldsmobile Bravada, and drove home.

CHAPTER TWENTY-TWO

September 9, 1945
Manila, Philippines

AS THE AIR FORCE CARGO PLANE dropped its landing gear over Manila Bay, Harold gazed yet again on a city he barely recognized.

Two years since he boarded the *Taga Maru* for Japan and five years since he bunked as a raw Army Air Corps recruit at Nichols Field, Manila wore another new face. Below him he could see airplanes parked in neat rows. There were hundreds of them, in all sizes and descriptions. More aircraft than Harold had seen in all his life, many of new design he did not recognize. The plane he was riding in was a new model, a B-24, one of many warplanes invented out of the necessity of war.

In the days since their liberation, Harold and the other former prisoners had been held spellbound by stories of huge planes capable of enormous military feats, about single bombs powerful enough to destroy entire cities, and about a United States military that was now second to none in the world. Stories almost not to be believed. The newspapers were full of reports about the atomic bombs dropped on the Japanese cities of Hiroshima and Nagasaki. The bomb on Hiroshima, dropped on August 6, 1945, killed an estimated sixty-four thousand people, while the Nagasaki bomb, dropped three days later, killed another forty thousand. An additional ninety-four thousand people were injured. On August 14, six days after the Nagasaki bombing, Emperor Hirohito capitulated to Allied surrender demands. The next morning was when Harold and the others at Toyama stopped going to the docks to work.

But the best and most undeniable proof that the stories were all true was the presence of American troops everywhere the former POWs went:

in Tokyo Bay, in the southern Japanese province of Okinawa, and then in Manila.

Harold and the rest of the liberated captives did not wear signs announcing that they had been prisoners of war, nor did they introduce themselves that way, but their very presence gave them away. They were nothing but bones held together by thin layers of transparent skin. They weren't walking wounded so much as they were walking ghosts. Everywhere they went, their healthy military counterparts parted and patted them on the back and hurried to find them chow.

At Toyama, Harold and the others had been escorted out of town on September 5, 1945, three days after formal surrender ceremonies had been held aboard the battleship USS *Missouri* in Tokyo Bay. A unit of U.S. soldiers trucked them to the railroad station. There the men boarded a train bound for Osaka. A number of Special Service Japanese soldiers were on the train to help escort the Americans to their destination. The Japanese soldiers were dressed in full military uniform, complete with swords at their sides. Still dizzy from the thrill of their new freedom and the total turnaround of the conflict, several of the U.S. soldiers boldly approached the Japanese soldiers and demanded pieces of their uniforms and their swords. "By the time that train landed those Japs were lucky to have their underwear," remembered Harold. "We took everything, and they didn't raise a finger about it. After the surrender there was no opposition, nothing. The soup was knocked right out of them."

The train let the men out at the edge of Tokyo Bay, where the hospital ship *Rescue* awaited them.

Aboard *Rescue* the first order of business was to strip the men of their Japanese military clothing and dump it, to loud cheers, over the side and into the sea. Fresh GI fatigues were issued, which the men put on after taking long hot showers. Then they were given a series of shots administered by genuine women nurses.

Harold would never forget his first look at American women in nearly four years. "A lot of them were just old, seasoned Army nurses," he said. "They were pretty tough looking and hardened, I'm sure, but doggone, they sure looked good to us. We didn't know how to talk to them it had been so long. They'd ask us what our name was and we'd just stand there. We couldn't remember."

Stripped to the waist, every rib showing, the men submitted to the nurses' needles willingly. "The shots didn't bother us none," said Harold. "We were just in awe of those women."

Those too ill to move on were left to convalesce aboard the hospital ship while the rest, including Harold, were transferred to a Navy destroyer farther out in the bay for more days of rest and recuperation.

"They had a cooked meal ready for us. I'll never forget it. We had pork chops, brown gravy and mashed potatoes, and rolls with butter. We just started eating and couldn't stop. If we'd stayed on the hospital ship, I'm sure we'd have had soup or something easy to start us back. But on the destroyer, those Navy cooks looked at us and said, 'They're hungry, let's feed them.'"

All that rich food colliding with digestive systems that were used to boiled rice and watery fish-flavored soup produced a war of another kind.

"We were in the head all the time and some of the crew got irritated about that," recalled Harold. After one lengthy stay, a Navy enlisted man asked Harold what he was doing in there. "I told him I had not seen a toilet with a seat for three and a half-years," he said, "and I was just sitting on it, enjoying it."

The destroyer eventually transported the men to the Atsugi airstrip near Tokyo where they were flown, thirty at a time, via cargo plane to the island of Okinawa. As they lifted off over Tokyo Bay and headed south, Harold did not even bother to glance back at the land that had served as his prison for the past two years.

From Okinawa, the B-24s transported the men to the Philippines. The majority of them were essentially retracing the route that had brought them to Japan, but everything about the return trip was better. The B-24 took five hours and covered roughly the same distance the *Taga Maru* hell ship had taken two weeks to cross.

Seeing Manila again through free eyes dramatically brought home the point that the war was indeed over—and that it had taken its toll. Beyond Nichols Field and the impressive display of warplanes, Harold and his compatriots could see that Manila was a shambles. Most of the city's landmarks had been reduced to rubble, including the Manila Hotel that had held MacArthur's once-luxurious penthouse.

MacArthur, the men learned, had returned to the Philippines in the spring to retake the islands with an Allied invasion force larger than the one that stormed the beaches of Normandy on D-day. When the general waded ashore at Leyte Island in October, he was flanked by two hundred thousand troops, a full press contingent, and plenty of photographers. The world took note when he made his predictable announcement: "I have returned."

When Harold and the rest of the POWs arrived at Nichols Field, the press was not alerted and no one took much notice.

But at that, the prisoners' return may have been more satisfying than the great MacArthur's, given where they had come from.

Aboard the flight to Okinawa, Harold echoed such thoughts of unbridled joy in a lengthy letter to his parents. He had managed to dash off a short note while on the destroyer, letting them know he was alive and liberated, but during the flight he had time to expand on how it felt to be free.

Using a U.S. Army issue pencil and Red Cross stationery he wrote:

On board C-54 Airplane
September 8, 1945
Dear Folks,

I finished my first letter in a hurry, as this plane was ready to go, leaving the field at 6:15 PM.

It's like a beautiful dream, flying in this big ship, it drones on through the night as smooth as silk. One can stroll around in its large cabin and never realize he is shooting through the air 140 mph and 8,000 feet above the ocean. I marveled at the ease the destroyer slipped through the water, the smoothest and fastest boat ride I have ever had, but this plane ride tops everything!

Man, but the Yanks sure treat us swell. They won't let you run out of gum or candy, and for the smokers, all kinds of cigarettes. We all have sailor clothes on, and what luxury it is to have shoes and socks, and all of it for that matter!

I know that one of your first questions would be, "How did the Nips treat you?" The worst treatment that can be inflicted upon man or beast is continued hunger and starvation. In Japan, all prisoners went hungry from the time they landed there, until the end of the war. On top of the work, we were forced to exercise in the mornings and drill after work at night, besides walking each way, rain or shine, every day.

Outside of being hungry and underweight, and the hard work, I could say they treated us fairly well. However, the least little thing that anyone did wrong, or out of turn, they would deal out punishment that sometimes put the men near death. The strict discipline that they forced on us could almost be excused, because that is the way they treat their own army. I have even seen them beat their own soldiers nearly to death for very small offenses, and I could show you where two of their soldiers are buried at Cabanatuan (Camp No. 1, PI) who had their heads chopped off for disobeying orders.

Of course there has been certain individuals, both army and civilians, who were very outstanding in their habitual cruelty to the prisoners. They are being rounded up now, and will no doubt be properly taken care of, the way these Yanks are doing things!

After landing at Okinawa at 11:10 PM that night, Harold ate, went to sleep, and then concluded his letter the next morning.

September 9, 1945
Okinawa

Again I am completely amazed at the progress and enormity of our forces, combined on land, sea, and in the air! Maybe it is because I have been in the dark for so long, but these war machines sure are an eyeful for me.

When we landed, we were taken in trucks from the plane to a Red Cross canteen, where they served coffee and doughnuts. The first doughnuts I had seen since before the war, and I ate a dozen of them without even looking up! I thought we would be put on a strict diet for a while after we were retaken but not so, they feed us all we want of nearly everything, and how we do eat!

I sure have felt good since I've been back on American chow again. I sure will enjoy eating some of mother's good home-cooked meals again . . . That long-awaited day of our reunion is about here now, and let us all join in giving our heartfelt prayers of Thanksgiving, to God, for our happiness, which never could have been accomplished without his all-powerful guidance and care. I'll be seeing you in the near future.

Love, Harold

Once they were on the ground in Manila, the men were loaded onto trucks and taken a few miles beyond Nichols Field to what the army called a replacement area.

Virtually all of the U.S. war prisoners coming out of the Far East—nearly twenty thousand of them—were collected here, conveniently placed next to the Pacific Theater's quartermaster supply headquarters. The men were housed in newly constructed barracks, with mattresses and soft pillows on their individual bunks. Hot showers were just down the hall, and the only drill was the eating drill. The mess was open around the clock, with Army cooks at the men's service.

"The idea was to fatten us up," said Harold. "The army didn't want us coming home looking like we looked."

To be sure, the men who stepped off the cargo planes in Manila hardly qualified as poster material to illustrate an Allied victory. Nearly 300,000 American fighting men had died in World War II, more than 225 men every single day of the nearly four-year war. The military was not anxious to send another 20,000 home who *looked* dead.

Not that the men minded.

"After what we'd been through," said Harold, "when we got to the Philippines we thought we had died, and it was heaven."

In Manila, a city that spent the war in captivity, men who had done likewise began to nurse their wounds, mend their minds, and begin making up for lost time and meals. The food and the good care quickly changed everyone's attitude.

"You know, I've gone without most everything for three and a half years," Harold wrote his folks from the replacement area, "but I haven't missed anything, I've just postponed them a while, that's all!"

No more than fifty miles from Cabanatuan, O'Donnell, and Bataan, the men ate as if there were no tomorrow. They had their appetites back, and their stomachs had expanded. They devoured massive piles of food: pancakes, bacon, and eggs at breakfast; Dagwood-style sandwiches at lunch, piled high with meats, cheeses, and all the trimmings; and at dinner, T-bone steaks and turkey and dressing and cheeseburgers and mashed potatoes and steamed corn topped off with apple pie a la mode for dessert. In between, they snacked on nuts, chocolate, fruit, cereal, and piles of ice cream. Practically overnight, the symptoms of beriberi, scurvy, dysentery, and dozens of other illnesses began to disappear.

Every night, the men watched first-run Hollywood movies made during the war years. No one complained about reruns. They hadn't seen a single one. They ate popcorn and watched John Wayne in *Tall in the Saddle*, Vivian Leigh in *Gone With the Wind*, Humphrey Bogart in *Casablanca*, and a popular new actor named Ronald Reagan in *For God and Country* and *This is the Army*.

"Man, did we enjoy ourselves," said Harold. "A movie every night and all we wanted to eat."

After three weeks of fattening up, Harold was sent again to Manila Harbor and loaded onto the *Joseph Dickman*, a large navy transport ship that would take more than two thousand American fighting men back home.

On October 5, 1945, he walked up the gangplank to board the ship, just slightly less than five years since November 23, 1940, when he walked off the USS *Washington* into Manila, his duffel bag over his shoulder, and gazed out on a future he could have never possibly imagined.

He was traveling lighter now, in every way. Besides the eighty pounds of muscle he had lost (he had already regained almost forty pounds, although virtually none of it muscle), he had lost his wide-eyed youthful innocence along with every physical possession he had brought with him to the Philippines. His clothes, camera, eyeglasses, and his father's pocket watch were all long gone, replaced by a bag for the return voyage that contained one change of uniform and his Bible. The *Joseph Dickman* took four days to get to Honolulu, where the returning troops were kept on board while the ship refueled and took on more passengers and cargo. As Harold speculated, "If they'd let all of us off that ship, they would never have rounded us all up again."

The lure of freedom was pulling hard on the men now: the freedom to chart their own paths and choose their own schedules, to do what they wanted under no one's command but their own. They all yearned for what they had been fighting for. With their stomachs full, and the world no longer at war, the prisoners of the Japanese wanted to taste their own individual freedom.

During the seven-day crossing from Honolulu to San Francisco, Harold had time to write a longer narrative about his experiences. Without any of the seasickness that plagued his crossing as a raw recruit, he wrote freely and almost continuously. This letter he addressed to himself. He started at the beginning, at Hamilton Field in California when he joined the 20th Pursuit Squadron and began his career in the United States Army Air Corps. Event by event, he put it all down on paper. He wrote of the first year of peacetime service in the Philippines, of the day the Japanese attacked Clark Field, of the siege of Bataan, of the surrender, of the Death March, of the prison camps at O'Donnell and Cabanatuan, of the work camp at Cabcaben, of the hell ship crossing to Japan, of the slave camps at the steel mill and the shipyard, of the end of the war, and of the final voyage home.

He had been a peacetime soldier for 465 days, a wartime soldier for 153 days, and a prisoner of war for 1,224 days.

He wrote seamlessly, with barely a word crossed out in the entire double-sided twelve-page handwritten chronicle. After years of not being able to write any of it down, of keeping it locked inside his brain, he listed dates, spelled places, and named names. The bulk of the diary dealt with his years of captivity as he detailed the torture, the brutality, the diseases, and the starvation.

"We were accustomed to death," he wrote. "It was part of our life, it was part of our existence."

But Harold also included remembrances of his days before he attained the rank of POW. He wrote with pride of the day he passed the AM (air mechanics) rating examination ten days after landing in the islands: "We had no technical schools in the Philippines, so we new recruits had to pick up our knowledge of these AMs the hard way." And he devoted almost a full page to shooting down the Japanese Zero the day the war began:

> I experienced the most exciting event that ever happened to me thus far in my life. Burning ammunition was going off in all directions, gasoline drums were exploding, everywhere there seemed to be fire and hell in general. On top of all this, the Jap planes were diving and strafing all over the field. I grabbed the machine gun and swung it into firing position. It was an old .30-caliber air-cooled Lewis Machine Gun, on a post set in the middle of this hole. I mashed the trigger down as a Jap plane came diving across the field within beautiful range, but the bomb had thrown dirt all through the gun's mechanism, and it was dead. This was awful, out there all around the ground I could see lifeless bodies

> and limbs of my buddies strewn around and me with a clogged-up gun, and Nip planes all around. I pulled the gun down off the mount and took it apart, wiped off the parts with a rag I had in my pocket, and reassembled it. I tested it, and this time it spoke beautifully! I clenched my teeth and centered the next on coming Jap plane in those ring sights, and felt the steady pounding of my gun as it returned the challenge that the Nips had made. He was on fire and burning fast, as the speed of his dive carried him through a cloud of smoke from one of our buildings, out of my sight. Observers farther up the line said he crashed and burned up, not far from the field.

He did not editorialize much in his nuts-and-bolts narrative, but when he wrote of the surrender of Bataan, he made an exception: "I personally believe we would have held out another four months if we had not run out of food," he wrote. "You can't fight on an empty stomach, and we were getting pretty run down with the slim rations we had been on."

His long months of captivity had neither diminished his clarity for dates nor his memory of how it began: "We started the Death March out of Bataan April 12, '42, and arrived at Camp O'Donnell April 18, '42. I teamed up with a good pal out of our outfit, Nelson Quast, and we helped each other through the march, which was a nightmare of starvation, thirst, and fatigue."

He detailed his move to Cabanatuan on June 2, 1942, his departure by boat to Japan on September 18, 1943, his arrival in Japan on October 5, 1943, the first day of no work at Toyama on August 15, 1945. His brief and understated descriptions reduced nearly unspeakable horrors and conditions to a simplicity that offered insight into how their author survived them. Of the hell ship journey, he wrote exactly forty-two words: "It was the roughest boat ride I have ever experienced, big waves dashing high over the decks and knocking us about like a cork in the storm. I guess the storm saved us in the long run, however, from our own submarines."

Of the steel mill at Hirohata where he spent six hundred days of his young life, he wrote the following: "The work was hard, handling ore and pig iron, etc., and the winters were hard on us in our run-down condition. Several men died here and they were cremated, which is the Japanese custom. We had to sleep with all our clothes on in the winter months. We had to drill, and learn Jap commands, and learn to count in Jap, and we exercised every morning before breakfast, and then had to drill up and down the road every night after returning from a hard day's work."

But, then, without missing a beat, he wrote sympathetically about his Japanese counterparts: "Their own soldiers sometimes were treated worse than us. They believe in beating a man for disobeying orders, rather than confine him for any given period of time like our own army."

Of his liberation, he wrote mostly of food: "In normal times soldiers and sailors think and talk about nothing other than women and liquor. After living on the starvation diet in Japan a short time, one forgets all else except food and combinations of food. Many of the men have notebooks with nothing in them except menus and concoctions."

He concluded his POW diary with a personal vow: "This past experience has been an education in itself. I wouldn't take a million dollars for it, and I wouldn't go through it again for a billion!

"I am ready to fight again if my country calls me, but I promise I will never again become a prisoner of war. T./Sgt. Harold W. Poole."

It was late afternoon on October 16, 1945, when the *Joseph Dickman* steamed within view of San Francisco. Straight ahead, basked in the sun's dying rays, stood the Golden Gate Bridge, and as the ship got closer the men on board could make out throngs of people standing on the bridge, waving and shouting at them, standing above a huge banner on the bridge's side that spelled out WELCOME HOME! A Navy Zeppelin hovered high above the bridge. On its side was the message, WELL DONE!

"I'll never forget the sight of the Golden Gate Bridge," explained Harold. "My first thought was that this is the gate to my backyard. On the other side of that, I'm home."

Because of the crush of troops returning to the West Coast in October of 1945, the government requested that families of servicemen wait to greet their loved ones when they arrived all the way home. In Harold's case, as with all prisoners of war, there was the additional wrinkle of medical examinations and treatments. Harold's family remained in Salt Lake City as he walked alone onto U.S. soil at the Presidio in San Francisco, one of thousands of World War II military men coming home that day.

Smiling broadly as he gazed toward the San Francisco skyline, Sergeant Poole—in the Philippines he had been informed that he had been upgraded two ranks during his captivity—drank in his first breath of free American air in five long years.

The next day the army put him in a truck and drove him to a hospital near Los Angeles, where Harold was assigned to a bed in a ward with other returning prisoners of war and poked and prodded by army doctors and nurses who set about reversing the ill effects of four years of malnutrition, insomnia, unsanitary living conditions, and cohabitation with bugs and vermin of all manner and description.

After a time the army granted Harold, who was in better condition than a majority of the recovering war prisoners, a leave to visit his older sister, Margaret, who had moved to the Los Angeles area. Harold put on his dress uniform and set off down the hospital corridor to meet Margaret, who, when she was notified Harold was coming, had jumped in her car and made a quick trip to the hospital. She was already in the building and was walking at the far end of the corridor when they recognized each other. "She was the first I saw of my family. I'll tell you, that was really something."

The oldest of his five sisters saw to it that Harold was instantly and sufficiently pampered, taking her brother home to introduce him to her husband Clare McMillen and their two-year-old son, Roger, Harold's first nephew.

Then Margaret, as only sisters can do, prodded the army into getting Harold home by Thanksgiving. Harold was told that he would be traveling to Utah by bus, but Margaret saw to it that he had a seat on a C-47 army transport airplane. She alerted the family that Harold was on his way, and when the C-47 landed at the Salt Lake Airport, sisters Vivian, Katherine, Afton, and Patsy were there with their parents, Stanley and Nina.

They were all straining to get a first look at Harold, but none more than Nina Poole. Above them all, it had been Harold's mother who had kept the home fires burning while her son was away. Theirs was a close bond that had only been strengthened during the long years of separation. Not long after he had arrived in the Philippines, before the war began, Harold had written the first and only poem of his life on his mother's birthday.

Happy Birthday Mother
This is a special little message
Just to let you know
That even though I am far away
May you have a pleasant birthday
And many more to come,
And that I may soon be with you
When my work here is done.
There may be an ocean between us,
But I never feel far from you
As there is no distance on this earth
That could alter my love for you.
Throughout my days of childhood
You loved me and taught me to do right
Now that I have outgrown my childhood
I am free to do as I like.
However because of your loving care,
I find as the months roll past
That all I can do is follow
In the straight and narrow path
I pray to the Lord to bless you
In all the things that you do
For if anybody always tried to do right
It most certainly has been you
All that I ever amount to
Or anything special that I might do
I know down deep in my heart
I owe it all to you!

"This is the only poem I have ever written, and as far as poems go, I guess it doesn't stack up very high," Harold scrawled at the bottom of the poem, which was sent from Clark Field and dated April 2, 1941, "but it portrays my thoughts to you at least. I hope you have a pleasant birthday and have lots of fun, even though some of your interests will not be there in person. We can always look forward to the day when we will all be together again."

Throughout the war, Nina Poole had held tight to that sentiment, and with a mother's heart she had fought any and all impulses that Harold would not return. During the long nine months of 1942 between the surrender of Bataan and verification that her son was alive, she refused to give up. When great gaps of time passed between letters from prison camp, she remained faithful. Sometimes well-meaning family and friends would suggest to her that it might be best to at least accept the possibility that Harold could be gone, but she would not have it. "No, Harold is alive," she would say. "He's alive and he will be coming home."

But privately, she knew that even her resolve was tested, and one night at the height of despair Nina Poole had sat down in her study to write a prayer.

> *Dear God,*
> *You gave your only Son to save the world,*
> *without a selfish thought of sacrifice.*
> *Now, God, I have given my son to fight*
> *for the things for which your Son so nobly died.*
> *If, when this war is won, you send my son home*
> *I'll hold him close to my heart.*
> *But, if it is thy will to take him,*
> *I'll know that he and your Son go on hand in hand,*
> *and, dear God, I'll understand.*
> *Amen.*

A fence kept family and friends a safe distance from the runway as the airplane came to a final stop and portable stairs were rolled to the side of the plane for the disembarking passengers.

A few soldiers walked down the steps first and made their way toward the exit.

Then Harold appeared at the top of the stairs, at which point Nina Poole, respectable wife and mother of six, consummate rule keeper, and faithful singer in the Mormon Tabernacle Choir, leaped the fence in her best dress and ran across the tarmac to embrace her son.

And no one made a move to stop her.

CHAPTER TWENTY-THREE

Winter 2002
Cabazon, California

WE WERE RUNNING OUT OF TIME. I knew it, and the veterans certainly knew it. I even got the impression the other side knew it. With World War II vets dying at the rate of nearly three thousand a day, the sad truth was that the JPOW case, if left to languish in the court system, would simply, to paraphrase MacArthur, fade away.

In three and a half years, the number of Pacific Theater POWs had gone from over six thousand to about five thousand. Our clients were dying faster than during the war. If we were going to do something meaningful for them while they were still alive, we needed to do it right away.

The problem was, I did not get the impression my colleagues in the mega-firm appreciated this basic urgency. A conference call with the legal team did not ease my anxiety. I had been with Dave Casey and Bonnie Kane at their office in San Diego for the call, which involved mega-team lawyers around the country.

The legal argument had basically boiled down to whether the individual rights of the JPOWs could be taken away by the treaty. Since that was a constitutional question, the focus of our call was on the need to keep appealing until we got in front of the United States Supreme Court. Each fall, the high court chooses cases to review on the basis of the constitutional issues they raise. It was why such landmark cases as *Brown v. Board of Education* and *Roe v. Wade* were heard.

All of our setbacks to date—including the recent affirmation of Judge Walker's dismissal of JPOW lawsuits by the Ninth Circuit Court of Appeals (the California Court of Appeals had yet to rule on the similar state appeal)—had been based on interpreting the treaty. With the prospects of getting a favorable interpretation of the treaty growing dimmer, our primary goal now was to get a majority of the nine justices on the Supreme Court to rule that the provisions in the treaty that took away individual rights were unconstitutional.

There were a number of inherent problems. The most troubling was that the Supreme Court might simply decline to hear the case. The high court agrees to hear an average of fewer than one hundred cases every year, out of more than five thousand annually submitted for review.

Another problem was that even if the Supreme Court heard the case, there was no telling how long a review could take. Given the age of our clients, it could be time we did not have.

Finally, there was no guarantee the Supreme Court would rule in our favor. A negative ruling would be the end of the game. There could be no more appeals and no further recourse. There would be nothing at all for the men.

Given these realities, I felt that instead of concentrating on the legal issues, we needed to shift our focus to the United States Congress. We had allies in Congress. Both the House and the Senate had held hearings on the JPOW question. Even the State Department agreed that Congress could and should do something appropriate for the JPOWs. Within the mega-firm, we had strong lobbying power with both Republicans and Democrats. If we were going to get anything for the men, including an apology for dealing away their rights, the best and quickest course of action seemed to be our own government.

I was not the only one of this opinion. Ron Kleinman and Alan Foster were others on the team who thought we should look to Congress. But the majority fell in line with Dave Casey and Maury Herman, who were adamant about staying the legal course and appealing to the Supreme Court.

On the drive from San Diego back to Palm Desert, I had ample time to get more and more agitated. Forty miles from home, I stopped at a convenience store, pulled out my cell phone, and started making calls. In turn, I called Maury Herman, Ron Kleinman, Joe Reeder, Alan Foster, and Dave Casey and pitched my plan, which is a euphemistic way to describe my begging. One at a time, I implored them to agree to an intensive lobbying of Congress. I would help coordinate it if they wished, which I hoped they would.

To my relief, everyone, including Dave Casey and Maury Herman, said go for it. We would still make our legal appeals, and we would still lay our case on the steps of the Supreme Court. But we would also aggressively seek a settlement with the United States government.

I first contacted Senator Orrin Hatch, still a strong supporter of the former JPOWs. After the Bush administration took over from the Clinton administration, Hatch had contacted Colin Powell, Madeleine Albright's successor as Secretary of State, to solicit Powell's support for the former JPOWs. Powell, as had Albright, was loyal to the 1951 treaty but indicated to Hatch there was room for diplomacy and compromise.

I made an appointment to fly to Washington, D.C. and meet with Hatch to discuss drafting a bill that would grant compensation to the World War II slaves of the Japanese similar to the bill that granted compensation to the World War II Japanese Americans held in internment camps. The senator said he would be happy to talk about such a bill, but told me over the phone, "This isn't a negotiation. I don't want to go back and forth about the compensation. Tell me what you think is fair and that's what we'll work with."

This of course was unfamiliar ground for PI lawyers, who routinely start high and work toward the middle. But as we laid out the parameters for the bill we were proposing, I told our lawyers that we needed to come in with exactly what we thought was fair and we could live with. That was what Hatch wanted.

After deliberation, the firm decided to ask for $30,000 for each surviving JPOW, $20,000 for the living spouse of a deceased JPOW, and $10,000 for designated heirs of all other JPOWs.

According to our research, there were 5,124 former JPOWs eligible for the $30,000 claims, 9,928 surviving spouses eligible for the $20,000 claims, and 4,934 heirs eligible to file for the $10,000 claims. In addition to the money, we proposed that the bill include an apology from the United States government for taking away the former JPOWs' rights with the 1951 treaty.

We also proposed that the bill include funding for a foundation that would further Japanese-American relations, memorialize those who participated in World War II, and establish a channel whereby the Japanese corporations and the Japanese government could choose to voluntarily contribute compensation to the JPOWs.

The payout ceiling for the bill was projected at or near $400 million. As for attorneys' fees, we proposed dropping our 28 percent contingency fee in favor of accepting any fee determined reasonable by mandatory outside arbitration.

Through Nancy Taylor at Greenberg Traurig in Washington, we forwarded these figures to Senator Hatch's office. Nancy had previously worked on Hatch's staff and was interfacing with his office on preliminaries for the JPOW bill.

My job was to seal the deal. I left the desert on a balmy afternoon and flew into a D.C. snowstorm, armed with a dossier that had been prepared by Bonnie Kane and others outlining all the reasons we believed this bill was past due. Besides facts and figures from the war, Bonnie put together quotes from representatives of the executive branch, including former Secretary of State George Shultz, State Department diplomat William Howard Taft IV, and Assistant Attorney General Robert McCallum, endorsing congressional aid for the former JPOWs.

I would leave all this material with the senator, but what I was most anxious to do was talk to Hatch in person. I prepared my speech in California, and practiced it on the flight and that night in Washington in front of a mirror until I had it down cold. It went like this:

> Senator, the United States of America took away the rights of thousands of its fighting men in 1951. You knew that instinctively the first time you heard of this case, and you wrote your letter to the State Department demanding justice. You also know we were initially optimistic of getting a favorable judgment in the courts, but unlike in the Holocaust case, the government intervened and argued against us. Because of that there is only one way this can be solved and that is if you step in and take care of it legislatively. We cannot go the statute of limitations route because that will take us through the courts all over again, and three years from now we will very likely be in the same place we are in today. Now please let me play you a tape.

The tape was from a message left recently on my answering machine by Marlene Agnes, who called from Everett, Washington, after her husband, Bataan veteran and JPOW case client Francis Agnes, passed away. "Jim, this is Marlene Agnes. I wanted to let you know that Fran died on Sunday. That beloved man who soared with the eagles is now flying with the angels. He's gone home now and he's safe."

I planned to tell the senator, This is one of the men who was in Salt Lake when the Tabernacle Choir sang the "Battle Hymn of the Republic" and everybody in the tabernacle stood and applauded. *Everybody.* Orrin, the whole nation is behind these men. Every newspaper and magazine article, every television news program, they all ask the same thing: where is the justice? We are running out of time. When I called Marlene Agnes and asked for her permission to play her tape for you, she said, "Please tell the senator that Fran has now died, let's get something done before they all die." The U.S. government took these men's rights away once, don't let them do it again. Only one United States senator has the power and ability to get this done quickly, to go to the State Department and the president and both houses of congress and finally get a measure of justice for these men, and I'm talking to that senator. Please, Orrin, make this happen for the men.

That was my memorized speech, one I never got to give.

A filibuster had taken over the Senate and our meeting wound up taking place in the long corridor that connects the Senate office buildings with the Capitol. Hatch needed to get back to the Senate floor and motioned for Nancy Taylor and me to walk with him from his office. I sensed he was displeased about something. We walked briskly toward the underground monorail that transports senators to the Capitol. When we climbed onto the train, Hatch leaned toward me, lowered his voice, and said, "Parky, $2.5 billion!"

"What?" I said.

"You want $2.5 billion to pay these men, and out of that you want your 10 percent cut. That's $250 million for the lawyers. That's ridiculous."

I was stunned. I did not know what to say. I asked him, "Where did you get the $2.5 billion?" afraid it had come from someone on our legal team.

Just then a legislative aide who was walking with us answered, "That's what it adds up to. I did the calculations myself." "Just don't bullshit me, Parkinson," the senator said. "Just quit bullshitting me," and then he walked into the Capitol to cast a vote.

I looked to Nancy Taylor for help. "I have no idea where the $2.5 billion came from," she said, reading my mind. She said the figures she sent Hatch's office were in the $400 million range, as we had discussed, and that was to be staggered over a two-year period. Relatively speaking, she reminded me, it was a modest amount, paling alongside the $1.25 billion appropriated for the Civil Liberties Bill for Japanese American internees, for example.

Hatch soon returned and we made the short trip back to his office in the Hart Building, where his legislative aide picked up a calculator to prove her math, while Nancy got busy with a pen and legal pad.

"Senator," said Nancy, "you know I was a math major," and within seconds she showed him figures that added up to $400 million, not $2.5 billion.

Meanwhile, over at the calculator came an audible "Oops!"

The senator's mood changed abruptly after the math error was realized. After rechecking the figures and confirming that $400 million was the maximum for the bill, he was back to his old self.

Hatch said to me, "What you're telling me is the State Department, *our* State Department, screwed these men?" I nodded.

"OK, if we caused the problem, let's solve the problem. It's time to make the State Department pay."

The senator turned to his aide and to Nancy. "Let's get this worked out on paper," he said, "and let's do it quickly. We need to get this thing passed."

He turned to me, said, "Thanks," and excused himself for another appointment. Just like that, with my speech notes still in my briefcase, our deal was done.

At the curb outside the Hart Building, I hailed a cab for the airport. The snowstorm was lessening. In the backseat I collected my thoughts. I understood why the senator had at first been so indignant. Hatch thought the lawyers were trying to highball him and secure a nice inflated fee for ourselves. To his credit, once he realized it was a simple arithmetic error, he recovered quickly. He did not even take it out on his staffer, which impressed me. I had to smile. A United States senator had just told me to stop the bullshitting. A lot of people had asked that of me, but never a United States senator, and never about a case that had less bullshit to it than any I had ever worked on.

I could not really blame the senator. As lawyers, especially PI lawyers, we paint our own perception, and it is usually shaded in green. Million-dollar verdicts not only make the pages of the *Washington Post*, they also make the walls of law firm corridors. Bragging is the way a PI attorney advertises. Nothing sells success like success. When I was starting out in Indio as a summer law clerk, the first thing I did was buy a two-hundred-dollar suit—and I was making four hundred dollars a month. For my first court appearance in the JPOW case, I had gone to Facconable in Beverly Hills and spent twelve hundred dollars for a suit. Perception is important in my business.

But if hustling money is the reputation a lawyer in twenty-first-century America has to bear, it is not always the reality. The driving force that kept the JPOW case going was not dollar signs, and everyone on the inside knew it. The case was kept alive because no one wanted to call up the men of the Greatest Generation and deliver the news that they had been surrendered again.

Three and a half years. That is how long the case had been going. No one expected that. Coincidentally, it was the same amount of time the soldiers who surrendered on Bataan remained in captivity. I pointed out that irony to Harold, and he answered, "But this time we've eaten much better."

As I left Washington with a serious JPOW bill on the drawing board, I felt encouraged. If all went well, at least a measure of respect and appreciation was coming our clients' way. It was something I wanted to do for the men; something I felt I needed to do.

But first, there was something I needed to do for me.

CHAPTER TWENTY-FOUR

December 8, 2002
Clark Field, Pampanga, Philippines

WEARING A SHORT-SLEEVED plaid sport shirt, dark blue cotton pants, and a pair of comfortable-looking leather oxfords, Harold Poole, twelve days from his eighty-fourth birthday, stepped spryly out of the side door of a Toyota van at the entrance to the Clark Field Holiday Inn.

Overhead a banner proclaimed "Mabuhay," the greeting of welcome in Tagalog, the traditional language of the Philippines. Below that, a sign read "Merry Christmas" in English, the modern language of the Philippines.

To the west, beyond the hotel and a golf course, the Zambales Mountains stood sentry just as they had when the Japanese bombers with the red dots on their wings suddenly appeared sixty-one winters ago.

This trip back in time was not Harold's idea. He had had a lifetime to return to the Philippines and had not. He exhibited no disdain for the land. On the contrary, his eyes lit up when he talked about the islands and the friendly people he had known there as a young man. He had scrapbooks full of photographs and a grainy black-and-white eight-millimeter movie he had taken of Manila before the war that he counted among his prized possessions. And he almost did come back, once, in 1968, when the U.S.–funded Pacific War Memorial was dedicated on Corregidor Island. Specially invited by the governments of America and the Philippines, many of the American defenders of Bataan and Corregidor made their way back for that ceremony. But Harold had a young family at the time, and a new house, and when he weighed the cost of traveling to the Philippines against adding home improvements, home improvements won.

Now, a bit past his best traveling years, Harold was content to visit the Philippines only in his memories—until I brought up the idea of this reunion trip. I wanted to see the place that shaped Harold and so many of the other veterans I had come to know and admire.

Over time, Harold warmed to the idea. Seeing Clark Field and Manila again had a certain draw to it, but what ultimately motivated him to agree to the trip was the thought of paying respects to his friends who had not made it home.

I invited Paul Warner to join us, and when I uttered the magic words "business class ticket," he agreed. For Harold's son-in-law and my good friend it would be a kind of reunion trip as well. From 1969 to 1971, Warner had spent two years as a Mormon missionary in the Philippines, living as the natives, in tin-roofed huts without air conditioning, and eating fish and rice. There were four thousand Mormons in the Philippines when Warner returned to America in 1971. Now there were five hundred thousand, a fact not lost on the bemused former missionary who observed just before we landed in Manila, "When I left I thought we'd baptized everyone who was interested."

As Utah's U.S. attorney, Warner was well aware of the dangers that go along with traveling in the modern Philippines. There are Muslim terrorists in the south and communist terrorists in the north. His friends at the FBI advised us to be especially careful around the Clark area, where an American hiker had been shot and killed on Mount Pinatubo by a communist rebel the past spring, at a spot not more than fifteen miles from the Clark Field Holiday Inn.

Under normal circumstances, such news would have been more than enough to turn me back. Anyone who knows me knows it is not my nature to court danger. As a PI lawyer, I prefer to leave high risk to my clients. Everything about my life is careful and controlled. But for me, the lure of actually setting foot on Bataan and trying to absorb what happened there overrode the reasons screaming at me why I should not go. So I took off my wedding ring for safekeeping, put my wallet in my front pocket, and we went.

A few more clouds hung in the air, Harold said as he looked into the noonday sky, but otherwise it was the climate of sixty-one Decembers ago, with the temperature in the mideighties and high humidity. It was hot, but it was not unbearable; it was about as nice as it ever gets on Luzon.

But if the climate had not changed appreciably over the decades, a lot of other things had. Hotels, swimming pools, and golf courses now stand where first the Americans, and then the Japanese, anchored their air forces. The Philippine Air Force still maintains one corner of the "field," whereas the rest has given way to the "Clark Field Economic Zone," a government-designated duty-free area meant to lure foreign businesses and tourists. The last U.S. Air Force planes departed years ago, after the United States' fifty-year lease on the airstrip expired in 1991. That same year, the volcano inside Mount Pinatubo erupted, ending six hundred years of dormancy and sending lava and hot liquefied *lahar* mud dozens of miles in every direction, significantly altering the landscape of the base and displacing a million people.

But scrape it all away and it is still Clark Field, the place where war hit the Philippines. Just after lunch, at 12:20 PM, Harold looked westward to the Zambales Range and paused to remember that fateful moment on that long-ago day. As Warner and I stood a respectful distance away, Harold silently paid his personal tribute to a time and place when he dove into a foxhole and shot down a Japanese dive-bomber with a .30-caliber machine gun.

No one disturbed our impromptu ceremony. If anyone else in the Clark Field Economic Zone was commemorating the start of World War II, they were doing it with a five-iron or a margarita by the pool. We were well aware that a few hours earlier, and in sharp contrast, commemoration ceremonies had taken place at Pearl Harbor in Hawaii, five thousand miles away, in front of TV cameras and worldwide attention. Every year groups gather on the island of Oahu to "Remember Pearl Harbor," where half the Pacific Fleet was destroyed only nine hours before, half the Pacific Air Force was wiped out at Clark Field. Now, as then, we could personally attest that the Other Pearl Harbor remained largely forgotten.

We had landed at the airport in Manila the day before and made our first stop at the American Cemetery, where 17,206 marble Christian crosses and Stars of David mark the final resting place of men who came to fight the war in the Pacific and never made it home. The markers stretch out over 152 acres of manicured green grass, the gravestones clipped as clean as a marine's haircut. On the edge of a city teeming with twelve million people, among the largest and most congested places on the planet, the American Cemetery is a serene place. At the center of the grounds stand long rows of towering marble columns that contain the name, rank, and home state of another 36,282 American fighting men who died in World War II but whose remains are either missing or unidentifiable. Few who walk the American Cemetery's hallowed corridors are not touched by the reverent spirit there.

Harold was pleased to find that the names of those members of the 20th Pursuit Squadron who died in the war were listed, and that their remains, along with the remains from all prison camp cemeteries in the Pacific, had been brought here. Harold had been unaware that the bodies he pitched into the makeshift grave below Cabanatuan, as well as those bodies he watched being carried out of Camp O'Donnell, had been given this proper burial.

Harold searched the thousands of names etched on the marble columns until he came to the surnames starting with *P*. Near the top of one of the markers, he found the names of Jack Pool and Everett Poole, "Cess" and "Whirl," his squad mates and namesakes from a lifetime ago. He stared for a long moment before moving on, shambling slowly among the names of men he once stood next to and fought alongside. None of them lived to see their thirtieth birthday.

After taking a seat on the grass and allowing the serenity of the place to settle around us, I asked Harold, "Do you ever think about why you made it?"

"I think about it a lot," Harold answered. "So many of the guys," he swept his hand across the green landscape, "didn't make it and I did. Why? I've never been able to answer that question completely. I honestly don't know why. God knows why, but I don't."

The visit to the cemetery delighted Harold. He had come to the Philippines for the express purpose to "see where some of my buddies are buried and say good-bye," and within hours of landing at the airport he was seeing where all of them were buried. He was able to pay his respects and say his good-byes at one time in one place. We wound up staying for hours.

The Philippines we saw was not the Philippines Harold left. So much had changed in six decades. A country of fifteen million people in 1941 was now a country of eighty million people, with one in seven residing in Manila. Almost all the landmarks from 1941 were gone. Our Philippine Airlines jet had landed at Manila's international airport at the very spot that was once Nichols Field, Harold's home and workstation the first nine months he was in the islands. The American Cemetery was built near what had been Nielson Field in the 1940s and was now part of the suburb of Makati, Manila's financial hub. There was no evidence of the old Allied airstrip or the hundreds of bombs the Japanese once dropped to destroy it.

From the cemetery we moved on to pay a visit to the Manila Hotel and the ancient walled-city section of Intramuras. The grand old hotel, opened in 1912 at the edge of Manila Harbor, was the epicenter of Manila when Harold was a buck private and General MacArthur sat on his balcony every evening to watch the sun set.

Amid the decay of Intramuras and garbage floating in the bay—evidence of a poverty the Philippines plunged into after the war and has not been able to shake since—the hotel stands as a kind of final defiant strand to the Manila of yesterday. Bombed and purposely gutted by the Japanese during the battle of Manila, it was rebuilt after the war. A high-rise tower was added and the MacArthur suite was replicated on the top floor of the old building, albeit a floor lower and a much smaller version of the original. MacArthur's suite had seven bedrooms, a den, library, dining room, and full balcony; the postwar version has two bedrooms, a den, dining room, and an abbreviated balcony. The hotel rented out this mini-MacArthur suite at two thousand dollars a night, including twenty-four hour butler service.

We declined the nightly rental (although Bill Clinton did not when he visited the Philippines during his presidency) but since the suite was vacant the afternoon of our visit, the hotel concierge gave us a guided tour. There are all sorts of MacArthur memorabilia in the suite, including dozens of photos and paintings and a trophy case filled with replicas of his many medals.

The opulence and braggadocio reinforced my feelings about Douglas MacArthur. I had read the MacArthur biography by Manchester and the various histories about his involvement in the war. The most recent such history, Richard Connaughton's scholarly *MacArthur and Defeat in the Philippines*, was the latest in a line of increasingly harsh treatments. The further World War II recedes, the more obvious and glaring are the exposés of MacArthur's excesses of ego and hubris, and his catastrophic failure in defending the Philippines.

And yet at the time it happened, MacArthur, through aggressive and proactive public relations, was able to spin a military disaster into a scenario that cast him as a hero who would return again to the Philippines, despite the fact that it was his incompetence that made him leave in the first place. Those who were in charge at Pearl Harbor were dismissed of their commands and to some degree blamed and disgraced. Even Masarahu Homma, the Japanese general who *won* the battle of the Philippines, was demoted in the aftermath—and executed after the war for his crimes. But MacArthur avoided all opprobrium and succeeded in turning his Bataan blunder into a Congressional Medal of Honor.

To me, the new MacArthur suite is an appropriate reflection on the general's true legacy. The suite is a fake, no matter what the hotel brochure claims, and so is the MacArthur legend.

From the balcony of the MacArthur Suite, Harold looked below at a wooden dock just beyond the hotel's grounds at the edge of the bay, and it was as if sixty years disappeared.

It was at that very dock, he pointed out, that the USS *Washington* arrived on November 23, 1940, and discharged him onto Philippine soil for the first time. It was at that very dock that the freighter *Taga Maru* left for Japan on September 18, 1943, with 850 POWs, Harold included, deep in the hold. And it was at that very dock that the troop ship *Joseph Dickman* departed for San Francisco more than two years later, on October 5, 1945, to take him home again.

There had been small articles written in the Salt Lake newspapers the week he had returned home from the war, and the congregation at his local Mormon ward had invited him to speak in a church meeting. But beyond that he did what most of America's sixteen million World War II veterans did—embraced the future and left the past in the past. There were careers to be started, fortunes to be made, and women to meet.

He met his wife-to-be at a church fireside talk soon after he became a civilian again. He had gone to the meeting with one girl, who introduced him to her friend, and before the week was out Harold had set up the first girl with his cousin so he could set himself up with the friend. Within the year, all four were married, just the way Harold paired them off. Harold and Kathleen Jowers, an Alabama girl who moved to Utah after her family converted to the LDS faith, were married in the Mormon temple in Salt Lake City in October of 1947. In 1952 Harold and Kathleen had a daughter they named Linda. In 1958 they had a son they named Stanley, after his grandfather. By 1964 the four of them had moved into a four-bedroom brick home on the east side of the Salt Lake Valley with a large yard, fruit trees, a darkroom for Harold in the basement, and a shop at the back of the garage for Harold's tools.

Harold pursued a career in photography, his first love, and worked for a time as a commercial photographer, shooting weddings, school graduations, and birthdays. Then one day he visited a friend's house and happened to notice a pail of fresh trout. "What kind of job do you have that lets you have the time to catch fish like that?" asked Harold. His friend replied, "I work for the post office. I'm a mailman."

"That's for me," said Harold, and his days and nights shooting weddings were over.

He carried the mail (and caught fish) for thirty years. This was in the days BC—Before Computer—when people wrote real letters to each other. "Everybody loved to see me coming," Harold said. Before, after, and in between mail runs, he hunted, fished, paid his taxes, and raised his family with Kathleen, the love of his life. The day the doctor said she had breast cancer was the worst day of both of their lives.

The doctors gave Kathleen two years to live; she held on for three and a half but still went much too early at fifty. Before she died, Linda had married Paul Warner and Stanley had been called to serve a two-year Mormon mission—in Japan.

Those aware of Harold's imprisonment at the hands of the Japanese wondered how the ex-POW would react to his son's missionary assignment. But Harold had made his personal peace with the Japanese long before, and he treated his son's call with as much enthusiasm as if it had been to England, his own father's homeland. "I have no animosity toward Japan or the Japanese people," Harold said. "A lot of them weren't much better off than I was during the war. I saw how they were living."

After Kathleen's death, Harold remained single for eight years. Then at the age of sixty-seven, he married a widow, Jeannette Harrison. They had been married eleven years when Jeannette died of a stroke in 1998. As with Kathleen, Harold was at Jeannette's side when she died, holding her hand.

It was about this time that interest in World War II began picking up. For the first time in his life, people were actively seeking Harold out, asking about the old days, hungry for details.

Years before, he had organized his photographs from the Philippines into a photo album and had written his war memoirs. Later he had added newspaper and magazine articles that contributed details and statistics about the Death March, hell ships, and prison camps. These, together with his own narrative, added up to fifty-two typewritten pages, double-spaced, which he put together with a title page, "Harold W. Poole, P.O.W." He made copies for each of his children and grandchildren.

"After all is said and done, our families are the most important things in our life," he wrote at the end of his book. "I want to thank my family, both present and past, for all they have done for me, and for how much they mean to me. To again testify that prayers are answered and that our Father in Heaven, and his son, Jesus Christ, live and are watching over us, and desire for us to live good and happy lives."

He concluded his memoir with this line: "I found out we can be as happy as we let ourselves be."

His war experiences were never secret and he was never secretive about them, but he was never the sort to bring them up unsolicited. Warner told me about the first time he sat in the living room of the Poole's home. He had driven Linda home from college one afternoon in 1971 when he met Linda's father. Paul mentioned that he had recently returned from his two-year Mormon mission to the Philippines. "I spent a little time in the Philippines," Harold said in response, and that was that.

What surprised everyone was how much Harold talked when he finally *was* asked. He told his war tales eagerly, with amazing clarity, detail, and enthusiasm. He pulled his cardboard box out of the basement with its photographs, maps, medals, the GI Bible, and the bullets he had saved—one .30-caliber and one .50-caliber. The stories he told were as happy and sad and true and unbelievable now as they were then. No embellishment was necessary. He talked and talked and talked. He told dinner groups he would be happy to speak to them for forty-five minutes and two hours later he would still be going strong. He entertained entire student bodies at schools, the kids spellbound. *You ate what?!*

The first time he talked to an elementary school, Paul and Linda went along to listen, and Warner remembered sitting in shock in the audience when Harold pulled out the Silver Star. As a colonel in the Army National Guard and a former JAG in the navy, Warner knows the military awards system. He knows the eminence of the Silver Star, and he had been married to Harold's daughter for twenty-five years and did not know he had one. "My jaw could have hit the floor," Warner told me. "I turned and whispered to Linda, 'Your dad got the Silver Star!' She said, 'I know.' She had no idea what that meant; what it takes to be awarded one."

On all the war holidays, especially, Harold became a man in demand. He was on TV and in the newspapers. Colleges honored him with citations and introduced him with other veterans at assemblies and during halftime at football games. People who knew Harold all his life stood in disbelief when they discovered where he had been and what he had gone through. They had no idea. A woman he had delivered mail to for twenty years called him on the phone after watching a story on the TV news about her former mailman's participation in the Bataan Death March. "All those years," she told him, "And I never knew you were a hero."

As with the war itself, the war revival had momentum of its own, and after the speeches and honors and squadron get-togethers, and finally, the JPOW lawsuit, it was that momentum that conspired to finally carry Harold back to the dock in Manila. A dock he admitted he never thought he would ever see or care to see again.

Warner and I watched as Harold looked in the distance at the sun approaching the horizon on the bay. As on so many occasions during our visit to the Philippines, we could only guess at what he might be thinking. A thin layer of clouds hung low in the sky, creating a truly spectacular sunset.

"The sunsets are beautiful here," Harold said presently, reaching for his camera. "They were always beautiful, you know, even during the war."

After a pause, he smiled and added, "That was something the Japs couldn't take away."

We drove through the streets of Manila at dusk, passing mile after mile of squatter shacks along the shoulders of the roads. The makeshift shanties, made of plywood and tin, presented a heartbreaking sight. There was no electricity for these houses, no plumbing, and clearly not nearly enough food. Skinny children were everywhere, running to the sides of cars in the slow-moving traffic, their tiny heads barely at window height, their hands out begging for pesos.

The Philippines had been poor when Harold was last here. A soldier back then could live well on army pay and hire a houseboy as well. But the poverty Harold had seen in 1941 was not anything like this. It would be a nice story to tell if the Philippines since World War II world had gone on to progress and prosperity. But the truth is, after the country gained its independence on July 4, 1946, a legacy of corrupt politicians and an uneven distribution of wealth has kept the country's economy and its democracy teetering near disaster. Almost all of the wealth sits in the bank vaults of only a few, whereas the Filipino people in general have become maids and servants to the rest of Asia.

Japan, on the other hand, has flourished since the end of the war. The Japanese have rebuilt their economy into a model of stability. In the process they have become the Philippines' biggest provider of foreign aid. The week we were there, Philippine President Gloria Macapagal-Arroyo was in Tokyo, soliciting the Japanese parliament for more assistance. Each year, more tourists visit the Philippines from Japan than from any other nation. The modern Philippines depends on Japan.

As we drove through Manila, everywhere we looked we saw cars and trucks built by Mitsubishi, motorcycles built by Kawasaki, and buildings made of Japanese steel, much of it undoubtedly Nippon Steel. When we stepped onto the elevator in our hotel I noticed the Mitsubishi logo (although Harold did not seem to). In Manila and throughout the Philippines we were surrounded, in essence, by the defendants in the JPOW lawsuit. I found the irony almost overwhelming.

As I accompanied Harold through Manila, I found myself wondering if I could have made it. Could I have handled MacArthur's orders to defend this place at all costs, without enough to eat and enough bullets? Would I have rebelled? How would I have reacted when MacArthur and the other officers left for Australia, leaving me behind? Most of all, I wondered how I would have held up under the brutality of the Japanese, the constant physical and mental abuse, the daily torment and deprivation. Would I have lasted three and a half years? Would I have lasted three and a half days? And if I had, would I have forgiven my tormentors, honestly forgiven them, when it was over? Would I have returned home a better man? Closer to God? At peace with myself and the world? Or would I have become a bitter man, cursing God and bent on revenge?

I honestly did not know the answers to those questions. For a man who does everything he can to avoid disaster, a man who requests lower floors in hotels and carries a flashlight in case the place catches fire or the electricity goes out, a man who does not believe in just buying insurance, but in buying too much insurance, it was difficult for me to even imagine being in such a position. In my world I had a lot of answers, but I did not have those answers.

We left Manila in a Dollar Rental Car van, a Toyota nine seater with our hired driver, a young Filipino named Benji, behind the wheel. After clearing the not insignificant sprawl of the Philippine capital, we merged onto Expressway One, a four-lane highway built long after the war, passing billboards that advertised Pizza Hut, Shell Oil, Aiwa Audio, and Yokohama Tires—signs that the competition between America and Japan had moved in a decidedly more peaceful direction. Later the Japanese van we leased from an American rental car company merged onto MacArthur Highway, a four-lane stretch of Filipino freeway that took us through the town of Angeles and to the entrance of the Clark Field Economic Zone. In Angeles, Benji and the Toyota had to dodge the usual swarms of pedal bikes, motorcycle sidecars the Filipinos call "tricycles," and the distinctive long-backed jeepney buses—versions of army-issue Jeeps that haul passengers for four pesos per kilometer. Occasionally, a hog or chicken had to be dodged as well.

After our understated observation of the 61st anniversary of the beginning of the war, we gave Benji directions to our next destinations. They were Harold's three addresses of incarceration: Cabanatuan, Camp O'Donnell, and Cabcaben.

Unlike Manila, which was all but unrecognizable to Harold, the countryside struck a familiar chord with him. He noted that except for more traffic, little had changed. Bumpy, narrow two-lane roads wind through flat land dominated by rice paddies and interspersed by barrios with shops and houses built to the edge of the pavement. Here, as in 1941, massive carabao still pull plows in the fields and air-conditioning remains nonexistent. Around the houses, livestock roams unchecked just as it had when Harold lived here six decades ago and when Warner lived here three decades ago. "I once asked a farmer if it was safe to travel, having all those chickens and pigs just running around loose," said Warner as the van swerved to miss some livestock in the center of a barrio. "He said it sure was, he hadn't lost a pig in fifteen years."

The traffic was heavy when we got to Cabanatuan City, an overgrown village of a million people where few buildings exceed two stories. The two-lane road that snakes through town was alive with pedabikes, motorcycle trikes, jeepneys, vans, trucks, and buses constantly moving over, around, and out of the way of the other. The rental van eventually cleared the city congestion and continued on the road to Palayan. After seven kilometers we came to the place where Prison Camp No. 1, the beginning of the infamous Cabanatuan compound, once stood. There were no buildings or significant landmarks remaining, just a small half-finished memorial at the end of a dusty lane, barely noticeable from the road. Flags of the United States and the Philippines flew above the memorial, and a cement mixer and several bags of cement littered the entrance.

Benji stopped the van and Harold stepped out, squinting into the sun. There was no brass band to greet him and he had to step around the bags of cement, but it was an infinitely better arrival than the last time he was dropped off at Cabanatuan.

"This is the place," Harold said, looking around panoramically at the farms and fields. "There's nothing here now, but yes, this is where it was."

Harold pointed toward a field in the distance and said it was the prison farm where he had worked. It was someone else's farm now, covered with sugarcane. Below and south of the farm he pointed out where they had buried the dead. More than three thousand men, a third of all the POWs who walked in Cabanatuan's front gate, ended up there. As we had learned in Manila, the remains had since been moved to the American Cemetery.

It was eerie, standing on ground where so much savagery took place, but with absolutely no verifying physical evidence. Harold did not say much, his normal expansiveness rendered silent by the setting and by his private thoughts (this happened a lot on our trip; usually talkative and forthcoming, in the Philippines, Harold turned pensive). In Manila and at Clark, he had experienced good times as well as bad, but at Cabanatuan it had all been bad. When he left Cabanatuan for Japan, it was because he believed the Japanese, never wanting what happened there to become public knowledge, would kill him before they would set him free.

The summer before, Hampton Sides had detailed in *Ghost Soldiers* the intent of the Japanese to do precisely what Harold predicted. In January of 1945, when two hundred and eighty thousand Allied troops invaded the west coast of Luzon to reclaim the Philippines, the prisoners at Cabanatuan were indeed marked men, a fact validated by Japanese military execution orders found after the war. There were just 513 left by then, the sickest and the weakest. A team of United States Army Rangers crawled thirty miles across central Luzon to rescue them. By then Harold was working at the steel mill in Japan.

As Harold poked around, a Filipino caretaker emerged from beyond the memorial. The man introduced himself as Teofilo Ongalon and explained that the U.S. Embassy in Manila had hired him to spruce up the place. He said there were plans to expand and enlarge the memorial and erect a wall that would list the names of those who perished at Cabanatuan. "It will be magnificent," he said.

"Here, please sign," asked Teofilo, producing a guest book.

We each wrote down our name and address, the first entries in the guest book in four days. The caretaker explained that the four barely visible cement footings lying in weeds just beyond the memorial were the only physical remains left of the camp. The footings had once held up the camp water tower, which, like the rest of the place, was long gone.

When Warner and I told Teofilo that Harold had been at Cabanatuan, the caretaker exclaimed, "Ahhhhhhhhh, you were here!" and rushed over to shake Harold's hand warmly and ask to take his picture, repeating over and over again, almost in disbelief, "You were here!"

Sixty miles west of Cabanatuan, we visited Camp O'Donnell. Here, at the place where the Death March ended and at least twenty-five thousand men died (even the markers at the memorial cannot agree on an exact figure; one puts the number of dead at twenty-five thousand, another at thirty thousand, and a third at thirty-one thousand), the Republic of the Philippines has set aside a huge expanse of land, preserving it in perpetuity as Capas National Shrine. Thirty-one thousand trees have been planted in honor of those who died at O'Donnell and separate memorials have been erected to the Philippine Army, the Philippine Scouts, and various branches of the U.S. military. The newest memorial we saw had been dedicated just two years earlier by the Battling Bastards of Bataan organization, listing every name of the 1,645 Americans who died at O'Donnell.

As at Cabanatuan, there is almost nothing physical left of the original camp, only wide open fields where a prison camp and barbed wire once existed. But at O'Donnell, in addition to the thousands of new trees, two guard towers and a barracks have been constructed in an attempt to replicate the wartime structures that were once there.

When Harold saw the guard towers and the barracks he immediately verified their authenticity. "This is how it was," he said as he walked into the stark, bamboo-thatched barracks. "But there was no cement floor, and ours were more run-down."

Despite the pain and torture the barracks and guard towers represented, Harold said he appreciated the attention to detail in reconstructing them, and the fact that they had been reconstructed at all. He saw it not only as a tangible reminder of what happened here, but a validation that it mattered. He felt similarly appreciative about the various memorials that paid tribute not just to the men who were held captive, but also to their various battalions, divisions, and regiments. He pointed proudly to a line on the American monument that read "20th Pursuit Squadron." In the museum building next to that monument, a black-and-white photograph of the Death March—one of only a few in existence—had been blown up to wall-size and greeted us as we entered. Harold studied the images of weary prisoners being prodded by Japanese bayonets and said, "I'd never seen that picture before, but that really captures it."

At the center of the Capas National Shrine stands a one-hundred-foot obelisk molded in the form, curiously, of a bullet. Divided into three sections, this towering structure serves as a memorial to the nationalities that once inhabited O'Donnell: Filipinos, Americans, and Japanese. A plaque at the bottom of the bullet states that the memorial is ecumenical and nonjudgmental to preserve harmony "in this era of global peace."

After I read the inscription I turned away in disgust, appalled that there could be any acknowledgment, let alone tribute, to the Japanese at a place where they violated so many basic rules of morality. Erecting a memorial to the Nazis at Auschwitz would be no less objectionable.

It reminded me of something I had read that morning in *To America: Personal Reflections of an Historian* by historian Stephen Ambrose: "My wife and I were in Bataan when the Battling Bastards of Bataan were having a reunion and we joined them for a few days. Their accounts of what the Japanese did to them are scarcely credible, except that they happened. One of them said that although most Americans during the war thought of the Japanese as beasts, they really were not. 'A beast,' he said, 'is an animal, and animals kill only to eat. The Japs killed for fun.'"

And yet now the Japanese were being granted a measure of respect in a place where not only had their benign neglect killed thousands, but in the war's aftermath they had never so much as acknowledged their atrocities. It reminded me of Ambrose's description in *To America* of the Japanese version of World War II: "The Japanese presentation of the war to its children runs something like this: 'One day, for no reason we ever understood, the Americans started dropping atomic bombs on us.'"

As we drove away from O'Donnell, I broached the subject about the Japanese memorial with Harold. How did he feel about the Japanese, after what they did, having any mention whatsoever at O'Donnell?

"Well," said Harold, searching for his thoughts on the subject, "It was a long time ago and a lot has changed. The Japanese have a big presence here in the Philippines. Almost every car you see is Japanese. People want peace. People want to get along with those they associate with. I suppose that's why they included Japan."

From the back van window, Harold took one last look as the Capas National Shrine and the bullet obelisk of O'Donnell faded in the distance, before giving me some measure of satisfaction.

"But it does kinda stick in your craw, doesn't it?" he finally added.

In their starkness, disrepair, and silence, the memorials at Cabanatuan and O'Donnell speak volumes about the state of the Philippines since World War II. At both places, Harold, Paul, and I were the only visitors, and as we wrote our names in the guest registers we not only noticed there were often several days between each entry, but also that most were written in English by other American visitors. It was obvious that in a country that wrestles every day with poverty, paying tribute to things that happened more than a half century ago does not rank high on many priority lists, particularly when that tribute memorializes the defeat of a country that is now among your primary benefactors.

America and Japan, two world powers, met here once and then they moved on. The land and the people the Americans and the Japanese fought over—land and people once considered pivotal to the future course of civilization—have long since returned to their normal routine.

From Camp O'Donnell we drove east to the village of Capas and what was once the train station there. We were on the Death March trail now, tracing it backward from the end of the line at O'Donnell. After exactly seven kilometers we turned half a block off the main road and arrived at a marker noting that this was the spot where the Death Marchers ended their thirty-five-kilometer train leg of the trip from San Fernando and began the relatively short walk to O'Donnell. The worn cement marker was damaged and covered with graffiti. We would find that to be typical of the various memorials and markers along the eighty-five miles of the Death March. There are numerous reminders that this is where the Death March took place, such as the garbage truck we saw in Capas with the town slogan on its side: "Death March Our History. Today's Progress Our Destiny." But most are in poor repair. Exceptions are the kilometer markers being placed by Filipino-American Memorial Enterprise (FAME), a Manila-based organization dedicated to preserving Death March history. Among other goals, FAME wants to post a marker at every kilometer along the original route, although a lack of funding keeps stalling the project's completion.

From Capas, we turned south toward San Fernando. The railroad line that hauled the prisoners in 1942 between San Fernando and Capas no longer exists and neither does the train station in San Fernando. One of the narrow-gauge freight cars that transported the Death Marchers was set aside a few years go by the people of FAME, but when they came back for it they discovered it had been sold for scrap.

For lunch, we stopped at a McDonald's in San Fernando, not far from where the train station once stood. Harold ordered a cheeseburger, fries, and a Sprite. The juxtaposition was almost not to be believed—that an eighty-three-year-old man could be eating lunch at a McDonald's in the same place where sixty-one years ago he had been forced to march without so much as a drink of water.

Warner joked by asking his father-in-law if he had had similar fare the last time he was here.

"The Japanese were in charge of lunch," Harold joked back, "and the service was lousy."

Continuing south, we soon crossed out of Pampanga Province: Harold had returned to Bataan.

With a full stomach and a bottle of water at his side, Harold guided us through Lubao, Abucay, Balanga, Pillar, Orion, Limay, and Tobang, the towns of the Death March. We drove past churches, petrol stations, rice drying on the asphalt, skinny dogs, roadside stands selling coconuts and bananas, kids playing basketball on hard dirt playgrounds, and a cockfighting arena. Mile after mile, we retraced the infamous march along the old National Road as Filipino life went marching past us.

Now, as then, it is not much to look at. Bataan has the feel of a forgotten place, its atmosphere foreboding. Still bordered on three sides by the sea and two sides by mountain ranges, still a geographical afterthought, still a dead-end land.

At the edge of the peninsula, just before the coastline angled westward, we stopped at the Cabcaben Elementary School and got out of the van. Harold could not tell for sure if it was the same school he once lived underneath for a month while salvaging scrap for the Japanese. If it was, the building had been rebuilt. But the village was and is small, so it easily might have been the same location.

I watched as a smile came across his face as he walked up and down the highway by the school.

From Cabcaben it was fourteen kilometers to the seaport town of Mariveles, where it all ended and all began.

The road turned into a sharp descent coming into Mariveles, the only stretch of the Death March with a significant change in elevation. I asked Harold if he remembered that the march began with such a severe uphill climb. He answered that he had no clear recollection of the hill whatsoever, but that he could remember that there were guns shooting from Corregidor. "I remember wanting to get away from those guns," he said. "The bullets were flying right over us."

We looked up and there, seemingly almost close enough to touch, was Corregidor Island.

The afternoon shadows were beginning to lengthen when we stopped at the Kilometer Zero marker at the Mariveles Death March Memorial, a small enclosed park that sits across the street from Manila Bay and marks the Death March starting line.

A dozen or so Filipino youths passed in front of the memorial, paying us no mind as we crossed the road. We stopped under the canopy of a banyan tree to read the marker, written in Tagalog on the left and English on the right. "More than seventy thousand Filipino and American troops left this spot on April 10, 1942," it reads.

From the doorway of her small combination store and house next to the memorial, a place where visitors could buy a pack of Marlboros for thirty pesos or a bottle of Pepsi Cola for ten pesos, a middle-aged Filipino woman named Zenaida Uchi surveyed the scene. I walked over and bought a soda from her and told her that the white-haired man standing by the Zero Kilometer marker was a Death March participant. "He looks very strong, strong and healthy," said Ms. Uchi. "I can see why he made it."

As I walked from the store to the park I considered the long odds Harold Poole had overcome just to be standing under that banyan tree in the twilight of his life. He was in good health at eighty-three. He wore a hearing aid in one ear, and he tired more easily than he once did, but he stood straight and he walked with no cane or walker. What were the odds? How many were left? I added the round numbers in my head. Of the nearly ten thousand U.S. soldiers who started on the Death March, about seven hundred died along the way. Of the nearly nine thousand who reached Camp O'Donnell, one thousand six hundred and forty-five died there. At Cabanatuan and other Philippine prison camps, another two to three thousand Death Marchers perished. Add close to another thousand who died at sea during hell ship crossings to Japan or during the years slaving in Japanese mines, factories, and mills, and it means that only somewhere between four and five thousand of those U.S. soldiers who started the Bataan Death March—less than half—even made it home to America at the end of the war.

That was almost sixty years ago. At the close of 2002, I guessed there could not be more than a thousand Americans left, probably less, who walked this walk, and fewer than that among the Filipinos, whose life expectancy is shorter. Harold Poole indeed represented the last of a special breed. There would be few of the Death Marchers who would endure the seventeen-hour airline flight from the States and then the endurance course of a drive from Manila to return to Bataan and stand once again at Kilometer Zero in Mariveles. There would be some, but not many.

But it was not making it to a ripe old age that mattered, I realized. It was making it to a ripe old age at peace with your world.

Throughout this return to what had been Harold's greatest shame and torture, where he was shot at, surrendered, starved, and worked as a slave, where his dignity was castigated and his friends died all around him, I watched for signs of the kind of deep-seeded bitterness that might be expected at such a reunion. I waited to hear railings against the injustice of what happened, for expressions of vengeance or at the very least some good old-fashioned self-righteous indignation. But even at the spot where the long march began, I saw and heard none.

CHAPTER TWENTY-FIVE

September 2003
Washington, D.C.

A HURRICANE NAMED ISABEL was moving across the southern Atlantic with winds reaching 160 miles per hour. No one knew where or even if Isabel would find land, but the entire eastern seaboard of the United States covered up just in case, including the houses of government in Washington, D.C. Three hundred and fifty thousand government workers were told to stay home for two days.

I got word of Congress's shortened work week late Tuesday afternoon, September 16, at my office in Palm Desert—about the last place Isabel would come calling. It was dry and hot when I answered the phone call from Karen Marangi, who was at her office in D.C. at Patton Boggs. She wanted to let me know that because of the hurricane, the Department of Defense appropriations bill would be coming up for a vote the next day. It was the second time the vote had been moved up. It had originally been scheduled the first week of October, and then, before Isabel, to this Friday, September 19. Now, Wednesday was the day.

Our interest in the defense bill, an enormous piece of legislation that annually appropriates money to the country's defense agencies, was because Senator Hatch had submitted his "Justice for Veterans" amendment as part of the bill. By filing the JPOW legislation as an amendment, rather than as its own separate bill, it was hoped that it would "fly under the radar," as one legislator put it, and make it through the system at a time when even the smallest of budget requests were under heavy scrutiny due to the high cost of maintaining troops in Iraq.

The rushed timetable did not help our chances. For one thing, the Wednesday vote meant that Orrin Hatch would not personally be able to be there. At a government conference in Mexico over the weekend, his back had gone out. He had returned to Washington with a herniated disc and emergency surgery had been scheduled for Wednesday.

The rush also gave us even less time to rally the last-minute support we all sensed we badly needed.

It had been a long hard campaign since the day I left Hatch's office, buoyed by the senator's commitment to "get this thing worked out." It had seemed so simple then. The senator would introduce the JPOW legislation, the mega-firm lawyers would work with Hatch's staff on the details of the compensation package, and the mega-firm lobbyists at Patton Boggs and Greenberg Traurig would work the Senate and House for sufficient support to get the bill passed. I had images, as did Senator Hatch, of a ceremony at the White House where Lester Tenney, Harold Poole, and other World War II veterans would be honored by President Bush. In a best-case scenario, I hoped we could get everything finalized so the ceremony could be held in the Rose Garden on April 9, the day Bataan fell.

The fantasy was not unfounded. Early on, support came, as we expected and hoped, from Republicans and Democrats alike. Maury Herman and I visited Joe Biden, the Democratic senator from Delaware who serves as the ranking Democrat on the Foreign Relations Committee, at his Washington office and he could not have been more enthusiastic. "This is Hatch's bill, so we'll stay in the background," he said, "but call if there's anything you need." Biden offered the full use of his staff, along with his own unqualified personal endorsement. Other influential Democratic senators, including Tom Harkin from Iowa and Dianne Feinstein from California, also quickly lined up in support of Hatch's bill. Bipartisan support would not be our problem.

Then the setbacks began. First, as the legislation took shape in early March, compromises with opponents succeeded in reducing the compensation package from $400 million to $300 million. Then on March 19, 2003, an American-led coalition attacked Iraq. The Iraqi war lasted only twenty-two days—Baghdad fell on April 9, of all days—but no soldiers were sent home as the democratization of Iraq began, at a cost of a billion dollars per day in the beginning. Suddenly, defense expense had become a huge concern.

Other hurdles got in the way, including a knee-jerk reaction in Congress to the trial lawyer's profession. Some legislators, we kept hearing from our lobbyists, did not want to pay the former JPOWs because they did not want to pay the lawyers who were helping them.

By July, when Senator Hatch formally introduced his amendment on the Senate floor, a number of opponents appeared ready to fight. Leading the opposition was Alaska Senator Ted Stevens, chairman of the Senate Appropriations Committee. Right behind him was Hawaii Senator Daniel Inouye, a World War II veteran who had been awarded the Congressional Medal of Honor, who was worried that the bill would not be well received by the Japanese community in Hawaii. Others worried about how a compensation package for the World War II vets would impact any number of victims' groups clamoring for attention, including those affected in the September 11 attacks, in the Oklahoma City bombing, and even African Americans seeking slave reparations.

After a shouting match between Hatch and Stevens on the Senate floor, the amendment was reduced yet again, this time from $300 million to $49 million: $10,000 per JPOW slave laborer still alive and nothing beyond that.

It was a big blow, but at least the amendment was still part of the Senate's defense appropriations package. As Hatch explained the process to us, as long as the amendment stayed in the defense bill there was always the possibility that its numbers could be elevated at a future point in time. The important thing was keeping it alive.

During Congress's traditional August recess, we had our lobbying work cut out for us. I talked personally to a number of legislators, starting with Californians John Dolittle and Duncan Hunter. Both pledged their support but Hunter added the ominous warning that with so much money going to Iraq, money in Washington was tight and hard to find. Hunter urged me to contact congressman Jerry Lewis, chairman of the House Defense Appropriations Subcommittee.

I made an appointment with Lewis at his office in Redlands, California, not far from my office, and arranged for Harold to fly to the meeting from Salt Lake City. I played an eight-minute video highlight of the case and then asked Harold to say a few words, which he did with his usual understated aplomb. I knew the congressman was preparing to take a trip to Iraq to meet with the soldiers, so with Harold sitting there, I took the opportunity to juxtapose the Iraqi conflict with what went on in the Philippines in World War II, contrasting just two hundred American deaths, at that time, in the Iraq war to a grave every thirty feet along the eighty-five-mile Bataan Death March.

"When you talk to the young soldiers in Iraq, thank them on behalf of the American people," I said, "and after you do that remind them that after the war is over that they will be taken care of."

I hoped the inference was obvious: all soldiers, from all wars, need to be thanked and need to be taken care of after the war is over.

In August, Orrin Hatch came to Utah for a two-day golf fundraiser for women's charities and I paid for a place in the tournament and then did not swing a club. I spent both days chauffeuring Hatch in his golf cart so I could talk to him about the legislation. I also lobbied Utah congressman Chris Cannon, who had been a supporter of Mike Honda's JPOW resolution in the House.

Around the country, members of our JPOW legal team lobbied hard, lining up votes, trying to ensure a political victory. It was like talking to members of a jury one at a time, and the jury had five hundred and thirty-five members.

The reception, to our surprise, was less than overwhelming. Although not a single legislator disparaged the Bataan veterans, many, including some who had earlier signaled their support for the separate JPOW Senate and House resolutions, now hedged. Whether this was because of the situation in Iraq, White House and State Department resistance, lobbying efforts of the Japanese, or some other factor, such as trial lawyer bias, was difficult to say. But overall, the wind seemed to be shifting.

I thought about the earthquake that preceded the surrender on Bataan. I remember thinking, *They had their earthquake, and we have our hurricane.*

I waited by my phone all day on Wednesday, hoping against hope that we would get word that the amendment survived. Maybe we would get a last-second reprieve simply because Congress would say, Wait a minute, we cannot trample on these guys again.

But they could. And they did.

Just before the close of Wednesday's session, with Isabel losing steam well before Washington, and with Hatch in the hospital, the Department of Defense appropriations bill was passed without a trace of the Justice for Veterans amendment. The conference committee met for twenty-three minutes. The JPOW legislation was tossed out without further discussion. And afterward, not a single congressman or senator complained about it publicly.

Congress was the first death knell. The final blow came two and a half weeks later, on October 6, the fabled first Monday in October when the United States Supreme Court traditionally announces the cases it will hear during the upcoming session.

The JPOW appeal was not one of them.

By declining to entertain the appeal to the earlier rulings of Judge Walker and the Ninth Circuit Court of Appeals, the clear implication was that the Supreme Court justices saw no compelling constitutional argument or any other reason to take the case. It was essentially the legal knockout punch for the cause, and a silent one at that. Even though a few POW cases remained in the California state system, it begged common sense that they would be heard after the highest court in the land turned away from the argument.

A number of senators and congressmen were quoted in the media decrying the Supreme Court's declination. In the Salt Lake City *Deseret Morning News*, the newspaper that landed on Harold Poole's porch, Hatch observed that now that the Supreme Court had let them down, "Congress is the last recourse for these POWs," and announced that he was sponsoring legislation to bring the men justice. The senator did not mention that two and a half weeks earlier similar legislation had already been defeated.

We could try again in the next congressional session, of course, a year down the road. But I knew that as much as the White House, State Department, Justice Department, federal courts, and Senators Stevens, Inouye, and the rest were against us, time was an even bigger obstacle.

What were we down to now, fewer than five thousand who slaved at the furnaces and the mines in Honshu? The men from the Pacific were on the real death march now. Every last man who fought in the Philippines was in his eighties. Their time was running out. Frank Bigelow died during the past year; so did Nelson Quast and Fran Agnes. Half the men who stood in front of Orrin Hatch's original congressional hearing in the summer of 2000 were gone. When Harold Poole attended the annual gathering of the 20th Pursuit Squadron in Washington State in September of 2003, only four men were healthy enough to attend, compared to eleven the year before.

It was hard to watch. Not because of the men; the men would be all right, no matter what. What was hard to watch were the leaders of the United States government doing nothing for the POWs. They could not do anything about the problem in 1942, and they could not do anything in 1951, either. Back then, their hands were tied. But now? A country that found $1.25 billion for the Japanese Americans it interned during World War II, that purposely stayed out of the German Holocaust fight so nearly two million wartime civilian slaves could split up $8 billion, that was spending billions of dollars in Iraq, *that* government could certainly afford to recognize and offer a token compensation to the men who held the Alamo in the Philippines, who stayed the course, fought the fight, and then saw their civil rights sacrificed for the public good at war's end.

It was not the money. Money, as Mike Honda would say, is simply a way to say thank you, you matter. Thank you for getting by on eight hundred calories a day, for sitting in languid prisons and taking repeated beatings, for burning up in the Philippines, for freezing in Japan, for riding hell ships in typhoons. Thank you for never forsaking America or what America stands for through all of it.

I found it ironic that a handful of soldiers held captive in Iraq received nationwide sympathy for enduring twenty-two days as prisoners of war. The most celebrated, nineteen-year-old Army Private Jessica Lynch, was in captivity nine days before she was rescued, and she became a national hero. There was no denying that these Americans went through a trying ordeal and deserved sympathy for their suffering and credit for their courage, but what about three and a half years of captivity, most of it without any contact with friends or family? Did not that deserve sympathy, too?

In light of the Iraqi captures, the media in Salt Lake sought out Harold to ask him about being a prisoner of war. He was asked how a soldier recovers from such an ordeal. How do you regroup and go on? "You come home and you forgive and forget," Harold answered. "Don't carry it with you, just let it go. It's the only way to find peace."

The situation in Iraq, along with the publicity the JPOW case generated, brought the Pacific Theater vets a measure of new attention. Among other honors, Harold received a Minuteman Award from the Utah National Guard for "outstanding service to freedom and country." At the banquet where the award was given, hundreds of guardsmen gave the old soldier a standing ovation.

At the grassroots level, it seemed that America always responded appreciatively and with appropriate respect. In four years working the case, I did not see one instance in which the World War II veterans were not publicly accorded dignity and respect. I was yet to read a media commentary that did not support their cause.

But government was where it had always been regarding the men of Bataan. They were a pawn in geopolitical maneuvering in the beginning, and still were at the end. In six decades, nothing changed. Forgotten soldiers then, forgotten soldiers now.

Just how forgotten was subtly pointed out to me during one of my lobbying trips to Washington. One afternoon I visited the Smithsonian Institute's Berring Museum of Natural History. In the section on wartime history, I came across a display that recounted the internment of Japanese Americans during World War II and described how that was a violation of their constitutional rights. I looked around the museum for a mention of the Philippines and the Bataan campaign and found nothing. I asked a docent if there was anything about Bataan. "We probably should have something," the docent said, "but we don't."

In a way, even my colleagues and I ended up making our own unwitting contribution to the Bataan veterans' continued problems. Part of the reason Congress turned a deaf ear to the JPOW case was because of the "money-hungry" trial lawyers they hooked up with.

And how choice was that? For four years, ever since Lester Tenney carried his grievance into Mike Goldstein's office, the "money-hungry trial lawyers" had picked up every dime of the JPOWs' legal expense. We organized a nationwide network of lawyers, we recruited the best specialists available, we collectively spent thousands and thousands of hours and millions of dollars, and never charged anyone anything.

I wanted to tell Harold in person. I drove from California to his house in Salt Lake City, giving me a day to think about how I wanted to deliver the news. We sat in the overstuffed chairs in his front room, where on numerous occasions he had detailed his war stories for me, and that is where I told him about the congressional defeat and the Supreme Court's decision not to hear the appeal. I explained that there were members of the legal team as well as Senator Hatch, Congressman Honda, and other lawmakers who wanted to carry on, but for the first time in four years, I confessed that I did not think we would prevail.

"I didn't think the war with Iraq and all the worry about terrorism was going to help," said Harold, which summed up his entire commentary on the subject. It had never been Harold's cause anyway. He always loyally supported the case. I know he sincerely wanted to see the men get some recognition, he wanted to pay tribute to those who had not made it out of the war, and he wanted to raise public awareness to help prevent similar war atrocities ever happening again. But the court battles, the legal maneuverings, and, especially, realizing financial compensation, that had always been my dream for Harold, not Harold's for himself.

"Come on out in the back and see what happened to my tree," Harold said, diverting my attention.

I walked with him to an apple tree in the backyard, the same tree Harold had picked apples from for Mike Honda a year ago. The limbs were so loaded down with fruit that the trunk of the old tree had snapped.

"Would you look at that," said Harold, acting as if he had just discovered the month-old break. "Too many apples this year."

He proceeded to pick fruit from the tree and load my arms with as much as they could carry. As we turned back toward the house, I looked at the ground beneath the tree, littered with overripe apples, and watched as Harold walked right past them. I remembered the stories of his near starvation in Cabanatuan, when such a sight invaded his sleep nightly. But times change, and so do dreams. What was once the end-all of a young man's fantasy was now just rotting fruit, left to lie unnoticed on the ground.

SOURCES

WHEN THE SUBJECT IS WORLD WAR II, it is an easy thing to stand on the shoulders of the many fine and thorough researchers who have, over the last sixty-plus years, recorded so much of the who, what, when, where, and how in detail and in context.

Among those sources drawn upon most extensively in this book are Linda Goetz Holmes's *Unjust Enrichment*, Gavan Daws's *Prisoners of the Japanese*, Gregory F. Michno's *Death on the Hellships*, Richard Connaughton's *MacArthur and Defeat in the Philippines*, William A. Bartsch's *Doomed at the Start*, and Louis Morton's seminal *The Fall of the Philippines*.

Most valuable were the verbal and written personal accounts of the war and Japanese captivity as told by the men who lived through it. The clarity of recall displayed by these veterans six decades after the fact was nothing short of astounding. Not the least of these were the oral and written war histories of Harold Poole, whose experiences stand, in this narrative, as proxy for them all.

The following is a bibliography of source books used for quotes, historical accounts, chronologies, and statistics. Additionally, a variety of Internet Web sites were consulted for spelling and statistical checks and to access previously published materials.

Alexander, Irvin. *Surviving Bataan and Beyond*. Edited by Dominic J. Caraccilo. Stackpole Books: Mechanicsburg, Fla., 1999.

Bartsch, William H. *Doomed at the Start: American Pursuit Pilots in the Philippines, 1941-1942*. Texas A&M University Press: College Station, TX, 1992.

Bradley, James. *Flags of Our Fathers*. Bantam: New York, 2000.

Clarke, Thurston. *Pearl Harbor Ghosts*. Ballantine Books: New York, 2001.

Connaughton, Richard. *MacArthur and Defeat in the Phillipines*. The Overlook Press: New York, 2001.

Daws, Gavan. *Prisoners of the Japanese: POWs of World War II in the Pacific*. William Morrow and Company: New York, 1994.

Dillman, Frank. *A Time in History*. Unpublished memoir, 2001.
Dyess, William E.. *The Dyess Story: The Complete Eye-witness Account of the Death March from Bataan*. G.P. Putnam and Sons: New York, 1944.
Eizenstat, Stuart E. *Imperfect Justice: Looted Assets, Slave Labor, and the Unfinished Business of World War II*. Perseus Books Group: New York, 2003.
Fitzpatrick, Bernard T., with John A. Sweetser III. *The Hike into the Sun*. McFarland and Company: Jefferson, North Carolina, 1993.
Goodwin, Doris Kearns. *No Ordinary Time*. Touchstone: New York, 1995.
Hibbs, Ralph Emerson. *Tell MacArthur to Wait*. Self-published, 1988.
History of the Defenders of the Philippines, Guam and Wake Islands, 1941-1945. Volume II. Turner Publishing: Paducah, Kentucky, 1998.
Holmes, Linda Goetz. *Unjust Enrichment: How Japan's Companies Built Postwar Fortunes Using American POWs*. Stackpole Books: Mechanicsburg, PA, 2001.
Knox, Donald. *Death March*. Harcourt Brace: Orlando, FL, 1981.
Martin, Adrian R.. *Brothers From Bataan*. Sunflower University Press: Manhattan, KS, 1992.
Michno, Gregory F.. *Death on the Hellships*. Naval Institute Press: Annapolis, MD, 2001.
Morton, Louis. *The Fall of the Philippines*. U.S. Army Center of Military History: Washington, D.C., 1953. Official U.S. Army history.
Parker, R.A.C.. *The Second World War: A Short History*. Oxford Press: New York, 1989.
Poole, Harold. *Harold W. Poole, P.O.W.* Unpublished memoir, 1946.
Saburo Ienaga. *The Pacific War: World War II and the Japanese, 1931-1945*. Pantheon Books: New York, 1978.
Sides, Hampton. *Ghost Soldiers*. Random House: New York, 2001.
Tenney, Lester I. *My Hitch in Hell*. Brassey's, Inc.: Washington, D.C., 1995.
Toland, John. *But Not in Shame: The Six Months After Pearl Harbor*. Random House: New York, 1961.
Towle, Philip, Margaret Kosuge, and Yoichi Kibata. *Japanese Prisoners of War*. Hambledon and London: London, 2000.
Waterfield, Van. *Prisoners of the Japanese in World War II*. McFarland & Company: Jefferson, NC, 1994.
Whitney, Courtney. *MacArthur: His Rendezvous With History*. Alfred A. Knopf, Inc.: New York, 1956.

INDEX

Note: Page numbers in italics refer to a map on that page.

ABOUT THE AUTHORS

JAMES PARKINSON received his law degree in 1976 from Brigham Young University and has been practicing law ever since. He is a member of numerous professional associations and has been the recipient of a number of awards, including the Association of Trial Lawyers of America Distinguished Service Award. He lives with his wife, Susan, in California, where he is in private practice.

LEE BENSON is a newspaper columnist for the *Deseret Morning News* in Salt Lake City and the author of a number of books on subjects as diverse as the Olympic Games and the kidnapping of Elizabeth Smart. A graduate of Brigham Young University and a Utah native, he makes his home in Park City.

THE NAVAL INSTITUTE PRESS is the book-publishing arm of the U.S. Naval Institute, a private, nonprofit, membership society for sea service professionals and others who share an interest in naval and maritime affairs. Established in 1873 at the U.S. Naval Academy in Annapolis, Maryland, where its offices remain today, the Naval Institute has members worldwide.

Members of the Naval Institute support the education programs of the society and receive the influential monthly magazine *Proceedings* and discounts on fine nautical prints and on ship and aircraft photos. They also have access to the transcripts of the Institute's Oral History Program and get discounted admission to any of the Institute-sponsored seminars offered around the country.

The Naval Institute also publishes *Naval History* magazine. This colorful bimonthly is filled with entertaining and thought-provoking articles, first-person reminiscences, and dramatic art and photography. Members receive a discount on *Naval History* subscriptions.

The Naval Institute's book-publishing program, begun in 1898 with basic guides to naval practices, has broadened its scope to include books of more general interest. Now the Naval Institute Press publishes about seventy titles each year, ranging from how-to books on boating and navigation to battle histories, biographies, ship and aircraft guides, and novels. Institute members receive significant discounts on the Press's more than eight hundred books in print.

Full-time students are eligible for special half-price membership rates. Life memberships are also available.

For a free catalog describing Naval Institute Press books currently available, and for further information about subscribing to *Naval History* magazine or about joining the U.S. Naval Institute, please write to:

Member Services
U.S. NAVAL INSTITUTE
291 Wood Road
Annapolis, MD 21402-5034
Telephone: (800) 233-8764
Fax: (410) 571-1703
Web address: *www.navalinstitute.org*

UNION OF SOVIET SOCIALIST REPUBLICS
MONGOLIA
Manchuria
Vladivostok
KOREA
JAPAN
Tokyo
CHINA
Shanghai
Ryukyu Islands
Okinawa
Iwo Jima
INDIA
Formosa (now Taiwan)
BURMA
Hong Kong
Pescadores Islands
Hainan
Mariana Islands
Luzon
THAILAND
South China Sea
Manila
PHILIPPINES
Bangkok
INDOCHINA (now Cambodia, Laos, and Vietnam)
Mindanao
MALAYA (now Malaysia)
Singapore
Borneo
Sumatra
Celebes
New Guinea
Dutch East Indies (now Indonesia)
Java
Timor
Indian Ocean
AUSTRALIA